MW00667889

Randolph L. Braham

ROMANIAN NATIONALISTS AND THE HOLOCAUST:

The Political Exploitation of Unfounded Rescue Accounts

The Rosenthal Institute for Holocaust Studies
Graduate School of the City University of New York

Distributed by
Columbia University Press
1998

HOLOCAUST STUDIES SERIES

Randolph L. Braham, Editor
The Institute for Holocaust Studies
The Graduate School and University Center
The City University of New York

Previously published books in the Series:
Perspectives on the Holocaust, 1982
Contemporary Views on the Holocaust, 1983
Genocide and Retribution, 1983
The Hungarian Jewish Catastrophe: A Selected and Annotated Bibliography, 1984
Jewish Leadership During the Nazi Era: Patterns of Behavior in the Free World, 1985
The Holocaust in Hungary — Forty Years Later, 1985
The Origins of the Holocaust: Christian Anti-Semitism, 1985
The Halutz Resistance in Hungary, 1942–1944, 1986
The Tragedy of Hungarian Jewry: Essays, Documents, Depositions, 1986
The Treatment of the Holocaust in Textbooks, 1987
The Psychological Perspectives of the Holocaust and Its Aftermath, 1988
Reflections of the Holocaust in Art and Literature, 1990
Studies on the Holocaust in Hungary, 1990
*Anti-Semitism and the Treatment of the Holocaust in Postcommunist Eastern
    Europe,* 1994
The Tragedy of Romanian Jewry, 1994
The Wartime System of Labor Service in Hungary, 1995
The Holocaust in Hungary: Fifty Years Later, 1997
The Destruction of Romanian and Ukrainian Jews During the Antonescu Era, 1997

The Holocaust Studies Series is published in cooperation with the Institute for Holocaust Studies. These books are outgrowths of lectures, conferences, and research projects sponsored by the Institute. It is the purpose of the Series to subject the events and circumstances of the Holocaust to scrutiny by a variety of academics who bring different scholarly disciplines to the study.

The first three books in the Series were published by
Kluwer-Nijhoff Publishing of Boston

Printed in the United States of America
1998

Contents

Contents

Contents

Contents

Introduction

The dissolution of the Communist system and the consequent disintegration of the Soviet bloc just 44 years after the defeat of the Third Reich had engendered considerable historical controversy. Perhaps the most vocal debate has followed from the provocative conclusions reached by Francis Fukuyama, a political scientist associated with a Washington think tank. Among Fukuyama's conclusions was the argument that the destruction of the two rival totalitarian systems of the twentieth century denoted not only the worldwide triumph of liberal democracy but also the end of history as we know it.[1] Unfortunately, Fukuyama's optimistic conclusions have proven unfounded. They have been negated, among other things, by the persistence of ethnic-nationalist political and military conflicts as well as the racial and religious animosities that continue to bedevil many parts of the world. While he correctly identified the defeat of the Axis in 1945 and the collapse of the Soviet system in 1989 with the bankruptcy of both Nazism and Communism, he failed to properly consider the continuing—and in many places increasing—vitality of nationalism, a social ideology that preceded the totalitarian doctrines of the Left and Right by more than a century.

The resurfacing of xenophobic nationalism in East Central Europe almost immediately after the collapse of the Soviet empire

---

[1] Francis Fukuyama, *The End of History and the Last Man* (New York: The Free Press, 1992).

is a case in point. The ethnic-national conflicts and territorial disputes that plagued this polyglot area during the pre-World War I and interwar periods had been suppressed during the Soviet era under the veneer of "proletarian internationalism." After the dissolution of the Communist system, these conflicts were rekindled with a vehemence that induced many scholars to observe correctly that the post-1989 political developments in East Central Europe denoted a *return back to history* and the *failure* of liberal democracy.[2] This regression in the political evolution of the area has been exacerbated by the social conflicts that were brought to the fore by the relatively rapid marketization and privatization programs initiated by the post-Communist regimes.

The political opportunities offered by the failure of the capitalist experiment to provide instant economic gratification were—and continue to be—exploited by xenophobic nationalist elements opposed to both liberalism and constitutional democracy. Reflecting the techniques used during the Fascist and Communist periods, these nationalists, including many "professional historians," are engaged in a political-ideological campaign designed to create an authoritarian future of their own liking. Identifying parliamentary democracy and liberalism as both "foreign" and undesirable, they are actively involved in what Arthur Schlesinger Jr. calls the writing of exculpatory history. With political habits formed during the nationalist-socialist regimes most of them had previously supported, these xenophobic nationalists are clearly involved in a calculated drive to carry out an ideologically defined political agenda. This includes the whitewashing of their countries' record during the Nazi era in general and their involvement in the Final Solution program in particular. Toward this end, they

---

[2] See, for example, Shlomo Avineri, "The Return to History and the Consequences for the Jewish Communities in Eastern Europe," in *The Danger of Antisemitism in Central and Eastern Europe in the Wake of 1989–1990*, Yehuda Bauer, ed. (Jerusalem: The Hebrew University, 1991), pp. 95–101.

exploit history—a formidable weapon for shaping history—by corrupting the truth and distorting the realities of the past. By their rewritings and reinterpretations, these practitioners of exculpatory history appear to be guided by the party slogan in George Orwell's celebrated work *1984*: "Who controls the past controls the future. Who controls the present controls the past."

Their treatment of the Holocaust is a case in point. Recognizing the significance of this tragic event in their national, Jewish, and world histories, extremist elements—ranging from the charlatans who call themselves "historical revisionists" to many elected party, government, and state leaders—have been engaged in a history-cleansing campaign designed to discredit the Holocaust. They are resolved not only to absolve their wartime leaders and their collaborators of all responsibility for the crimes committed against the Jews, but also to blur the historical record—and memory—and make the world forget the nature and consequences of their involvement in the Nazis's war against the Jews. By denigrating, distorting, or actually denying the Holocaust, these extremists, who are pursuing different and often conflicting political-ideological objectives, have reinforced both the traditional religious and the more modern racial components of anti-Semitism with new, and perhaps even more virulent, strains of intolerance.

Subdued and controlled during the Communist era, when it was camouflaged under the guise of anti-cosmopolitanism and anti-Zionism, this new form of anti-Semitism was brought to the fore after the collapse of the Soviet system. Although the scope and intensity of the campaign has varied from country to country, xenophobic intellectuals, nurtured and trained under the discredited Fascist and Communist regimes, have launched a seemingly concerted campaign to whitewash their countries' wartime genocidal record.

While the history-cleansing campaign is clearly discernible in all countries formerly dominated by the Third Reich, it is particularly intense in Croatia[3] and Romania—the two countries that tried to "solve" the Jewish question on their own terms even before the Nazis launched their Final Solution program. In Romania, ultra-nationalist intellectuals have dedicated themselves to convincing the Romanian people—and the world—that there was no Holocaust in their country. They distort the historical record of the wartime era in general and falsify the anti-Jewish policies of General (later Marshal) Ion Antonescu in particular. Dedicated to the rehabilitation of the Marshal, who was executed as a war criminal in 1946, these history-cleansers "overlook" the singlemindedness with which the Antonescu regime tried to "solve" the Jewish question in Romania during the euphoric phase of the anti-Soviet war. They emphasize the Marshal's policies of the post-Stalingrad era, when his regime, no longer convinced that the Axis Powers would win, began to look upon the Jews as possible sources of revenue and as a potentially useful bargaining chip in a postwar settlement.

The basic objective of this study—the eighteenth volume in the Holocaust Studies Series—is to protect the integrity of the historical record of the Holocaust—an objective also shared by many Romanian Jewish and non-Jewish scholars. It attempts to pursue this objective by unmasking the drive of sundry "historical revisionists" and chauvinistic nationalists to refurbish the past and cleanse the historical record of the Antonescu era. Contrary to these chauvinistic revisionists who wrap themselves in the mantle of nationalism, the historical quarrel is not with Romania or the Romanian people. The study aims exclusively at exposing the falsehoods advanced by the historical revisionists who glorify the record of the Antonescu regime, distorting, if not actually denying, the tragedy that befell Romanian Jewry during the Second World War. Toward this end it (a) presents a critical overview of

---

[3] The treatment of the Holocaust in Croatia and elsewhere in the former Soviet bloc is beyond the scope of this monograph.

the basically propagandistic historical positions of the revisionists
bent on bringing about the rehabilitation of Marshal Ion Antonescu;
and (b) demonstrates that one of their main arguments in support
of the rehabilitation drive—the large-scale rescue of Jews across
the Hungarian-Romanian border during the war—is basically
false, having been based on increasingly grandiose accounts of
rescue advanced since 1985 by two individuals motivated primarily by personal interests.

While the falsifiers of history constitute but a minute fraction
of the Romanian people, they represent a potential danger not only
to the few thousand—mostly elderly—Jews still living in Romania,
but also to the country's political evolution. Although the extremist political parties of the Left and Right suffered a devastating
defeat in the elections of November 1996, revealing the maturity
of the post-Ceauşescu Romanian electorate yearning for the establishment of a constitutional, effective parliamentary democracy, the
damage caused by the falsifiers of history will be difficult to undo.
Unless the regime of President Emil Constantinescu, a learned and
enlightened statesman, takes resolute action in confronting the historical truth of the Antonescu era, the falsehoods spread by the distorters and deniers of the Holocaust will continue to be circulated
and, like computer viruses, will end up affecting every segment of
Romanian historiography.

This volume consists of 8 chapters. The anti-Jewish policies
of the Romanian regimes since 1937 in general and the crimes
committed against the Jews during the Antonescu era in particular
are succinctly described in chapter 1. The chapter also provides an
overview of the role played by anti-Semitism in the country's
political and popular culture and describes the murderous phase of
the anti-Jewish drive spearheaded by the Iron Guard and the
Antonescu regime.

Chapters 2 and 3 describe the reaction to the Holocaust during
the immediate postwar period and its treatment during the Communist era, differentiating between its various phases. It demon-

strates that the "revisionist" reinterpretation of the Holocaust in Romania began during the nationalist-socialist regime of Romanian dictator Nicolae Ceauşescu, who launched the history-cleansing campaign in the early 1970s. Ceauşescu's version aimed not only to strengthen Romania's position against Hungary and change its image around the world by juxtaposing the country's wartime "humanitarianism" with Hungary's "barbarism," but also to bring about the gradual rehabilitation of Marshal Ion Antonescu. Chapter 3 reveals the role played by Iosif Constantin Drăgan, a former Iron Guardist and wealthy neo-Fascist, in advancing these objectives, and the way the xenophobic national-ists exploited—and continue to use—the uncorroborated wartime rescue accounts advanced by two octogenarians. Finally, it demonstrates how the history-cleansing campaign gained momen-tum after the fall of Ceauşescu in late December 1989.

The uncorroborated wartime accounts of rescue across the Hungarian-Romanian border are described and analyzed in chap-ter 4, which provides details on the two main proponents of the exaggerated rescue claims and the commonality of interests that bound Dr. Moshe Carmilly-Weinberger, the former Chief Rabbi of the small Neolog Jewish community of Kolozsvár (Cluj in Romanian) and Dr. Raoul Şorban, a painter and art historian asso-ciated with the University of Bucharest, with regard to these claims. Chapter 5 focuses on the tragedy that befell the family of Éva Semlyén, Şorban's fiancée. It details the unsuccessful attempts by a group of anti-Fascist Romanians to save the family and the arrest of Şorban soon after the liberation of Northern Transylvania by the then allied Soviet-Romanian troops. It also reviews the merits and political undertones of the case against Şorban, which was largely based on allegations that he had "betrayed" the Semlyén family.

Chapter 6 describes the drive for the identification of Şorban as a Righteous Among the Nations, focusing on the background and personal interests of the main backers. It also analyzes the background of Yad Vashem's controversial decision, demonstrating that it reflected a deviation from the standards generally employed in other cases.

Chapter 7 details the strategies pursued by the two leading protagonists and their supporters to achieve their different yet intertwined personal objectives. It also details the personal rewards and the nationalists' political windfalls associated with Şorban's recognition as a Righteous Among the Nations. Chapter 8 provides a succinct overview of the dangers represented by the sundry history-cleansers and comments on the current situation with regard to the furthering of historical memory and historical truth.

The Transylvanian towns and villages mentioned in this work are mostly identified by their official geographic names in 1944, but in a few cases the Romanian and Hungarian names are used interchangeably.

The permission by Oxford University Press to reproduce certain sections of my study on "Romanian Nationalists and the Holocaust. A Case Study in History Cleansing," which appeared in the Winter 1996 issue of *Holocaust and Genocide Studies*, is gratefully acknowledged. I also acknowledge with thanks the permission by *East European Quarterly* to reproduce several sections of my articles "A TV Documentary on Rescue During the Holocaust" and "The Jews of Transylvania: Opportunistic Historical Accounts," which appeared in the summer 1994 and fall 1997 issues of the journal, respectively.

This work could not have been completed without the support and encouragement of many friends and colleagues. I am indebted to Dr. Frances Degen Horowitz, the President of the Graduate School and University Center of the City University of New York, and Dr. Alan Gartner, Dean for Research and University Programs, for their consistent support of the Rosenthal Institute for Holocaust Studies at the Graduate Center. For their generosity and commitment to the advancement of Holocaust studies at CUNY, I am very grateful to Marcel Sand, the chairman, and Gizella and Arie Edrich, Valerie and Frank Furth, Eva and Norman Gati, Irene and Paul Greenwald, Sheba and Jacob Gruber, Ann and Gaby Newmark, and Elizabeth and Jack Rosenthal, members, of the Advisory Committee of the Rosenthal Institute for Holocaust Studies. I am especially grateful to Gábor Várszegi of Budapest for his consistent and most generous support of Holocaust-related research and publications. The Gábor Várszegi Endowment at the Graduate Center Foundation of CUNY's Graduate Center will ensure the continuance of the "J. & O. Winter Fund," which he established at the Graduate Center in memory of his beloved parents and which has become a leading source of support by the Graduate Center for Holocaust-related research in Hungary and other countries.

For their comments and helpful suggestions, I want to express my gratitude to Dr. Eva Fogelman, Senior Research Fellow at the Center for Social Research at CUNY's Graduate Center, Dr. Radu Ioanid, an expert on the Holocaust in Romania associated with the U.S. Holocaust Memorial Museum in Washington, D.C., Clara Knopfler, a member of the Advisory Committee of the Rosenthal Institute for Holocaust Studies, Professor Egon Mayer, Director of the Center for Jewish Studies at CUNY's Graduate Center, and Dr. Michael Shafir, Senior Regional Specialist at Radio Free Europe/Radio Liberty in Prague. For their invaluable contribution to the preservation of the historical record of the Holocaust, I am indebted to Eszter Goro (Fränkel) and Éva Pamfil (Semlyén), whose personal testimonies shed light on one of the most controversial chapters of the tragedy that befell Hungarian Jewry. Finally, I would like to thank Leslie Bialler, my friend and colleague at Columbia University Press, and my wife Elizabeth for their valuable editorial contributions.

New York, NY   Randolph L. Braham
July 1997

CHAPTER 1

The Jews of Romania: An Historical Overview

THE INTERWAR PERIOD, 1918–1939

Anti-Semitism has been an essential ingredient in Romania's political and popular culture since the mid-nineteenth century.[1] The nationalist movement forged during the drive for the unification of the Romanian principalities of Wallachia and Moldavia (1859) and the subsequent struggle for the attainment of national independence (1878) was guided by an ideology that included anti-Semitism and xenophobia among its basic elements.[2] Exploiting the trauma caused by centuries of foreign domination, Romanian nationalists continued to cling to these ideological tenets even after they had achieved their ultimate objective: the creation of Greater Romania (*România Mare*) in 1918.[3]

---

[1] The pre-World War I contrast between Hungary and Romania on the treatment of the Jews is startling. Whereas the Jews of Hungary enjoyed a "Golden Era" between 1867 (the year of their emancipation) and 1918, those of Romania were subjected during the same period to no less than 196 anti-Jewish acts. See Radu Ioanid, "Romania," in *The World Reacts to the Holocaust* (Baltimore: The Johns Hopkins Press, 1996), p. 229. (Cited hereafter as Ioanid, "Romania.")

[2] For some details on the characteristics of Romanian nationalism, see Leon Volovici, *Nationalist Ideology and Antisemitism: The Case of Romanian Intellectuals in the 1930s* (Oxford: Pergamon Press, 1991).

[3] Following the disintegration of the Austro-Hungarian and Romanov empires, Romania acquired—and retained under the postwar treaties—Bessarabia from Russia, Bukovina from Austria, parts of Dobrudja from Bulgaria, and Transylvania from Hungary.

9

The tradition of anti-Semitism and the generally xenophobic policies of successive Romanian governments induced the Great Powers to impose certain domestic and international legal obligations on Romania. This was the case at the Congress of Berlin in 1878 and at Versailles following the end of World War I. Under the provisions of the Peace Treaties and of the Minorities Treaty of 1920, Romania agreed to assure full and complete protection of life and liberty to all its inhabitants regardless of their origin, race, language, or religion. These obligations were duly incorporated in the Constitution of 1923 under which the Jews and the other minorities in the new multinational state were assured full civil rights and liberties. Although the protection of these rights was made a responsibility of the League of Nations, its implementation was rather *pro forma*. Chauvinistic nationalists consistently maintained that the obligations imposed under the constitution and the international treaties were an infringement on the national sovereignty of Romania. Guided by ever changing perceptions of national interests, which were often determined by both domestic and international pressures, successive Romanian governments followed an inconsistent policy toward the Jews.

As a result of the territorial acquisitions, census figures indicate that Romania's Jewish population increased from around 365,000 before 1918 to 760,000 or 4.3 percent of the total by 1930.[4] In the absence of a liberal tradition of tolerance, pluralism, and respect for minority rights, the provisions of the constitution, like those of the international treaties, were gradually eroded. With no genuine roots, the institutions of democracy transplanted from the West had no chance to succeed. They could not with-

---

[4] For an overview of the background and characteristics of the Jewish community, see Raphael Vago, "Romanian Jewry During the Interwar Period," in *The Tragedy of Romanian Jewry*, Randolph L. Braham, ed. (New York: The Rosenthal Institute for Holocaust Studies of the City University of New York, 1994), pp. 29–56. (The volume is cited hereafter as Braham, *Tragedy*.)

stand the pressures caused by the great economic crises and political upheavals that swept across Europe during the 1930s. Romania gradually abandoned the pretenses of democracy and, responding to both domestic and foreign Right radical influences, adopted increasingly authoritarian positions. Following the victory of the Nazis in Germany, the political climate of the country changed dramatically. While in foreign affairs Romania continued to rely on the Western democracies and the Little Entente for the protection of its territorial integrity, in domestic policies it gradually yielded to the pressures of the radical Right. The Jewish question was brought to the forefront of Romanian politics, especially after the formation of two virulently anti-Semitic Fascist movements—the League of National Christian Defense (*Liga Apărării Național Creștine*) and the Iron Guard (*Garda de Fier*). The latter emerged in 1927 as the political arm of the Legion of Archangel Michael (*Legiunea Arhanghelului Mihail*), an offshoot of the League founded and led by Corneliu Z. Codreanu, a notorious anti-Semite.[5]

Xenophobic nationalists exploited the socioeconomic dislocations caused by the depression and reinforced their traditional anti-Semitic ideology with new racial elements. By the end of 1937, they managed to bring about the establishment of the first openly anti-Semitic government. Led by Octavian Goga, a well-known poet,[6] and Alexandru C. Cuza,[7] a highly regarded historian

---

5 For some details on these and other Fascist political movements and parties, see Radu Ioanid, *The Sword of the Archangel. Fascist Ideology in Romania* (Denver: East European Monographs, 1990). See also Z. Ornea, *Anii treizeci. Extrema dreaptă românească* (The Thirties. The Romanian Extreme Right) (Bucharest: Editura Fundației Culturale Române, 1995), and Leon Volovici, op. cit.

6 A rabid anti-Semite, Goga urged that the Jews of Europe be "resettled" in Madagascar as early as 1938. In 1987, Mircea Mușat, the chief ideologue of the Ceaușescu regime, expressed his admiration for Goga, foreshadowing his full rehabilitation a short while thereafter. Ioanid, "Romania," p. 230.

7 Mușat also called for the cultural rehabilitation of Cuza. Ibid., p. 238.

associated with the University of Jassy (Iaşi), this short-lived government adopted a series of anti-Jewish laws, depriving, among other things, tens of thousands of Jews of their citizenship.[8] The anti-Semitic trend continued after the replacement of this government by King Carol II's personal dictatorship in February 1938. Influenced by the Nazis, the government of Ion Gigurtu was responsible for the adoption of many other anti-Jewish laws, including the so-called Statute of the Jews (August 8, 1940), the Nazi-type racial law under which Jews, including some categories of baptized ones, were prohibited from entering into mixed marriages.[9]

THE ANTONESCU ERA

The Anti-Jewish Drive. The situation of the Jews changed drastically for the worse in the summer of 1940. With the disintegration of the Little Entente following the dismemberment of Czechoslovakia in March 1939 and the collapse of France in June 1940, Romania's international security system collapsed. It had no alternative but to yield to a Soviet ultimatum of June 26, 1940, under which it surrendered Bessarabia and Northern Bukovina. (The ultimatum was based on the terms of a secret protocol attached to the Hitler-Stalin Pact of August 23, 1939.) Two months later, Romania had to agree to the transfer of Northern Transylvania to Hungary in accord with the Axis-imposed Vienna arbitration of August 30. On September 7, it had to return Southern Dobrudja to Bulgaria.

---

[8] Royal Decree No. 169 enacted under King Carol's signature on January 21, 1938. According to some sources, approximately 120,000 Jews had lost their citizenship as a result of the decree. Raul Hilberg, *The Destruction of the European Jews* (Chicago: Quadrangle Books, 1961), p. 487. (Cited hereafter as Hilberg, *Destruction*.)

[9] For an overview of the racial legislative record of Romania, see *Martiriul evreilor din România* (The Martyrdom of the Jews of Romania) (Bucharest: Hasefer, 1991), pp. 1–21. (Cited hereafter as *Martiriul*.)

Romanian anti-Semites, including elements of the Romanian army, vented their anger against the Jews, blaming them for their national misfortunes. Joined by Iron Guard zealots, soldiers and gendarmes expressed their frustrations by killing Jews, especially in the territories yielded to the Soviet Union. They rationalized their involvement in mass murder by identifying the victims as Communists or pro-Soviet sympathizers.[10] By far the greatest massacre during this period occurred in Dorohoi (June 30, 1940).[11]

Following the forced abdication of King Carol on September 6, 1940, power gradually shifted to General (later Marshal) Ion Antonescu. Enjoying the support of the Iron Guard, he immediately replaced the royal dictatorship by a National Legionary State (*Stat Naţional Legionar*). The alliance between the two forces of Romanian Fascism proved shortlived. The anti-Semitic measures adopted during the brief Fascist coalition era[12] were overshadowed by the murderous campaign the Iron Guardists waged against the Jews during their rebellion of January 21–23, 1941. Led by Horia Sima, the guardists rose in an attempt to overthrow General Antonescu. Crushed by the army, which remained loyal to the General, the leaders of the Iron Guard found refuge in the Third

[10] The idea that elements of the Romanian army and gendarmerie killed Jews in self-defense is accepted by many Romanians, nationalists and "moderates" alike. For a typical explanation, see Constantin Hlihor, "Calvarul retragerii armatei române din Basarabia şi Bucovina de Nord" (The Calvary of the Romanian Army's Withdrawal From Bessarabia and Northern Bukovina), *Revista de Istorie Militară* (Review of Military History), Bucharest, no. 1 (12) 1992, pp. 13–17.
[11] For some details, see Radu Ioanid, "The Antonescu Era" in Braham, *Tragedy*, pp. 121–122. (Cited hereafter as Ioanid, "The Antonescu Era.") See also *Martiriul*, pp. 25–39.
[12] Between September 11, 1940, and January 21, 1941, the National Legionary State passed 41 anti-Jewish racial decrees and ministerial decisions. For some details, see Eduard Mezincescu, *Mareşalul Antonescu şi catastrofa României* (Marshal Antonescu and the Catastrophe of Romania) (Bucharest: Editura Artemia, 1993), p. 17. See also *Legislaţia antievreiască* (Anti-Jewish Legislation), Lya Benjamin, ed. (Bucharest: Hasefer, 1993). *Evreii din România între anii 1940–1944* (The Jews of Romania Between 1940–1944), vol. 1. (Cited hereafter as Benjamin, *Legislaţia*.)

Reich. Though sympathizing with the ideological purity of the guardists, the Germans preferred the stability offered by the General to the chaos that would have ensued from Sima's victory. They were, above all, interested in the smooth and uninterrupted supply of Romanian resources, including the oil that fueled their war machine.[13] During their reign of terror, the Iron Guardists set synagogues afire and destroyed or looted Jewish-owned enterprises. They murdered more than one hundred Jews in and around Bucharest alone, hanging many of the victims in municipal slaughterhouses like carcasses of cattle. The savagery of the Iron Guardists shocked even many of the Germans who had witnessed their rampage.[14] After the crushing of the rebellion, Romania was transformed for all practical purposes into a *Führer* state, with Antonescu wielding dictatorial powers as *Conducător* (Leader).

During the interim between the crushing of the Iron Guard and the launching of the anti-Soviet war on June 22, 1941, the Antonescu regime continued its anti-Jewish policies by adopting a new series of laws aiming, among other things, at the Romanianization of the economy, i.e., the confiscation of Jewish wealth. The instigator of many of the anti-Jewish measures was Radu Lecca, Antonescu's Commissar for Jewish Affairs (*Împuternicitul Guvernului Pentru Reglementarea Regimului Evreilor din România*), who acted in close cooperation with *SS-Sturmbannführer* Gustav Richter, the SS expert on the Jewish question in the German Legation in Bucharest.

Concurrently with the virtual expropriation of the Jews, the Antonescu regime also launched an ethnic cleansing campaign

---

[13] For some details on the Germans' attitude, see Ioanid, "The Antonescu Era," pp. 122–123.

[14] For details, see Matatias Carp, *Cartea neagră. Suferinţele evreilor din România, 1940–1944* (Black Book. The Suffering of the Jews of Romania, 1940–1944), vol. 1. *Legionarii şi rebeliunea* (The Legionnaires and the Rebellion), 2d ed. (Bucharest: Editura Diogene, 1996). See also Hilberg, *Destruction*, p. 489. For some additional details, see *Martiriul*, pp. 41–83, and Ioanid, "The Antonescu Era," pp. 124–130.

aimed at the "dejewification" of the country. Eager as he was to bring about the ethnic purification of Romania, Marshal Antonescu could not act unilaterally during the Hitler-Stalin pact period. He expressed his ideas on this issue at the Council of Ministers' meeting of February 7, 1941:

> If these had been normal times, I would have proceeded to a mass expulsion of all Jewish elements, i.e., by banishing them over the borders.... But this is a problem the Romanian nation cannot resolve alone, as it has continental and intercontinental ramifications; so we shall see how this problem can be resolved in time.[15]

Until the arrival of the opportune time for the physical "solution" of the Jewish question, the Marshal sought to prepare the psychological ground for the operation. He amplified on these sentiments at the Council of Ministers meeting of April 8, 1941:

> We have to inspire the Romanians with hatred against the enemies of the nation. This is how I grew up, with hatred against the Turks, the kikes, and the Hungarians. This sentiment of hatred against the enemies of the nation must be pushed to the ultimate extreme. I take responsibility for this.[16]

[15] Lya Benjamin, "Anti-Semitism as Reflected in the Records of the Council of Ministers, 1940–1944," in *The Destruction of Romanian and Ukrainian Jews During the Antonescu Era*, Randolph L. Braham, ed. (New York: The Rosenthal Institute for Holocaust Studies of the City University of New York, 1997), pp. 1–18. (Cited hereafter as Benjamin, *Anti-Semitism*; the volume is cited hereafter as Braham, *Destruction*.) For the complete text of the minutes, see Doc. 92 in Benjamin, *Legislația*.

[16] Cabinet Meetings, Dossier 474/1941, File 65 as quoted by Chief Rabbi Rosen in his TV talk of February 3, 1994. For text, see *Revista Cultului Mozaic* (Review of the Jewish Religion), Bucharest, February 8, 1994.

The opportune time came after Antonescu's meeting with Hitler in Munich on June 12, 1941. The Marshal, who enjoyed the confidence of the Führer, was informed about the impending attack on the Soviet Union. The Romanians immediately began to plan not only for the reacquisition of the lost territories, but also for the incorporation of Transnistria, the area between the Bug and the Dniester. Their plan also called for the ethnic purification of all the territories to be conquered. These sentiments for ethnic cleansing were forcefully expressed by Deputy Prime Minister Mihai Antonescu (not related to the Marshal) during the Council of Ministers meeting of June 17, 1941. Talking about the issues relating to the organization and administration of the territories to be acquired, Mihai Antonescu emphasized that the greatest problem involved their inhabitants. He said:

> What I can tell you is that the Romanian nation, having arrived at this historical moment, which I don't think will again come across in centuries, must use this hour to cleanse the population.... As to the ethnic populations, let me assure you that it is not just the Jews but all the ethnic minorities — we shall apply a policy of full and violent removal of the foreign elements.[17]

The opportunity for the implementation of an indigenous version of the Final Solution program came with the launching of the war against the Soviet Union five days later. Romania provided the second largest army to fight alongside the Nazi forces all the way to Stalingrad, where it was virtually destroyed in January 1943.

[17] Benjamin, *Anti-Semitism*. For the minutes of the Council meeting, see Doc. 93 in *Problema evreiască în stenogramele Consiliului de Miniştri* (The Jewish Question in the Minutes of the Council of Ministers), Lya Benjamin, ed. (Bucharest: Hasefer, 1996). (*Evreii din România între anii 1940–1944*, vol. 2.) (Cited hereafter as Benjamin, *Problema*.)

Flushed by their early military successes and driven by feelings of revenge, Romanian Fascists, as well as many army and gendarmerie units, vented their hatred by killing thousands of Jews along the invasion routes. Occasionally these units acted in concert with the *SS-Einsatzgruppen*, the German mobile killing units, decimating the Jewish populations of the liberated cities and villages. In many cases the Romanians outdid the Germans in their brutality. The brunt of the Romanians' fury was felt by the Jews of the reconquered territories and the areas of the Ukraine occupied by the Romanian army. They committed particularly odious massacres in Bălți, Cernăuți (Czernowitz), and Chișinău (Kishinev).[18]

During the early phase of the war, atrocities were also committed in some of the communities of Old (i.e., pre–1918) Romania. By far the most heinous crimes were committed in Jassy, where many thousands of Jews were killed during the pogrom of June 29–30, 1941, the estimates ranging from 4,000 to 8,000. Thousands of Jews died in two sealed freight trains that were moved aimlessly for days on end for genocidal purposes. One of the first major massacres of the Holocaust era, the drive against the Jews of Jassy and its environs, was carried out on the excuse that the Jews had possessed arms and shot at the Romanian and German soldiers.[19] That the accusation was unfounded had been confirmed by the Romanian officers ordered to investigate the "disturbances." In his memorandum of July 2, 1941, addressed to Marshal Antonescu, General Emanoil Leoveanu, Director General of the Police, reported:

[18] For some details, see Hilberg, *Destruction*, pp. 199–200. See also Paul A. Shapiro, "The Jews of Kishinev (Chișinău): Soviet Withdrawal and Romanian Reoccupation," in Braham, *Destruction*, pp. 135–192.

[19] For details on the pogrom, see Carp, *Cartea neagră* (Black Book), vol. 2: *Pogromul de la Iași* (The Jassy Pogrom), 2d ed. (Bucharest: Editura Diogene, 1996). For a gripping eyewitness account, see Curzio Malaparte, *Kaputt* (New York: E. P. Dutton, 1946). See also Radu Florian, "The Jassy Pogrom," in Braham, *Destruction*, pp. 63–84.

...We have found no weapons and we have discovered no foreign fighters.... There was not a single casualty among the Romanian units which were fired on, and no traces of bullets on the walls of the houses, not even a window broken ... nor did the Germans experience any dead or wounded; the attack was thus a sham carried out with the aid of stage pieces [blanks fired from this kind of replica weapon were found on the ground] and of firecrackers which imitated the sound of automatic weapons.[20]

The massacres were perpetrated by local Romanian army and police units, acting in conjunction with elements of the Gestapo stationed in Jassy.[21]

There is no doubt that a number of Jews sympathized with the Soviet Union, naively believing that it was a country that had solved the problem of anti-Semitism along with all other ethnic-national and religious conflicts. Impoverished and subjected to discrimination, they suffered the social and economic consequences of the endemic anti-Semitism that characterized the area under the Romanians. Most of these Jews, moreover, were unaware of the realities of Stalinism and its own brand of anti-Semitism. But they were not alone in their sympathy for the USSR. As the many books of the early Communist era testify, there were tens of thousands of ethnic Romanians who had collaborated with the Soviets during that same time for ideological or opportunistic reasons. According to documentary evidence submitted to Marshal Antonescu, there were at least 40,000 such ethnic-Romanian pro-Soviet collaborators. Yet, even though the Antonescu authorities could not provide any specific proofs about Jewish involvement in the killing of Romanian forces during their

[20] Carp, op. cit., Doc. 45, pp. 118–122.
[21] Ibid., Doc. 14, pp. 61–62. For further details, see also *Martiriul*, pp. 85–136, and Ioanid, "The Antonescu Era," pp. 131–144, 153–157.

withdrawal from Northern Bukovina and Bessarabia, the virulently anti-Semitic perpetrators, acting on unfounded rumors, vented
their rage only against the innocent Jews. With respect to the ethnic Romanian collaborators, Antonescu followed the approach he
had earlier used against the Legionnaires who had revolted against
him in January 1941: he pardoned them.[22]

The Jassy pogrom was just the prelude to the systematic
"Romanian solution" of the Jewish problem in the reacquired and
conquered territories. The design to cleanse these areas of all
"alien" elements was revealed by Mihai Antonescu during the
July 8, 1941, meeting of the Council of Ministers:

> At the risk of not being understood by some of the tradi-
> tionalists that may still be among you, I am for the forced
> migration of the entire Jewish element from Bukovina
> and Bessarabia, which must be hurled across the border.
> I am also for the forced migration of the Ukrainian ele-
> ment, which has no business being here at this time....I
> am indifferent if we will be identified in history as bar-
> barians....I don't know in how many centuries will the
> Romanian nation once again have the total freedom of
> action, the possibility for ethnic purification and national
> revision, which were thwarted through many centuries by
> a series of infiltrations.[23]

The ethnic purification of the conquered territories proceeded
at a fast and bloody pace. The atrocities committed by the Romanian
army and gendarmerie units within Romanian territory were
exceeded only by those perpetrated in the "liberated" parts of
Ukraine. Antonescu's frustrations over the failure of the Romanian
army to advance toward Odessa as quickly as originally planned

---

[22] See Chief Rabbi Rosen's February 3, 1994 talk cited in footnote 16.
[23] Document 99 in Benjamin, *Problema*, p. 266. See also *Martiriul*, pp. 140–141.

were vented on the Jews. In a directive of September 5, 1941, addressed to Mihai Antonescu, the Marshal attributed the resistance of the "Slavs" and the delay in the capture of Odessa to the power wielded by Jewish Commissars in the Soviet armed forces. He called for the internment of Jews, concluding that the war was being fought against the Jews and not the Slavic peoples. Borrowing a term from Hitler, he called the Jew the real Satan with whom the Romanians were involved in a life and death struggle.[24]

Convinced of the ultimate victory of the Axis,[25] the Antonescu regime became eager to "solve" the Jewish problem independently, i.e., without the direct involvement of the Germans. General Antonescu was reportedly informed by Hitler about the impending "solution of the Jewish question in the East" during their meeting of June 12, 1941. On September 15, 1941, Antonescu ordered that the close to 150,000 surviving "alien" Jews of Northern Bukovina and Bessarabia be transferred to Transnistria, the Romanian-occupied part of the Ukraine between the Dniester and the Bug. The well-planned and effectively organized mass deportation began in the fall of that year, i.e., well before the Final Solution program was worked out at the Wannsee Conference (January 20, 1942), and continued through the spring and summer of 1942. According to some sources, at their peak the various concentration camps established in Transnistria contained approximately 185,000 Romanian and Ukrainian Jews. Except for approximately 10,000 Jews who were "mistakenly" picked up in Dorohoi County in Old Romania, the deportees were almost all from Bessarabia, Northern Bukovina, and the Herta Region.

---

[24] The handwritten directive and its transcript may be found in the Archives of the United States Holocaust Memorial Museum, Washington, Reel 19. Record Group 25.002 M, Council of Ministers Fond, Romanian State Archives.

[25] For some details on Antonescu's pro-Axis and pro-Nazi activities, see Radu Florian, "The Antonescu Regime: History and Mystification," in Braham, *Tragedy*, pp. 77–116.

Life in many of the concentration camps of Transnistria was not basically different from that endured by the Jews in many other parts of Nazi-occupied Europe. Aside from periodic executions, thousands upon thousand of Jews died of hunger and disease.[26]

At the Council of Ministers meeting of October 6, 1941, Marshal Antonescu provided the following racially based explanation for his anti-Jewish drive:

As for the Jews I have taken steps to remove them for good and completely from these regions.... Unless we use the opportunity given us nationally and internationally to cleanse the Romanian nation, we shall miss the last chance history provides. I can bring Bessarabia back and Transylvania, but I will have achieved nothing unless I cleanse the Romanian Nation. Because the borders do not make the strength of a nation, but the homogeneity and purity of its race. This has been my paramount goal.[27]

The goal was also extended to the Ukrainian territories occupied by the Romanian forces. Acting in conjunction with pro-Nazi

[26] For some details on the ordeal of Jews in Transnistria, consult Carp, *Cartea neagră*, vol. 3, *Transnistria*, 2d ed. (Bucharest: Editura Diogene, 1996). See also *Martiriul*, pp. 137–244; Ioanid, "The Antonescu Era," pp. 146–152, 157–160; Avigdor Shachan, *Burning Ice. The Ghettos of Transnistria* (Boulder: Social Science Monographs, 1996); and Jean Ancel, "The Romanian Way of Solving 'the Jewish Problem' in Bessarabia and Bukovina, June–July 1941," in *Yad Vashem Studies*, vol. 19 (Jerusalem: Yad Vashem, 1988), pp. 187–232. See also *Documents Concerning the Fate of Romanian Jewry During the Holocaust*, Jean Ancel, comp. and ed. (New York: The Beate Klarsfeld Foundation, 1986–1987), 12 vols.

[27] Benjamin, *Anti-Semitism*. For the minutes of the Council meeting, see Doc. 113 in Benjamin, *Problema*. See also Ioanid, "The Antonescu Era," pp. 146–149. For a detailed account documenting Marshal Antonescu's personal responsibility for the mass murder of Jews, see Jean Ancel, "The Romanian Campaigns of Mass Murder in Transnistria, 1941–1942," in Braham, *Destruction*, pp. 87–133.

Ukrainian volunteers and *SS-Einsatzgruppen* units, the Romanians murdered a large number of Jews in the "liberated" areas as well. By far the greatest massacre perpetrated by the Romanian occupation forces was in Odessa. The calvary of the Jews of Odessa began shortly after Soviet partisans blew up the Romanian army's headquarters in the city on October 22. The reprisals ordered by Antonescu[28] resulted in the mass murder of close to 60,000 Jews, including all the Bessarabian Jews found in the city. In Dalnic, a suburb of the city, between 25,000 and 30,000 Jews were shot or burned alive on October 23 and 24.[29]

At the Council of Ministers meeting of November 13, 1941, Antonescu assumed personal responsibility for the massacres perpetrated in Odessa. After learning from Gheorghe Alexianu, the Governor of Transnistria, that his reprisal orders had been carried out, the Marshal stated:

> I am responsible before the country and history. Let the Jews of America come and hold me responsible!... The Jews must not be spared.... Don't think they will not take revenge when given the opportunity. But, in order to leave no one to take revenge, I shall finish them first. And I do not do this for myself, but for the people of this country.[30]

[28] Marshal Antonescu's order called for the execution of 200 Jews for each Romanian who died in the blast and 100 Jews for each wounded Romanian. The order was transmitted by Col. Radu Davidescu on September 24, 1941, with the instruction that it be destroyed after reading. Three days later, a top officer of the Romanian Fourth Army informed Antonescu's office that the "order was carried out as instructed." See Record Group 25000M, Reel 12, Archives of the U.S. Holocaust Memorial Museum. The documents originated from Romanian Ministry of National Defense, Fourth Army Fond.

[29] Ioanid, "The Antonescu Era," p. 150. See also Hilberg, *Destruction*, p. 201 (2d ed. New York: Holmes & Meier, 1985, vol. 1, pp. 306–307), and Ioanid "Romania," pp. 233–234. According to Dora Litani, Romanian units massacred between 60,000 to 80,000 Jews in Odessa. See her "The Destruction of the Jews of Odessa in the Light of Romanian Documents," in *Yad Vashem Studies*, vol. 6 (Jerusalem: Yad Vashem, 1967), pp. 135–154.

[30] Doc. 118 in Benjamin, *Problema*. See also Benjamin, *Anti-Semitism*.

Romanian army and gendarmerie units were also involved in many other mobile killing operations, often acting in conjunction with the *Einsatzkommandos* of *Einsatzgruppe D* and Ukrainian hirelings. During the first phase of the military operations, these units killed approximately 160,000 Jews.

Acceptance and Rejection of the Final Solution. The Germans were aware that the ultimate objective of the mass resettlement of the Jews from the eastern parts of Romania was their eventual liquidation.[31] While visibly delighted with the Romanians' anti-Jewish initiatives, the Germans were quite concerned about the anarchic and unsystematic approach the Antonescu regime was following in the "solution" of the Jewish question. The Romanian system for murdering Jews was criticized, among others, by officers of *Einsatzgruppe D*:

> The way in which the Romanians are dealing with the Jews lacks any method. No objections could be raised against the numerous executions of Jews, but the technical preparations and the executions themselves were totally inadequate. The Romanians usually left the victims' bodies where they were shot—without trying to bury them. The Einsatzkommandos issued instructions to the Romanian police to proceed somewhat more systematically in this matter.[32]

Shortly after the end of the Wannsee Conference, they approached Romania to get involved in the European-wide Final Solution program. While the Antonescu regime eventually aban-

[31] See, for example, Gustav Richter's memorandum of October 17, 1941, in Hilberg, *Destruction*, p. 493. See also Jean Ancel, "German-Romanian Relations During the Second World War," in Braham, *Tragedy*, pp. 57–76.
[32] Nuremberg Document NO–2651 as quoted by Ancel, "The Romanian Campaigns of Mass Murder in Transnistria," op. cit.

doned most of its Jewish nationals living in the German sphere of influence, allowing them to be subjected to the anti-Jewish drive in accord with the consent given by Deputy Prime Minister and Foreign Minister Mihai Antonescu in November 1941,[33] it ultimately decided to retain its sovereignty over the solution of the Jewish question at home.

For a short while at least, the Romanian plan for this "solution" also called for the possible "resettlement" of the Jews of Old Romania across the Dniester[34] concurrently with the deportation of those of Southern Transylvania to German-controlled concentration camps. In mid-1942 the Germans were still convinced that the Romanians were ready to go along with the Nazi approach. According to a communication from Martin Luther, the head of the *Inland II* section of the German Foreign Office, addressed to his superiors on August 17, 1942, both Marshal Antonescu and Mihai Antonescu had given their consent to the implementation of the Final Solution. Shortly thereafter, Lecca visited Berlin to discuss details, but was apparently snubbed by Luther and others. Already in possession of the consent by the two Antonescus, these top-ranking officials of the Foreign Office were not too enthusiastic about meeting a lower-rank Romanian official.[35]

Mihai Antonescu acknowledged his and the Marshal's involvement in the general deportation plans at the Council of Ministers meeting of September 29, 1942. Expressing his bewilderment over the "spread of rumors" to this effect, he stated:

> At a certain point, the issue of sending some Jews from our country elsewhere was discussed. Nobody except the Marshal, me, and a liaison with the Reich's government

---

[33] For some details on this issue, see Radu Ioanid, "The Fate of Romanian Jews in Nazi-Dominated Europe During World War II," in Braham, *Destruction*, pp. 217–236.

[34] Hilberg, *Destruction*, p. 498.

[35] Ibid., p. 501.

had known about this. Only three lines were written, very vague, and the only one to know about this problem was somebody in the German SS.[36]

Changing Course. The Nazis were under the impression that, in accord with the agreement signed by Mihai Antonescu in August 1942, the Romanians would begin the first phase of the general deportation program on September 10, 1942. The plan called for the roundup of the Jews in Arad, Timişoara, and Turda—three major Hungarian-speaking Jewish centers in Southern Transylvania—during the first phase of the operation.[37] To the great dismay of the Germans, however, the Romanians changed their minds about the Final Solution program shortly after they had given their consent. The Antonescu regime, moreover, decided to halt the further deportations to Transnistria as well. Mihai Antonescu at the Council of Ministers meeting of October 13, 1942, explained the change in policy:

Lately a whole lot of discontent arose and especially a very unfavorable atmosphere was created in connection with the treatment of the Jews.... I am not a philosemite ...but because of the international situation and the fact that the Jews elsewhere are treated differently than in Romania ... we must not create a situation to look as if it is all the same to us if, on the level of civilizing measures, the Romanian government contributes to the prestige of the Army or, on the contrary, works against it.... We must examine Romanian economic positions and

---

[36] See Doc. 145 in Benjamin, *Problema.* See also Benjamin, *Anti-Semitism.*
[37] The plans for the deportation of the Romanian Jews were revealed, *inter alia*, in two Reich Security Main Office (*Reichssicherheitshauptamt*—RSHA) documents dated July 26, 1942. See Jean Ancel, "Plans for Deportation of the Rumanian Jews and Their Discontinuation in Light of Documentary Evidence (July–October 1941," in *Yad Vashem Studies*, vol. 16 (Jerusalem: Yad Vashem, 1984), pp. 381–420.

realities.... I do not undertake an anti-Semitic reform for
the Germans ... whatever European threat Jewish communism or Judaic ideology might still represent. I am interested in Romanian nationalism.... From our anti-Semitic
reform we must also produce a creative reform.... For the
time being, all transfers of Jews across the Dniester are
suspended.[38]

The change in the handling of the Jewish question was motivated neither by philosemitism nor a sudden commitment to pluralism or tolerance, but instead by a variety of personal, domestic,
and international considerations. While the alleged snubbing of
Radu Lecca during his visit to Berlin and the reported illness of
Marshal Antonescu (he suffered from syphilis) may have played a
role, the determing factor was the gradually changing perception
of the military fortunes of the Axis. The Romanian leaders also
came to understand that, their enthusiastic involvement in the anti-
Soviet war notwithstanding, the Third Reich would not cooperate
in the reacquisition of Northern Transylvania and was primarily
interested in the exploitation of Romania's economic and military
resources. Moreover, by abandoning the deportation plans and
changing course on the handling of the Jewish question, the
Romanian leaders undoubtedly also sought to advance Romania's
economic interests, acquire a new image abroad, ingratiate themselves with the Allies, and accumulate a record of goodwill to save
themselves.[39]

The crushing of the German and Romanian armies at
Stalingrad early in 1943, induced the Antonescu regime to radically change its policies toward the Jews. The Romanian authorities gradually eased the lot of the surviving Jews of Transnistria

[38] Doc. 147 in Benjamin, *Problema*. See also Benjamin, *Anti-Semitism*.
[39] See Ancel's "Plans for Deportation of the Romanian Jews...," op. cit. See also
Ioanid, "The Antonescu Era," pp. 160–162.

and, with the rapid approach of the Soviet forces, initiated plans to repatriate many of them. The Jews of Old Romania and Southern Transylvania fared even better. Although they were subjected to great economic hardship and deprived of many of their basic civil rights and liberties, around 90 percent of them survived the war.

The Romanian authorities became increasingly interested in schemes for Jewish emigration to Palestine—schemes that not only helped the affected Jews but also generated considerable income for the Romanians and contributed to their ideological objectives of ridding the country of its Jews. The latter objective was admitted by Mihai Antonescu during the Council of Ministers meeting of July 2, 1942:

> I am in agreement if the Romanian state can undertake an emigration policy that would remove from the country as many foreign elements as possible. It is all the same to me if these elements are taken beyond the Bug, in Transnistria, or beyond the Mediterranean to Palestine; the essential thing is that these elements leave our territory.[40]

The economic and foreign political objectives of the Romanian leaders in changing their policies on the Jewish question was also noted by the Germans. On December 12, 1942, Manfred von Killinger, the German Minister in Bucharest, reported to the German Foreign Office that, according to Lecca, Marshal Antonescu was ready to allow 75,000 to 80,000 Jews to emigrate to Palestine in return for a payment by the Jews of 200,000 lei (approximately $1,336.00) per emigrant. According to Killinger, Antonescu was eager to collect 16 billion lei ($107 million) for the Romanian State,

---

[40] Doc. 139 in Benjamin, *Problema*. See also Benjamin, *Anti-Semitism*, and Dalia Ofer, "Immigration and Emigration: The Changing Role of Romanian Jewry," in Braham, *Destruction*, pp. 19–43.

and get rid of a large number of Jews "in a comfortable manner."

Realizing that the Axis would lose the war, Marshal Antonescu became increasingly concerned with the postwar consequences of his policies. The inveterate anti-Semite that he was, Antonescu accepted the Nazi thesis about the Jews' leading role in both Soviet Bolshevism and Western capitalism. At the Council of Ministers meeting of April 20, 1943, discussing, among other things, the Jews' responsibility for the economic and financial difficulties of the country, the Marshal stated:

> One of the most radical [solution] would be for me to take all Jews and send them across the border. But we are a small country, not a big country like Germany. I am fighting to win the war, but it may happen that the democracies will win it. And we know what democracy means; it means Judeocracy. So, why should I expose the future generations of the nation to being punished for my decision to get the Jews out of the country?[41]

The German Foreign Office and the Reich Security Main Office (*Reichssicherheitshauptamt*), Heinrich Himmler's agency, were fully informed about the change in Romania's handling of the Jewish question and did everything in their power to bring about a reversal of the course, but to no avail. On January 14, 1943, Heinrich Müller, the head of the Gestapo, assessed the situation in Romania very pessimistically. Six days later, Himmler himself concluded that nothing else could be done in Romania and suggested the recall of Gustav Richter from Bucharest.[42]

---

[41] Doc. 166 in Benjamin, *Problema*. See also Benjamin, *Anti-Semitism*.

[42] For some details see Randolph L. Braham, *The Politics of Genocide. The Holocaust in Hungary* (New York: The Rosenthal Institute for Holocaust Studies of the City University of New York, 1994), pp. 1037–1048. (Cited hereafter as Braham, *Politics*.) See also Jean Ancel, "German-Romanian Relations During the Second World War," op. cit.

By the spring of 1944, when various Romanian political and military figures were actively seeking an effective and reasonably quick way out of the Axis Alliance, Romania also became a haven to many Jewish refugees from neighboring countries, especially Hungary.

The ordeal of the surviving Jews of Romania came to an end on August 23, 1944, when Romania managed to extricate itself from the Axis and fought for the remainder of the war on the side of the Allies. The losses of Romanian Jewry were enormous even though Romania rejected the German-style "solution" of the Jewish question by refusing to deport any of its Jewish nationals to Auschwitz or any other German-controlled extermination camp. According to most reliable accounts, the Antonescu regime was responsible for the murder of close to 270,000 Romanian and Ukrainian Jews.[43]

Romania as a Haven for Hungarian Jews. After the German occupation of Hungary on March 19, 1944, and the ensuing implementation of the Final Solution program,[44] Romania (and for a while Slovakia) emerged as a potential place of refuge. The Germans were fully aware of this possible avenue of escape and, on March 30, alerted all their agencies to be on guard to prevent the "illegal flight" of Hungarian Jews.[45] Concurrently, they also launched a campaign to persuade the Romanians to take effective countermeasures. The Antonescu government complied on May 29 by adopting a stiff law that mandated the death penalty for Jews entering the country fraudulently and for those aiding them.[46]

---

[43] For further details, see Radu Florian, "The Antonescu Regime: History and Mystification," in Braham, *Tragedy*, pp. 100–111; Ioanid, "The Antonescu Era," pp. 117–171; and Hilberg, *Destruction*, pp. 485–509.

[44] For details on the destruction on Hungarian Jewry, see Braham, *Politics*.

[45] Documents dated April 20, 1944, from the files of Gustav Richter (Roll 3, vol. 18), in possession of this author.

[46] *Monitorul Oficial* (Official Gazette) (Bucharest), May 29, 1944. On June 6, Richter informed the SIPO and SD leader in Berlin about the enacment of this law. Richter Files.

However, at that stage of the war, the Romanians, with a few exceptions, continued to treat incoming refugees with a considerable degree of indulgence. According to a report addressed to the U.S. Secretary of State by Leland Harrison, the American Minister in Bern, the Romanians had in fact issued confidential instructions to their border authorities to facilitate the admission of Jewish refugees from Hungary.[47]

The historical record on Marshal Antonescu's attitude toward the incoming Hungarian Jewish refugees is not clear. According to the postwar nationalists interested in the rehabilitation of the Marshal and his pro-Nazi regime, the Marshal, his orders notwithstanding, tolerated their entry into Romania and provided refuge for them. According to Lecca, however, the Marshal was not even aware of the presence of Hungarian Jewish refugees in the country. Had he been, the former Commissar on Jewish Affairs emphasized, Antonescu "would have given the order to shoot them [in accordance with the law then in effect] in order...to prevent other Hungarian Jews from trying their luck in Romania."[48]

The change in Romania's attitude toward the refugees is reflected in the June 2, 1944 communication by Mihai Antonescu to the Romanian delegate to the International Red Cross that he might give formal assurances that Jewish refugees from Hungary would be allowed to enter the country notwithstanding formal declarations to the contrary, and that "their safety would be looked out for by the Romanians."[49] The Romanians' level of tolerance continued to increase until August 23, when Romania extricated itself

---

[47] See his Telegram 3867 dated June 17, 1944.

[48] See his *Eu i-am salvat pe evreii din România* (I Saved the Jews of Romania) (Bucharest: Roza Vânturilor, 1994), p. 289. On the background and character of the publication, see Lya Benjamin, "Radu Lecca şi salvarea evreilor din România" (Radu Lecca and the Saving of the Jews of Romania), *Revista Cultului Mozaic*, November 16, 1994.

[49] *Summary Report of the Activities of the War Refugee Board with Respect to the Jews of Hungary* (Washington, October 9, 1944), p. 14 (typescript).

from the Axis Alliance and, switching sides, began to fight side by side with the Soviet forces. From that time on, the status of the Jews, both indigenous and foreign, changed radically for the better.

In the interim between the German occupation of Hungary and Romania's extrication from the Axis Alliance, the initiative for the rescuing of Hungarian Jews was taken by the Hungarian-speaking Jews of Southern Transylvania and the Hungarian-Jewish refugees in Bucharest. The latter acted in close cooperation with the Budapest-based Relief and Rescue Committee (*Vaada Ezra ve'Hazalah*), the International Red Cross, and the Zionist and traditional leaders of the Jewish community of Romania.

During the early phase of the Jewish persecutions in Hungary (March–June 1944), the rescue effort was carried out mainly by the leaders of the Jewish communities of Southern Transylvania bordering Hungary. Some of the largest ghettos in Hungarian-held Northern Transylvania, for instance those of Nagyvárad (Oradea Mare), Kolozsvár (Cluj), and Marosvásárhely (Târgu Mureş), were relatively close to the Romanian border. Nevertheless, only a few thousand Jews availed themselves of the opportunity to escape into Romania. Among the reasons for this were the absence of most able-bodied males (who were in forced labor service companies), the reluctance of the physically fit to leave behind the very young and the older members of their families, the risks associated with the illegal border crossings, and the failure of many of the Jewish leaders who were acquainted with the secret of Auschwitz to share that information with the masses.

The few thousand Hungarian Jews who did manage to escape successfully into Romania, mostly on their own initiative, used various means. Some were well-off and bribed both guards and smugglers; others had good contact with Romanian diplomatic officials or political leaders; still others followed the leadership of Zionist couriers (*shlichim*). A considerable percentage of those who dared cross the borders illegally were Jews of Southern Transylvanian background.

The main crossing points to the rescue centers in Romania were Arad, Beiuş, Braşov, Ginta, Sighişoara, Timişoara, and Turda. Of these, Arad and Turda[50] were the busiest ones. The major problems confronting those involved in the rescue operations were the lodging and protection of the refugees at the crossing points, and their subsequent transfer to Bucharest. These problems were largely solved through Jewish officials' well-established contacts with local Romanian authorities and through skillful illegal activities, including the production of forged documents.[51] In addition to the smugglers who were paid and many of the officials who were bribed, the refugees were also helped by several leading figures of the Transylvanian branch of the National Peasant Party (*Partidul Naţional Ţărănesc*).[52] Despite the benevolence of these Romanians, crossing the borders was a risky affair. For one thing, there were a considerable number of anti-Semitic Romanian officials who were opposed to the Jewish refugees. Romania was still an ally of the Third Reich and, occasionally, Romanian gendarmes extradited Jewish refugees to the Hungarian Fascist authorities, who subsequently deported them to Auschwitz.[53] Some of the Jews were caught while still on Hungarian territory.

While the Jewish rescue committees in the border towns were busy helping the escapees during their first few days and provid-

---

[50] Among the leaders of the Turda-based rescue committee were Arnold Finkelstein, Arieh Hirsch (later Eldar), and Eszter Goro. For some details on their wartime activities, see chapter 4.

[51] For details on the activities of the rescue committee in Turda, see Arnold David Finkelstein, *Fénysugár a borzalmak éjszakájában* (A Ray of Light in the Night of Horrors) (Tel Aviv: P. Solar and J. Nadiv, 1958), 400 p. See also Asher Cohen, *The Halutz Resistance in Hungary, 1942–1944* (New York: The Rosenthal Institute for Holocaust Studies of the City University of New York, 1986), 277 p.

[52] One of the leaders of the Romanian rescue campaign in Kolozsvár was Aurel Socol, the head of the local branch of the party. See his *Furtună deasupra Ardealului* (Storm Over Transylvania) (Cluj: Revista "Tribuna," 1991), 103 p.

[53] See, for example, the case of Éva Semlyén and her family detailed in chapter 5.

ing them with documents, a Committee for the Aid of Jewish Refugees from Northern Transylvania (*Comitetul de asistență a refugiaților evrei din Ardealul de Nord*) was organized in Bucharest under the aegis of the Zionist *Aliyah* Office. The Committee was headed by Ernő (Ernest) Marton, the former editor-in-chief of *Új Kelet* (New East—the Hungarian-language Jewish daily of Kolozsvár that had been shut down by the Hungarian authorities), and a former member of the Romanian Parliament.[54] The Committee acted in close cooperation with the leaders of Romanian Jewry, including A. L. Zissu and W. Filderman. During the pre-armistice period, its primary functions were to look after the personal safety of the escapees, ensure the departure of many of them for Palestine, and establish and maintain contact with major Jewish organizations abroad for the acquisition of funds and other material support.

Following the anti-German coup of August 23, 1944, the Committee acquired legal status. From that time, it concentrated its efforts on legalizing the status of the refugees and providing them with monetary and material assistance. Late in October, when almost all of Transylvania had been liberated by the Soviet and Romanian forces, the Committee was consolidated into a General Jewish Consortium of Northern Transylvania (*Curatoriu general evreesc al Ardealului de Nord*).[55]

Contrary to postwar claims advanced by self-motivated "rescuers" and sundry history-cleansers during and especially after the Ceaușescu era,[56] the number of Hungarian Jewish refugees in

---

[54] Marton himself had escaped to Romania in May 1944 with the aid of a Romanian consular official shortly after Rudolph (Rezső) Kasztner (see chapter 4) had visited Kolozsvár and informed the city's Jewish leaders about the realities of the Nazis' anti-Jewish measures.

[55] For details on the Committee and its activities, see Bela Vago, "Political and Diplomatic Activities for the Rescue of the Jews in Northern Transylvania," in *Yad Vashem Studies*, vol. 6 (Jerusalem: Yad Vashem, 1967), pp. 155–171.

[56] See chapters 4–7.

Romania was relatively small. According to a December 28, 1944 report by G. Bertrand Jacobson, the Bucharest representative of HIAS-HICEM, the two American-based Jewish rescue organizations, approximately 1,500 Hungarian Jews had clandestinely crossed the Hungarian-Romanian border that year.[57] Moreover, most of these escapees managed to cross into Romania without the aid of so-called rescue committees operating within Hungary.

The Reaction of the Germans. Although reluctantly reconciled to Marshal Antonescu's opposition to the Final Solution program, the Germans were quite upset about the Romanian government's position on refugees and its plans concerning the emigration of Jews to Palestine, fearing their impact on German-Arab relations and, above all, the successful continuation of the Final Solution program in Hungary. To correct the situation, German Foreign Office officials in Berlin and Budapest waged an intensive campaign in June and July 1944 but to no avail.[58]

Following the frequent complaints by Edmund Veesenmayer, Hitler's Plenipotentiary in Budapest, Eberhard von Thadden, a leading official of the German Foreign Office, approached Killinger on June 30, 1944, requesting confirmation of the news allegedly emanating from the Romanian Consulate General in Kolozsvár that the Hungarian Jewish escapees in Romania were being treated as political refugees and allowed to leave for Palestine.[59] Killinger confirmed this on July 14.[60] The day before, Horst Wagner, Thadden's immediate superior in the German Foreign Office, had approached both Killinger and Gestapo chief Heinrich Müller, complaining that the Romanian government con-

---

[57] Braham, *Politics*, p. 1040.
[58] Randolph L. Braham, comp. *The Destruction of Hungarian Jewry. A Documentary Account* (New York: The World Federation of Hungarian Jews, 1963), 1963), Docs. 194, 196, 197, 282, 284.
[59] Ibid., Doc. 316.
[60] Ibid., Doc. 317.

doned the emigration of Hungarian Jews to Palestine. On July 26, Killinger verified that Jews were indeed being allowed to leave Romania with the consent of Marshal Antonescu, that Hungarian Jews were moving around freely in the country, and that tolerance toward the Jews was generally on the increase. On August 8, Wagner approached Foreign Minister Joachim von Ribbentrop, proposing to forward through Killinger a request to the Marshal for the full application of the anti-Jewish laws enacted in Romania.[61] However, by the time the request was forwarded, Romania was already on the verge of quitting the Axis.[62]

In summary, Marshal Antonescu and his regime not only pursued the anti-Semitic policies of their predecessors, but also aimed to carry out—without any German coaxing—their own version of the Final Solution program during the early phase of the war against the Soviet Union. They changed course only after they realized that the Axis might not win the war and decided instead to free Romania of as many Jews as possible by "selling" them. As a result of their policies, close to 270,000 Romanian and Ukrainian Jews were killed in 1941–1943, mostly by units of the Romanian army and gendarmerie. The beneficiaries of their changed policies were the Jews of Old Romania and Southern Transylvania. However, in these territories, too, the Jews were not only subjected to many discriminatory measures, but also lost close to 10 percent of their population due to pogroms and a variety of anti-Jewish individual and collective operations.

[61] Ibid., Docs. 196, 318, 319.
[62] Braham, *Politics*, pp. 1037–1048. See also Radu Ioanid, *Evreii sub regimul Antonescu* (The Jews Under the Antonescu Regime) (Bucharest: Hasefer, 1997).

CHAPTER 2

The Drive to Refurbish the Past:
The Communist Era

THE PRE-COMMUNIST ERA

The details relating to the destruction of close to 270,000 Romanian and Ukrainian Jews during the Legionary and Antonescu periods were revealed during the major war crimes trials that were held shortly after the war. They were also described in many memoiristic narratives and several documentary collections. By far the most important of these was the three-volume documentary account by Matatias Carp, the Secretary of the Federation of Jewish Communities of Romania. Published between 1946 and 1948, the volumes deal, respectively, with the pogroms that took place during the Legionary rebellion of January 21–23, 1941, the Jassy (Iași) pogrom of June 29–30, 1941, and the destruction of Romanian and Ukrainian Jews in Transnistria.[1]

---

[1] See his *Cartea neagră. Fapte și documente. Suferințele evreilor din România, 1940–1944* (Black Book. Facts and Documents. The Suffering of the Jews of Romania, 1940–1944) (Bucharest: Socec, 1946–1948), 3 vols. During the Communist era, the volumes disappeared even from the so-called restricted sections of libraries. An abbreviated English version was published in Budapest in 1994 under the title *Holocaust in Rumania, 1940–1944*, presumably with some political objectives in mind. A new Romanian edition was brought out in 1996 under the original title (Bucharest: Diogene) through the cooperation of Lya Benjamin and Radu Florian. For some details on the fate of the Carp books, see Radu Ioanid, "Romania," in *The World Reacts to the Holocaust*, David S. Wyman, ed. (Baltimore: The Johns Hopkins University Press, 1996), pp. 236–237. (Cited hereafter as Ioanid, "Romania.")

One of the most important and insightful analyses of the background and characteristics of Romanian Fascism and its devastating impact on the Jews during the Second World War was provided by Lucreţiu Pătrăşcanu, an eminent Marxist intellectual. A national Communist, Pătrăşcanu played a leading role not only in the overthrow of the Antonescu regime, but also in several postwar governments as Minister of Justice. A staunch opponent of both the Soviet and Romanian versions of Stalinism, he was eliminated from the leadership in 1948 and executed in 1954. His analysis of the socioeconomic and cultural forces that shaped Romanian Fascism demonstrated the central role the Right radicals had attached to anti-Semitism. He cogently described how Judeophobia—the ideological backbone of Rightist political mass movements and, after 1940, Antonescu's official state policy—led to the systematic extermination of the Jews.[2] In language not repeated by an ethnic Romanian leader since then, Pătrăşcanu stated:

> From the individual and collective assassinations committed by the Legionnaires they proceeded to the systematic and methodical mass extermination of the Jewish population. Official pogroms were organized, with soldiers and state organs entrusted with their execution.[3]

[2] See his *Problemele de bază ale României* (The Basic Problems of Romania) (Bucharest: Editura de Stat, 1946). See also his autobiographical *Sub trei dictaturi* (Under Three Dictatorships) (Bucharest: Forum, 1945), which also contains an evaluation of the Romanian characteristic of Fascism.

[3] As quoted by Victor Eskenasy. "The Holocaust and Romanian Historiography: Communist and Neo-Communist Revisionism," in *The Tragedy of Romanian Jewry*, Randolph L. Braham, ed. (New York: The Rosenthal Institute for Holocaust Studies of the City University of New York, 1994), p. 176. (Cited hereafter as Eskenasy, "Historiography"; the volume is cited hereafter as Braham, *Tragedy*.)

THE STALINIST PERIOD

The first postwar years proved merely a temporary "liberal" interregnum. Under Soviet tutelage, the minuscule Communist Party was gradually transformed into a formidable force that replaced the monarchy with a "people's republic" at the end of 1947. Romania, a former Axis satellite, soon became a full-fledged Soviet satellite state. During the Stalinist era, the Holocaust was essentially buried in the Orwellian black hole of history. Historiography, like all other fields of humanities and the social sciences, became an appendage of Party propaganda guided at first by Marxist-Leninist tenets and then by nationalist-socialist orthodoxy. It was practiced almost exclusively by historians associated with or guided by the Institute of History of the Communist Party and the equally subservient Center for Military History and Theory.[4] The "historians" had not only to follow the guidelines but also to obtain the approval of their publications by the Party's Agitation and Propaganda ("Agitprop") Section—a practice that remained in effect until the overthrow of the regime in December 1989.[5] Although the Jewish question itself was officially taboo, anti-Semitism was subtly kept alive—as it was in the entire Soviet bloc—under the guise of anti-Zionism and anti-cosmopolitanism.

[4] Established in 1951, the official name of the Institute was "Institute for Historical and Social-Political Studies of the Central Committee of the Romanian Communist Party" (*Institutul de Studii Istorice şi Social-Politice de pe lîngă Comitetul Central al Partidului Comunist Român*). During the Ceauşescu era, the Center for Military History and Theory (*Centrul de Istorie şi Teorie Militară*) was headed by General Ilie Ceauşescu, the dictator's brother. Many of the "historians" associated with these institutions continued their work under the auspices of various governmental organizations even after the overthrow of the Ceauşescu regime in December 1989.

[5] During the latter part of the Ceauşescu regime, the Agitprop section was headed by Mircea Muşat. For further details, see below.

THE CEAUȘESCU ERA, 1964–1989

Following the policies of Gheorghe Gheorghiu-Dej, his immediate predecessor and mentor, Nicolae Ceaușescu gradually shifted Romania's domestic and foreign policies along nationalist-socialist lines. This change in direction was also noticeable in the treatment of the Jewish question. Eager to advance Romania's national interests and change the country's image abroad, Ceaușescu decided to tone down the anti-Zionist and anti-cosmopolitan campaign that continued to rage in the other Soviet bloc nations. Later, he demonstrated Romania's autonomy by refusing to join his allies in breaking diplomatic relations with Israel after the Six-Day War and by rejecting pressures to support the 1975 UN resolution that equated Zionism with racism.

The wartime tragedy of Romanian Jewry reemerged as a public topic in the mid-1970s, presumably in response to a political decision taken by Ceaușescu's nationalist-socialist regime to cleanse the wartime historical record of Romania. The decision was apparently designed to further both domestic and foreign political objectives. Domestically, it aimed, above all, to bring about the gradual rehabilitation of Marshal Ion Antonescu, the wartime pro-Nazi dictator. In the foreign political sphere, the history-cleansing campaign was designed to improve the country's image abroad by contrasting Romania's self-proclaimed wartime "humanitarian" record on the Jews with the "barbarism" of the Germans and, above all, the Hungarians—the Romanians' traditional enemy.

The history-cleansing decision appears to have been based on Ceaușescu's resolve to strengthen his political power base by orchestrating an agreement early in the 1970s between his ideological lieutenants and the chauvinistic faction of the ethnic Romanian intelligentsia. Under the agreement, the latter reportedly consented to support the regime in exchange for being allowed to engage in "nationalist cultural activities," including the propagation of xenophobic and anti-Semitic ideas. While not officially endorsed, anti-Semitism was in fact condoned and occasionally overtly displayed during Ceauşescu's rule. Among the leaders of the chauvinistic neo-Fascist group were Eugen Barbu, Corneliu Vadim Tudor, and Adrian Păunescu—all Ceauşescu hagiographers. Barbu and Tudor frequently expressed their anti-Semitic and anti-Hungarian ideas in the weekly *Săptămâna* (The Week); Păunescu purveyed the same views in *Flacăra* (The Flame), a weekly he edited.[6] As part of the agreement, Communists of Jewish origin were gradually purged from top party and government positions, continuing a process that had begun under the leadership of Gheorghiu-Dej.[7]

The broad policy guidelines for the Holocaust-related history-cleansing campaign were provided by Ceauşescu himself. In a policy statement that dealt indirectly with the wartime ordeal of the Jews along with other subjects, Ceauşescu completely distorted Romania's record on the destruction of nearly 270,000 Romanian and Ukrainian Jews. He minimized the number of "persons" (a term he used rather than "Jews") killed in Jassy as well as the number of those "interned" in the "occupied Soviet territory." (The latter was a bleak reference to Northern Bukovina, Bessarabia, and Transnistria, the Romanian-occupied territory between the Dniester and the Bug, where Romanian army and gendarmerie units murdered a large number of Jews.) In contrast,

---

[6] For some details, see Ioanid "Romania," pp. 239-240. See also Michael Shafir, "The Revival of the Political Right in Post-Communist Romania," in *Democracy and Right-Wing Politics in Eastern Europe in the 1990s*, Joseph Held, ed. (Boulder: Social Science Monographs, 1993, pp. 153–174. Cited hereafter as Shafir, "The Revival of the Political Right.")

After the fall of Ceauşescu in 1989, Barbu, Tudor, and Păunescu became associated with viciously anti-Semitic papers and parties. See chapter 3.

[7] Among the top Communists of Jewish origin purged by Gheorghiu-Dej were Ana Pauker and Iosif Chişinevschi. The last such leader, Leonte Răutu, once the chief ideologue of the regime, was purged by Ceauşescu in 1981.

Ceauşescu emphasized that "during the Horthyist and Nazi occupation, 170,000 citizens [*sic*] from Northern Transylvania were sent as forced laborers to Germany to concentration camps, and of these more than 100,000 were killed."[8]

Guided by these directives, the Communist Party-supported "official historians" undertook in an exculpatory fashion to distort the tragedy that had befallen Romanian and Ukrainian Jewry during the Antonescu era. Their accounts of the Jassy pogrom, like those related to the destruction of the Jews of Northern Bukovina and Bessarabia and the horrors of Transnistria, are distorted or falsified.[9] The Party-historians' portrayal of Antonescu's Romania as a "wartime oasis of humanitarianism"—a country that not only prevented the Holocaust, but also afforded haven to thousands of foreign Jews, allowing their emigration to Palestine—is both distorted and politically motivated. Their methodological approach is as sophisticated as it is scientifically flawed. Specifically, this approach:

- Generally minimizes or distorts the anti-Semitic policies and anti-Jewish laws that were adopted by successive Romanian governments, beginning with those initiated by the Goga-Cuza regime in late 1937 and culminating by those enforced during the Antonescu era (1940–1944);
- Virtually ignores or rationalizes Romania's role as an Axis ally which provided the second largest army in the war against the Soviet Union—an army that was largely destroyed at Stalingrad—and emphasizes the country's contribution to the Allied war effort after August 23, 1944, when Romania switched sides;

---

[8] Nicolae Ceauşescu, *România pe drumul construirii societăţii socialiste multilateral dezvoltate* (Romania on the Road of Building the Multilaterally Developed Socialist Society), vol. 11 (Bucharest: Editura Politicâ, 1975), p. 570.

[9] For a fully documented overview, see Eskenasy, "Historiography," pp. 173–236. See also Ioanid, "Romania," pp. 240–252.

– Distorts the role played by King Michael and the leaders of the anti-Fascist parties in the *volte face* and identifies the punitive measures taken against Marshal Antonescu as acts of "treason";
– Fails to acknowledge the murder of close to 270,000 Romanian and Ukrainian Jews mostly by units of the Romanian army and gendarmerie in parts of Moldavia, Bukovina, Bessarabia, and Transnistria;
– Focuses on the opportunistic, "moderate" anti-Jewish policies the Antonescu government pursued starting in late 1942, and especially after the crushing defeat of the Romanian army at Stalingrad, emphasizing its refusal to go along with Germany's final solution program in Old Romania and Southern Transylvania;
– Fails to acknowledge or adequately deal with the fact that even in these areas close to ten percent of the Jews were killed primarily by Romanians loyal to the Iron Guard and Marshal Antonescu, and that the survivors, grateful as they were for escaping with their lives, were not only deprived of their livelihood but also of their civil rights and liberties;
– Identifies Romania's wartime record with that of Bulgaria and Denmark, contrasting the country's "humanitarian" record with that of Hungary's barbarism;
– Lays ultimate responsibility for some of the admitted anti-Jewish excesses in Romania proper on the Germans and "a few misguided and over-zealous Iron Guardists";
– Rationalizes the mass murder of the Romanian Jews of Bukovina and Bessarabia as actions of self-defense against Judeo-Bolsheviks and Soviet collaborators; and
– Emphasizes and exploits the tragedy of the Jews in Hungarian-ruled Northern Transylvania as an integral part of a calculated political campaign against Hungary and the Hungarians.

The historical accounts by xenophobic nationalist intellectuals aim at the exploitation of the Holocaust for political ends.

Incorporating a deductive approach, these accounts are devoid of any meaningful objectivity and critical analysis. The political objectives of these "historians" include the whitewashing of the crimes committed by Romanians and the contrasting of the wartime "humanitarian" record of Romania with the anti-Romanian and anti-Jewish "barbarism" of Hungary.

With respect to the first of these two objectives, the historical accounts are generally exculpatory in nature. They offer an idealized portrayal of the Romanian people in general and provide an uncritically positive evaluation of the wartime positions and policies of the Antonescu regime. In a romantic, idealized fashion the nationalists characterize the Romanians as a gentle, kind, and magnanimous people whose humanitarianism was manifested toward the Jews during World War II. They make no attempt to differentiate between the three wartime attitudinal categories of Romanians—categories that were also clearly discernible among the peoples in all the other Nazi-dominated states: (1) The relatively large number of collaborators who were motivated by ideological convictions or, as was most often the case, by rapacious instincts;[10] (2) The pitifully low number of those who dared to save their Jewish friends or neighbors; and (3) The overwhelming majority who, for a variety of reasons, remained basically passive.

The nationalists are also dedicated to defending the integrity of the wartime leaders by denying or rationalizing their anti-Jewish policies. They are particularly brazen in "explaining" the campaigns of mass murder against the Jews as acts of self-defense, ignoring the evidence that the Romanian version of the Final Solution was in fact initiated by the Antonescu regime and

---

[10] Many objective historical accounts and eyewitness testimonies provide gruesome details about the involvement of Romanians, Gypsies, and others in the murder of Jews and especially in the looting of their property. Perhaps the most vivid account was provided by Curzio Malaparte in his *Kaputt* (New York: E. P. Dutton, 1946) in connection with the Jassy pogrom of June–July 1941.

generally carried out by units of the Romanian army and gendarmerie. Their more sophisticated but equally distorted accounts attempt to minimize the tragedy of the Jews by shifting the blame almost exclusively to the Germans and "a few misguided Iron Guard radicals."[11]

The second major political objective is pursued through accounts demonstrating Romania's alleged wartime "humanitarian" record, emphasizing—not always without any justification—the brutality with which the Hungarians collaborated with the SS in the implementation of the Final Solution program in 1944.[12] These accounts fail to note, however, that the Jews of Hungary, while subjected—like the Romanian Jews—to many discriminatory measures, survived almost intact until the German occupation of March 19, 1944.[13]

This distortion of history is also reflected in the nationalists' contradictory portrayal of the Jewish communities of Bukovina

---

[11] A classic example in this category is Maria Covaci and Aurel Kareţki, *Zile însingerate la Iaşi* (Bloody Days in Iaşi) (Bucharest: Editura Politică, 1978). The preface by Nicolae Minei contains a "historical revisionist" interpretation of the wartime plight of Jews in Romania. See also Mihai Pelin, "Aproximaţiile unui reporter frenetic" (The Approximations of a Frenetic Reporter), *Almanahul "Săptămâna"* (The "Week" Almanac), Bucharest, 1986. The latter is a distorted review of Curzio Malaparte's *Kaputt*, cited above.

For a critical review of Pelin's position, see the piece by Tudor Bugnariu in *Societate & Cultură* (Society & Culture), Bucharest, no. 32 (I), 1996, pp. 33–38. For some details on Covaci, Kareţki, and Pelin, see Eskenasy, "Historiography," pp. 185–186.

[12] The Holocaust in Hungary and the responsibility of the Germans and Hungarians in the destruction of Hungarian Jewry are detailed in Randolph L. Braham, *The Politics of Genocide: The Holocaust in Hungary*, 2d ed. (New York: The Rosenthal Institute for Holocaust Studies of the City University of New York, 1994). (Cited hereafter as Braham, *Politics*.)

[13] For some details on the destruction of the Jews of Northern Transylvania, see Braham, *Politics*, chapter 18. See also Randolph L. Braham, *Genocide and Retribution. The Holocaust in Hungarian-Ruled Northern Transylvania* (Boston: Kluwer-Nijhoff, 1983), and *Martiriul evreilor din România* (The Martyrdom of the Jews of Romania) (Bucharest: Hasefer, 1991), pp. 245–290.

and Bessarabia, which fell to Soviet control in June 1940, and of those of Northern Transylvania, which came under Hungarian jurisdiction two months later. Although all of these communities were part of Greater Romania between 1918 and 1940, the former are portrayed in antagonistic terms, while the latter are viewed as victims who shared their plight with the Romanians. While the Jews of Bukovina and Bessarabia, victims of the Romanian Holocaust, are portrayed as anti-Romanian, pro-Communist, and pro-Soviet "aliens," those of Northern Transylvania, victims of the Hungarian Holocaust, are depicted as having been united in a veritable symbiosis of suffering with the Romanians. Disregarding the fact that the Hungarians' discriminatory measures were directed almost exclusively against the Jews, Romanian nationalists portray the suffering of the Romanians in Northern Transylvania as having been even more intense than that endured by the Jews. One of them, in fact, claimed that "the main feature of the Holocaust in Northern Transylvania was anti-Romanian and not anti-Semitic."[14] A high-ranking military officer appears to have "confirmed" it by claiming that "after the entry of the Horthyite troops in the northwestern part of Romania special camps were established for the extermination of Romanians." He added that by October 1940, i.e., within a month after the Hungarian annexation of Northern Transylvania, these camps included 13,359 Romanians, including Raoul Şorban, Emil Haţieganu, and Tudor Bugnariu.[15]

The Political Exploitation of the Holocaust. The history-cleansing works devoted to whitewashing the crimes committed

[14] See the review of *Teroarea Horthisto-fascistă în Nord-Vestul României* (The Horthyite-Fascist Terror in Northwestern Romania), Mihai Fătu and Mircea Muşat, eds. (Bucharest: Editura Politică, 1985) in *Luceafărul*, Bucharest, June 21, 1986.
[15] Ion Şuţa, *Transilvania: himera imperialismului iredentist* (Transylvania: Chimera of Irredentist Imperialism) (Bucharest: Editura Academiei de Înalte Studii Militare, 1995), p. 131. The author is a retired lieutenant-general.

by the Romanians in Bukovina, Bessarabia, and Transnistria are coupled with those dedicated to juxtaposing Romania's wartime "humanitarianism" with the "barbarism" of the Hungarians. These works, too, have a clearcut political objective. They are conceived as part of the political campaign against Hungary over the issue of Transylvania, including the contemporary treatment of the Hungarian minorities in the region—the basic source of conflict between the two traditional enemies. The campaign acquired considerable momentum in the mid-1980s, when a relatively large number of sophisticated history-cleansing works appeared with the support of the Ceauşescu regime. These slanted accounts on the Holocaust deal primarily with the destruction of the Jews of Hungary with emphasis on those of Northern Transylvania, the area held by Hungary between September 1940 and October 1944. One of the most popular pamphlets in this category was published under the authorship of the Central Jewish Federation.[16] Several wartime accounts and semi-fictionalized narratives were published in the same genre by survivors of the Hungarian Holocaust.[17]

---

[16] See *Remember. 40 de ani de la masacrarea evreilor din Ardealul de Nord sub ocupaţia horthystă* (Remember. Forty Years Since the Massacre of Jews in Northern Transylvania Under Horthyite Occupation) (Bucharest: Federaţia Comunităţilor Evreieşti din Republica Socialistă România, 1985).

[17] See especially the writings of Oliver Lustig, including *Blood-Bespotted Diary* (Bucharest: Editura Ştiinţifică şi Enciclopedică, 1988)—the English translation of *Jurnal însîngerat* (Bucharest: Editura Militară, 1987). He is also listed as one of the writers of *Horthyist-Fascist Terror in Northwestern Romania*, Mihai Fătu and Mircea Muşat, eds. (Bucharest: Meridiane, 1986). One of Lustig's articles in this category originally published in the May 1987 issue of *Magazin Istoric* (Historical Magazine) was republished as a separate pamphlet in English translation ("Distortions and Misrepresentations that Bring Insults and Desecrate the Memory of the Victims of Horthy's Reign of Terror") in 1995 in *Romanian Historical Studies* of Hallandale, Florida. Lustig's many personal and fictionalized accounts about the tragedy of North Transylvanian Jewry had earned him the appreciation of many Romanian nationalists. See László Fey, "Előítélet és karrierizmus" (Prejudice and Careerism), *Szabadság* (Freedom), Cluj-Napoca, May 22, 1996. For some comments about Lustig's work, see Ioanid, "Romania," pp. 241–242, and 245.

Others, and especially those written by ethnic Romanians, emphasize not only the Hungarians' responsibility for the destruction of nearly 570,000 Jews, including more than 100,000 Jews of Northern Transylvania, but also the "equally vicious" anti-Romanian policies of the Horthyite regime. Many of the latter accounts also focus, not without justification, on the revisionist policies Hungary had pursued against Romania during the interwar period.[18]

The history-cleansing campaign aimed at juxtaposing Romania's wartime "humanitarianism" with Hungary's "barbarism" received a boost in 1986. Pro-Ceaușescu propagandists began to take advantage of the basically unfounded accounts of mass rescue of Hungarian and other Jewish refugees across the Hungarian-Romanian border during World War II. These accounts were advanced by two elderly individuals who were motivated by their particular personal interests, Moshe Carmilly-Weinberger, the former Chief Rabbi of the small Neolog community of Cluj (Kolozsvár), and Raoul Șorban, a painter and art historian.[19] The first public disclosure of their rescue accounts, emphasizing the generosity and selflessness of the Romanians, appeared under the signature of Adrian Riza, a man identified by several scholars as a Ceaușescu propagandist.[20] This was followed by pub-

---

[18] See, for example, *Teroarea Horthysto-Fascistă în Nord-Vestul României*, op. cit. Interestingly, many of the Romanian historical accounts focusing on Romania's "humanitarian" record on the Holocaust occasionally rely for their "documentation" on this author's works, including *The Politics of Genocide* and *Genocide and Retribution* cited above. The quotations used, however, are quite selective and generally out of context, ignoring the "negative" sections dealing with the Romanian involvement in the massacre of Jews in Romania and the Romanian-occupied parts of the Soviet Union.

[19] For details, see chapters 4–7.

[20] See his "România pământ al speranței. Fascism și antifascism pe meleaguri Transilvane. Rețeaua omeniei" (Romania. Land of Hope. Fascism and Anti-Fascism in Transylvanian Regions. The Network of Humanity), in *Almanahul "Luceafărul" 1986* (Luceafărul Almanac 1986) (Bucharest, 1986), pp. 63–92. For some details on this work and its author, see chapter 6.

lished versions of the lectures and interviews given since 1986 by both elderly protagonists of the "rescue operation." These, in turn, emerged as sources for numerous other exculpatory writings.[21]

The Drive for Antonescu's Rehabilitation. The anti-Hungarian history-cleansing political campaign has been coupled with a well orchestrated drive to bring about the gradual rehabilitation of Marshal Ion Antonescu along with many other Romanian "national heroes," including Octavian Goga and Alexandru C. Cuza, the fathers of Fascist anti-Semitism. In 1987, Mircea Muşat, the head of the Communist Party's "Agitprop" Section and official "historiographer," offered a historical reinterpretation of both Cuza and Goga, calling the former "a Romanian intellectual of the first rank." He identified Goga as "a Romanian in the deepest dimensions of his soul ... a profound symbol of his people."[22] In retrospect, Muşat's affiliation with the neo-Fascist Right radicals almost immediately after the collapse of the Ceauşescu regime appears quite logical (see below).

The main effort since the mid-1980s has been directed toward the rehabilitation of the Marshal. Supported, if not publicly encour-

[21] See, for example, Moshe Carmilly-Weinberger, "1940–1944. În acele vremuri grele, poporul român şi-a păstrat demnitatea şi omenia" (1940–1944. During Those Difficult Times, the Romanian People Retained Their Dignity and Humanity), *Magazin Istoric* (Historical Magazine), Bucharest, vol. 13, no. 10 (271), October 1989; Constantin Mustata, "Convorbire cu Moshe Carmilly-Weinberger fost Şef-Rabin al Clujului" (Discussion with Moshe Carmilly-Weinberger, the Former Chief Rabbi of Cluj) in *Almanahul "Flacăra" 1989* (Flacăra Almanac 1989) (Bucharest, 1989), pp. 140–148; "Salvarea evreilor din teritoriul de nord-vest al României, 1940–1944" (The Rescuing of Jews in the Northwestern Territory of Romania, 1940–1944) in *Almanah "Luceafărul" 1989* (Bucharest, 1989), pp. 114-38 (A round-table discussion involving Carmilly-Weinberger, Raoul Şorban, Adrian Riza, and Mihai Ungheanu); and Adrian Riza, "Arhivele încep să vorbească" (The Archives Begin to Talk), ibid., pp. 139–162. The three journals were established and supported by agencies of Ceauşescu's Communist Party. See Eskenasy, "Historiography," p. 196, and Ioanid, "Romania," p. 245.
[22] Ioanid, "Romania," p. 238.

aged, by Ceauşescu's nationalist-socialist regime, the history-cleansers began to portray the former pro-Nazi dictator as:

> – A patriot who strove to reestablish the territorial integrity of Greater Romania;
> – A hero who waged war against the Soviet Union for the reacquisition of Northern Bukovina and Bessarabia and for the protection of Christian Europe from the menace of Bolshevism;
> – A diplomat-soldier who strove to reacquire Northern Transylvania from the Hungarians; and
> – A humanitarian who not only saved the Jews of Romania, but also gave refuge to thousands upon thousands of Hungarian and other Jews, enabling them to go on to Palestine.

The depiction of Antonescu as a "savior of Jews" is part of the nationalists' political campaign against Hungary and the Hungarians. Falsified and distorted, the tragedy of the Jews of Hungary and Romania is exploited as a weapon for domestic and foreign political ends. The history-cleansers are as silent about the Marshal's personal involvement in the mass murder of the Jews of Northern Bukovina and Bessarabia as they are neglectful in providing the historical context under which the great majority of the Jews of Old Romania and Southern Transylvania were actually saved. They conveniently ignore the Romanian leaders' original agreement with the SS to subject these Jews to the Nazis' Final Solution program and overlook the circumstances under which they had changed their minds.[23] These chroniclers also fail to remember that many of Romania's wartime humanitarian

---

[23] See Jean Ancel, "Plans for Deportation of the Romanian Jews and Their Discontinuation in Light of Documentary Evidence (July–October 1942)," in *Yad Vashem Studies*, vol. 16 (Jerusalem: Yad Vashem, 1984), pp. 381–420.

actions—such as the smuggling of Hungarian Jews and other refugees across the Hungarian-Romanian border, their permission to leave for Palestine, and the repatriation of the surviving Jews from Transnistria—were greatly abetted by the venality of various Romanian officials, payoffs by foreign Jewish organizations, and, above all, Marshal Antonescu's realization that the Axis would lose the war.[24]

In recent years, Antonescu has also been credited with the saving of large numbers of Hungarian Jews by granting them refuge in Romania and permitting their emigration to Palestine.[25] He did all this, they emphasize, despite the law of May 29, 1944, which mandated the death penalty for Jews entering the country illegally. However, their account goes counter to the recollections of Radu Lecca, Antonescu's Commissar on Jewish Affairs, who claimed that the Marshal was not even aware of the presence of Hungarian Jewish refugees in the country.[26]

The Drăgan Factor. One of the leading forces behind the resurgence of anti-Semitism and the drive for the rehabilitation of Marshal Antonescu has been Iosif Constantin Drăgan, an Iron Guardist who amassed a fortune in Italy allegedly by fraudulently

---

[24] For details on the distortions by Romanian historians, including those formerly associated with the now defunct Institute of History of the Central Committee of the Romanian Communist Party, see Eskenasy, "Historiography." See also Ioanid, "Romania." As Eskenasy demonstrates, many of the Ceauşescu-supported "Communist historians" have switched their allegiance to the post-Ceauşescu chauvinistic nationalist and ultra-Right forces.

See also Michael Shafir, "Marshal Ion Antonescu and Romanian Politics," *RFE/RL Research Report*, vol. 3, no. 6, February 1994, pp. 22–28.

[25] See, for example, "Mareşalul Antonescu i-a salvat pe evreii din România. Un dialog Raoul Şorban-Adrian Păunescu, Bucureşti, 17 Ianuarie 1996" (Marshal Antonescu Saved the Jews of Romania. A Raoul Şorban-Adrian Păunescu Dialogue, Bucharest, January 17, 1996). *Totuşi Iubirea* (Love Nevertheless), no. 2, January no. 4, February 1–8 no. 5, February 8–15 1996. (The titles of the last two segments of the interview vary.) The patently false assertions by Raoul Şorban, a Righteous Among the Nations, are detailed in chapter 7.

[26] See chapter 1.

appropriating Romanian state assets immediately after the war. A leader of the Iron Guard youth movement in Cluj, Drăgan fled to Fascist Italy soon after the crushing of the Legionary rebellion in January 1941. During the war, he reportedly was engaged in small-scale business deals through the Romanian Embassy in Rome and the Consulate General in Milan. Taking advantage of the chaos that prevailed during the immediate postwar period, Drăgan "fraudulently appropriated the financial assets of the Italo-Romanian Petroleum Association (*Asociația Petrolieră Italo-Română*—APIR), amounting to six to seven million dollars." These funds were then transferred to Vienna, where he founded the "Butangaz" Company. Romania's postwar security services tracked him down as one of the "escapees and traitors." He was also denounced by a fellow Romanian in Paris who had been disturbed by Drăgan's expropriation of state assets. Unmasked, Drăgan yielded to blackmail and became an informer of the Romanian *Securitate*—a service in exchange for which the Romanian secret police agency attributed his wealth to his wife's inheritance.[27]

Drăgan became an influential personality in Romanian domestic politics shortly after Ceaușescu acquired power in 1965. He ingratiated himself with Ceaușescu by bringing out a special edition of the dictator's works through his Venice-based NAGARD (Drăgan spelled backward) publishing house. He was, in return, reportedly appointed associate professor at the Academy of Economic Sciences (*Academia de Științe Economice*) of Bucharest and at the University of Timișoara. In the late 1960s, Drăgan established the Drăgan European Foundation (*Fundația Europeană Drăgan*) with headquarters in Milan.[28] Though a for-

[27] Cornel Ivanciuc, "Dacă Virgil Măgureanu este agent K.G.B., atunci I. C. Drăgan este agent al securității" (If Virgil Măgureanu is a KGB Agent, Then I. C. Drăgan is a Secret Police [*Securitate*] Agent), *Academia Cațavencu*, Bucharest, no. 9, March 7–13, 1995.
[28] Ibid.

mer Legionary who had to escape from Antonescu's wrath, Drăgan gradually emerged as the most enthusiastic leader in the drive for the rehabilitation of the Marshal—a leadership position he reportedly assumed at the "urging" of Ceaușescu. With top secret documents placed at his disposal by the regime, Drăgan published a three-volume documentary account of the Marshal.[29] Drăgan's interpretation of Antonescu's position on the Jewish question has been accepted as "correct" by the Party-affiliated historical revisionists. In his preface to the third volume, for example, Drăgan stated:

> It is known that the Jews were not loyal to the authorities and the Romanian army when Bessarabia and Northern Bukovina were handed over to the Soviets in June 1940, and the persecutions they had to endure afterwards were due to justified resentment that could not be suppressed under the given circumstances.... The Jews of Romania during the war did not have to share the tragedy of their coreligionists in the other parts of Europe.[30]

In line with this thesis, nationalist history-cleansers have identified the suffering of Romanians during the Soviet occupation of Northern Bukovina and Bessarabia as a "Holocaust." This suffering, they emphasize, was exacerbated by the activities of anti-Romanian, pro-Communist Jews in the area.[31]

---

[29] *Antonescu. Mareșalul României și războaiele de reîntregire* (Antonescu. The Marshal of Romania and the Wars for Reunification), I. C. Drăgan, ed. (Venice: Nagard, 1986–1989), 3 vols. The fourth volume appeared in 1990, reflecting the systemic change in Romania. The documents stemmed from the highly restricted holdings of the Ministry of the Interior and the Central Committee of the Communist Party.

[30] As cited by Eskenasy, "Historiography," p. 193.

[31] See Gheorghe Buzatu, *Așa a început holocaustul împotriva poporului român* (This Is How the Holocaust Against the Romanian People Began) (Bucharest: Editura Magadahonda, 1995), 56 p.

CHAPTER 3

The Drive to Refurbish the Past: The Post-Communist Era

Drăgan's influence in Romanian domestic politics has become especially visible after the overthrow of the Ceaușescu regime in December 1989. Taking advantage of the opportunities provided by the new system, Drăgan has been playing a leading, if not determining, role in the creation of a new political map, the resurgence of anti-Semitism, the distortion and denigration of the Holocaust, the exacerbation of anti-Hungarianism, and, above all, in the drive for the rehabilitation of Marshal Antonescu. He has been pursuing these objectives through various pro-Antonescu groups and the many publishing, media, and other enterprises he owns.[1]

THE NEW POLITICAL MAP

The spiritual and material support provided by Drăgan is reflected in the doctrines and policies of the many national and

[1] He owns, for example, the *Națiunea* (Nation) and the Timișoara-based *Renașterea Bănățeană* (Banat Rebirth) papers, the Europa Nova and the European Institute (*Institutul European*) publishing houses, several local TV stations, and a number of other commercial enterprises. Michael Shafir, "Marshal Antonescu's Postcommunist Rehabilitation. *Cui bono?*," in *The Destruction of Romanian and Ukrainian Jews During the Antonescu Era*, Randolph L. Braham, ed. (New York: The Rosenthal Institute for Holocaust Studies of the City University of New York, 1997), pp. 349–410. (The volume is cited hereafter as Braham, *Destruction*.)

local ultra-Rightist, pro-Iron Guard political movements and parties that sprung up after 1989.[2] Although their political power is overshadowed by the reorganized traditional historical parties[3] and the political parties and groupings that emerged after the overthrow of the Ceauşescu regime,[4] the many xenophobic ultranationalist parties continue to wield considerable influence. Taking advantage of the new democratic freedoms and the relative lack of civic awareness in the country, the Right extremists exploit the economic hardships and political turmoils caused by the systemic change. Their political message appears especially appealing to those frustrated by the negative consequences of privatization and marketization, aggravated by the ubiquitous nature of red tape and corruption. They exploit the deep disillusionment among virtually all sectors of society with the policies of the post-Ceauşescu governments that brought about declining living standards—a disillusionment coupled with anger by the realization that a coterie of former Communists and *Securitate* agents contin-

---

[2] For some details on the resurgence of Iron Guard activities, see Michael Shafir, "Anti-Semitism Without Jews in Romania," *Report on Eastern Europe*, June 28, 1991, pp. 21–23.

[3] The parties that dominated political life in prewar Romania were the National Liberal Party (*Partidul Naţional Liberal*) and the National Peasant Party (*Partidul Naţional Ţărănesc*). During the post-Ceauşescu era, the latter—reflecting the spirit of the time—renamed itself National Peasant Party—Christian and Democratic (*Partidul Naţional Ţărănesc*—Creştin şi Democrat). During the elections of the early 1990s, these parties united with 16 other smaller parties to form a center-right coalition—the Democratic Convention of Romania (*Convenţia Democratică Română*)—to oppose the Communist-derived forces that governed the country since the ouster of Ceauşescu.

[4] The dominant party that emerged after the ouster of Ceauşescu was the National Salvation Front (*Frontul Salvării Naţionale*), headed by Ion Iliescu and other former top Communist leaders. The party split in March 1992, with Petre Roman, the former prime minister, retaining leadership of the party, and Iliescu forming a new ruling party—the Democratic National Salvation Front (*Frontul Democratic al Salvării Naţionale*). In July 1993, the latter changed its name to the Party of Social Democracy of Romania (*Partidul Democraţiei Sociale din România*).

ues to prosper. Ironically, among the latter are a number of nationalist extremists who had been members of Ceauşescu's nationalist-
socialist nomenklatura. They appear to have retained their position of power and influence in virtually every segment of the new
state apparatus, including the dreaded secret police.

The ideological roots of the extremist nationalist political
groupings may be found in the doctrines and policies of the
viciously anti-Semitic Fascist movements and parties of the interwar period as well as in the nationalist-socialist party of
Ceauşescu. The linkages and continuities in Romania's Right radical tradition have been explained by Michael Shafir, an astute
scholar of Romanian affairs, as follows:

> The presence of the radical Right on the country's politi-
> cal map following the collapse of Communism is hardly
> surprising. The Ceauşescu version of "national Communism"
> was probably unmatched elsewhere in the region in its
> efforts to entrench the legitimacy of both the party and its
> ruler based on nationalist symbols and on a political dis-
> course that, for all practical purposes, resurrected the
> inter-war political credo of the extreme Right.[5]

The linkage between the Ceauşescu regime and the prewar and
post-Communist manifestations of Right radicalism has been
noticed by many other students of Romanian politics as well.
Vladimir Tişmăneanu, a Professor of Political Science at the
University of Maryland, for example, analytically demonstrated
that the resurgence of nationalist, xenophobic ideology in the post-
Ceauşescu era was not an accident. He revealed the continuities
between the Communist uses of nationalism and the post-

---

[5] Shafir, "The Revival of the Political Right in Post-Communist Romania," in
Democracy and Right-Wing Politics in Eastern Europe in the 1990, Joseph Held, ed.
(Boulder: Social Science Monographs, 1993), pp. 158–159.

Communist ethnonationalist discourse, hypothesizing that the Ceauşescu regime incorporated in its ideology the main themes of the extreme Right of the interwar period—themes that xenophobic nationalists tended to preserve and even exacerbate during the post-Ceauşescu era.[6] The Right radical continuity is reflected in the ideology and politics of several political parties.

One of the most influential ultra-nationalist parties representing this continuity is the Party of Romanian National Unity *(Partidul Unităţii Naţionale Române*—PUNR), a fiercely anti-Hungarian party headed by Gheorghe Funar, the Mayor of Cluj-Napoca. Founded in early 1990, it is the political arm of *Vatra Românească* (Romanian Hearth), the equally anti-Hungarian "cultural organization," whose honorary chairman is Drăgan. The party's ideological position is reflected in *Naţiunea* (The Nation), the Drăgan-owned organ of the *Vatra Românească*. PUNR reportedly expresses the political will of the Romanian Information Service *(Serviciul Român de Informaţii*—SRI), the "new" *Securitate.*[7]

The other party in this category is the Greater Romania Party *(Partidul România Mare*—PRM), founded in May 1991. Its viciously anti-Semitic and xenophobic policies are reflected in the contents of its weekly—*România Mare* (Greater Romania). The

[6] Vladimir Tişmăneanu, "Anti-Semitism and Myth-Making in Post-Communist Romania," in Braham, *Destruction*, pp. 303–348.

[7] Cornel Ivanciuc, "Dacă Virgil Măgureanu este agent K.G.B., atunci I. C. Drăgan este agent al securităţii" (If Virgil Măgureanu Is a KGB Agent, Then I. C. Drăgan Is a Secret Police [*Securitate*] Agent), *Academia Caţavencu*, Bucharest, no. 9, March 7–13, 1995. For some details on PUNR and Funar, see "Nationalist Transylvanian Mayor Kindles Romanian-Hungarian Animosity," *Research Bulletin* (Radio Free Europe), March 2, 1993. See also Shafir, "The Revival of the Political Right," pp. 159–162. In the November 1996 elections, Funar, who ran for the presidency, received 3.22 percent of the votes. His party, however, received 4.22 percent of the votes for the Senate and 4.36 percent for the Chamber of Deputies, managing to acquire 7 (out of 143) and 18 (out of 328) parliamentary seats, respectively. *Curierul Românesc* (Romanian Courier), October–November, 1996, and *Cronica Română* (Romanian Chronicle), November 8, 1996.

linkage between the party, its weekly, and the *Securitate* is reflected in the following comment by Silviu Brucan, an early ally of former President Ion Iliescu: "*România Mare* [is] not just the mouthpiece of the *Securitate* but the *Securitate* itself."[8] The party is headed by Corneliu Vadim Tudor, a Ceauşescu hagiographer and brazen Holocaust denier. One of its leading figures until his death in 1995 was Mircea Muşat, the former head of the Romanian Communist Party's "Agitprop" Section and, together with his colleague and co-author, Ion Ardeleanu, Ceauşescu's official historiographer. Muşat, a distorter of the Holocaust in Romania, severely criticized President Iliescu's participation in the inauguration of the U.S. Holocaust Memorial Museum in Washington in April 1993, and his attendance at Holocaust commemorative meetings in Bucharest.

Like the PUNR, PRM is not only anti-Semitic, but also anti-Hungarian and anti-Gypsy. *România Mare*—launched in June 1990—links the Hungarians and Jews as "aliens" opposed to the Romanian nation. Its anti-Semitic diatribes often rival those published in the Iron Guard press of the 1930s. Ironically, the paper was originally supported by the government of Petre Roman, who later became its chief target "as a Jew." The same viciously anti-Semitic and anti-Hungarian views are echoed in *Europa*, a weekly edited by Ilie Neacşu, which was launched in March 1990 reportedly with the support of the SRI.[9] The realities of the Ceauşescu

---

[8] Michael Shafir, "Anti-Semitism Without Jews in Romania," *Report on Eastern Europe*, June 28, 1991, p. 23. See also his "The Greater Romania Party," *Report on Eastern Europe*, November 15, 1991, pp. 25–30.

In the elections of November 1996, Corneliu Vadim Tudor, who ran for the presidency, received 4.72 percent of the vote. In the Senate race, the PRM received 4.54 percent and in the race for the Chamber of Deputies 4.46 percent of the votes, obtaining 8 and 19 parliamentary seats, respectively. *Cronica Română* and *Curierul Românesc*, op. cit.

[9] See Michael Shafir, "Marshal Antonescu's Postcommunist Rehabilitation. *Cui bono?*" See also his "The Revival of the Political Right," pp. 162–166.

era notwithstanding, the papers often identify the Jews as Judeo-Bolsheviks who brought the catastrophe of Communism on Romania. They have consistently attacked Chief Rabbi Mozes Rosen, various American and Israeli Jewish organizations, and American agencies, including the CIA. To expiate Ceaușescu's nationalist-socialist regime they so loyally served, the collaborators of these neo-Fascist organs focus their ire against their former colleagues of Jewish origin. Toward this end, they posthumously also "Judaized" a number of ethnic Romanian officials, including Elena Ceaușescu. The dictator's wife was identified as a "coreligionist of Pauker, Răutu, and Chișinevschi," the purged top Communist leaders of Jewish origin.[10]

A third ultra-nationalist political organization in this category is the Movement for Romania (*Mișcarea Pentru România*—MPR) established in December 1991. Led by Marian Munteanu, a former member of the Communist youth movement who also served the *Securitate*, MPR follows in the footsteps of the Iron Guard. The movement's political agenda is reflected in *Mișcarea* (The Movement), its official organ, and in *Gazeta de Vest* (Western Gazette), a Timișoara-based weekly financed from abroad by the followers of Horia Sima, the late exiled leader of the Iron Guard.[11]

Reflecting the spirit of the times, chauvinistic nationalist positions are also echoed by the Socialist Party of Labor (*Partidul Socialist al Muncii*—PSM), a theoretically Leftist party. The heir of Ceaușescu's Communist Party, the PSM is led by Ilie Verdeț, a former prime minister and influential Politburo member. Although he pays lip service to the interests of the working class, Verdeț often reveals his sympathies with the Greater Romania Party with which he, in fact, once established a parliamentary fac-

---

[10] Shafir, "Anti-Semitism Without Jews in Romania," p. 25. See also his "The Revival of the Political Right," pp. 162–163.

[11] For further details on the Movement for Romania, see ibid. pp. 166–171.

tion known as the National Bloc.[12] Among the leading figures of this Left-Fascist party are Adrian Păunescu, a former Ceauşescu hagiographer and editor of *Totuşi Iubirea* (Love Nevertheless), and, to a lesser degree, Raoul Şorban.

A common denominator that links these parties, movements, and press organs is the pursuit of chauvinistic nationalist objectives, including the rehabilitation of Marshal Ion Antonescu, the opposition to ethnic-national minorities, especially Hungarians and Gypsies, and the distortion, denigration, or denial of the Romanian chapter of the Holocaust.[13]

THE POST-CEAUŞESCU DRIVE ON BEHALF OF ANTONESCU

Begun during the Ceauşescu era, the campaign to rehabilitate Marshal Antonescu has gained momentum. The rehabilitation campaign has, among other things, involved the glorification of the Marshal and the pressuring of the authorities for a judicial review of his conviction. Hailing him as an anti-Soviet hero, the Romanian Parliament, including its few Jewish members, observed a minute of silence in tribute to the Marshal (May 1991). On October 22, 1993, one day after the U.S. Congress granted Romania most-favored-nation trade status, a statue of Antonescu was unveiled in front of the local police headquarters in Slobozia, a city east of Bucharest on the Ialomiţa River. The unveiling ceremony was attended by Mihai Ungheanu, the State Secretary in

---

[12] *East European Reporter*, November–December 1992, p. 8. In the elections of November 1996, Păunescu received only 0.68 percent of the vote. His party gained no parliamentary seats, having failed to obtain the required minimum of three percent of the votes: it only received 2.16 percent and 2.15 percent of the votes in the Senate and Chamber races, respectively. *Curierul Românesc* and *Cronica Română*, op. cit.

[13] In addition to the press organs mentioned above, there are a large number of smaller publications, including *Oblio* and *Arena Magazin*, that pursue the same objectives. For some details, see Ioanid, "Romania," pp. 246–247.

the Ministry of Culture who was formerly Ceauşescu's aide, and several members of the Parliament, including Corneliu Vadim Tudor. Ungheanu's presence, which reflected the then President Iliescu's tacit consent, aroused considerable controversy both in Romania and abroad. In a letter addressed to President Iliescu, 50 members of both houses of the U.S. Congress emphasized that "the presence of Ungheanu cannot but lead to the conclusion that the ceremony had benefited from the official support of the Romanian government."[14]

Another statue of Antonescu was erected in Piatra Neamţ (November 12, 1994). The inaugural ceremony was marked by the parade of a military unit and the laying of a wreath sent by the prefect, the representative of the central authorities. On June 1, 1996—the fiftieth anniversary of Marshal Antonescu's execution as a war criminal—a monument, consisting of a large cross on a marble base, was "secretly" unveiled in his memory within Jilava, a prison near Bucharest. Erected on the spot where the Marshal was executed, the monument was presumably authorized by the Ministry of Justice which has jurisdiction over prisons. Containing patriotic references to the Marshal, the monument reportedly emerged as a popular pilgrimage site for neo-Fascists. In August 1997 still another statue was erected in the town of Sărmaş, where the Hungarian military forces massacred 126 Jews in September 1944.[15] One of the most controversial—and clearly anti-Hungarian—plans relates to the erection of an Antonescu monument in Cluj-Napoca,

---

[14] As quoted by Shafir in his "Marshal Antonescu's Postcommunist Rehabilitation." For a reference to President Iliescu's tacit consent, see Andrei Codrescu, "Fascism on a Pedestal," *The New York Times*, December 7, 1993.

[15] The statue was inaugurated by Andrei, the Romanian Orthodox Bishop of Alba Iulia. The unveiling festivities were organized by the Romanian Orthodox Church, the representatives of the extremist parties and organizations, and the Historical Museum of Mureş County, which is subordinated to the Ministry of Education and Culture. For some additional details, see Zoltán Tibori Szabó, "Antonescu szobrára" (On Antonescu's Statue), *Szabadság* (Freedom), Cluj-Napoca, August 23, 1997, p. 3.

the capital of Transylvania. Spearheaded by Gheorghe Funar, the fiercely anti-Hungarian mayor and PUNR leader, the plans for the erection of a 10-meter high bronze statue were discussed on January 25, 1996, at a meeting attended by some 60 people, including Iosif C. Drăgan and Raoul Şorban.[16] Streets and squares were—and continue to be—named after the Marshal in many towns and cities. Chief Rabbi Rosen incurred the wrath of many xenophobic nationalists when he noted in one of his speeches that while on a visit to Budapest he had seen no streets named after Miklós Horthy, the Hungarian Regent of the Nazi era.[17]

In addition to statues and street names, the Marshal is also glorified in state-owned media and films. Sergiu Nicolaescu, a senator belonging to former President Iliescu's party and formerly official film director of the Ceauşescu regime, produced a motion picture—The Mirror (*Oglinda*)—in which Antonescu is depicted as a martyr. Another film—The Marshal's Destiny (*Destinul Mareşalului*)—was produced and distributed in December 1994 by state-controlled companies. The film portrays Antonescu "as a great patriot and justifies the massacre of the Jews during his rule with the claim that the victims were Communists and Russian sympathizers."[18]

Concurrently with the glorification of the Marshal, early in 1993, Romanian extremists also succeeded in publishing and dis-

---

[16] K. J., "Törvényen kívüli szobor és zsűrije" (Illegal Statue and Its Jury), ibid., January 1996. According to a May 8, 1996 report by *Azi* (Today), a Romanian daily, a statue of Antonescu was also being planned in Bacău in conjunction with the establishment of a "Ion Antonescu Museum." However, according to a July 5, 1996, communication by Dr. Mircea Dan Geoana, the Romanian Ambassador to Washington, the *Azi* report was incorrect: the museum is being dedicated to someone named "Iuliu Antonescu."

[17] Shafir, "Anti-Semitism Without Jews in Romania," p. 28.

[18] For details on the post-Communist glorification of Antonescu, see Shafir, "Marshal Antonescu's Postcommunist Rehabilitation," op, cit. See also Ioanid, "Romania," pp. 251, 253.

seminating a Romanian translation of Hitler's *Mein Kampf* with the authorization of Vasile Manea Drăgulin, the Prosecutor General.[19] This was coupled with the serialization of the *Protocols of the Elders of Zion*, the notorious forgery, by *Europa*, *România Mare*, and *Oblio*, a tabloid. A few years later, the viciously anti-Semitic works of Corneliu Zelea Codreanu and Horia Sima were also republished.[20] In 1997, the nationalist extremists headed by Şerban Şuru, the Holocaust denying Legionary leader, erected a monument to the Iron Guard at the Black Sea resort town of Eforie with the cooperation of the local deputy mayor.[21]

A short while earlier, the Prosecutor General was requested by sundry patriotic and xenophobic nationalist groups to help bring about the *judicial* rehabilitation of Marshal Antonescu by initiating extraordinary proceedings toward this end. The initiative was taken by the Pro-Marshal Antonescu League (*Liga Pro Mareşal Antonescu*), an anti-Drăgan "patriotic" group set up by sundry vet-

[19] Chief Rabbi Mozes Rosen lodged a protest with the Minister. *Revista Cultului Mozaic* (Review of the Jewish Religion), Bucharest, no. 760, June (1), 1993.

[20] Corneliu Z. Codreanu, *Pentru legionari* (For the Legionnaires) (Timişoara: Editura Gordian, 1993); Horia Sima, *Doctrina legionară* (The Legionary Doctrine) (Bucharest: Editura Majadahonda, 1995). Romanian nationalists also published a Romanian translation of Jan von Helsing's anti-Semitic work on the alleged conspiracy of the Jews to dominate the world: *Organizaţiile secrete şi puterea lor în Secolul XX* (The Secret Organizations and Their Power in the Twentieth Century) (Bucharest: Editura ALMA, 1996), 168 p. Early in 1998, the Legionnaires also launched *Permanente*, a Bucharest-based monthly edited by Professor George Manu. Dedicated to the propagation of the ideas of Horia Sima, the monthly is envisioned to be also distributed among the Legionnaries living in Germany. Sima's successor, Mircea Dimitriu, lives in Stuttgart. On January 20, 1998, Romanian TV broadcast a program relating to the Legionary movement, which, according to a protest note addressed to Stere Gulea, the head of Romanian TV by the *Liga Pro Europa* (Pro- Europe Ligue), had portrayed the movement in an "almost idyllic fashion."

[21] This and many other anti-Semitic incidents in many parts of the country which were not counteracted by the local authorities induced the leaders of the Romanian Jewish community on August 27, 1997, to contact György Tokay, the head of the Department for the Protection of National Minorities (*Departamentul pemtru Protecţia Minorităţilor Naţionale*). *Realitatea Evreiască* (Jewish Reality), Bucharest, September 1–15, 1997.

erans on June 1, 1990.[22] In September 1992, this League appealed to the Prosecutor General and to other governmental agencies for a retrial of the Marshal. The same objective has been pursued by a rival group—the Marshal Antonescu League (*Liga Mareşal Antonescu*), which was set up (together with a foundation bearing the same name) on October 16, 1990, by Drăgan and his neo-Fascist cronies, including Corneliu Vadim Tudor, Gheorghe Buzatu, Radu Theodoru, and Ilie Neacşu, with Drăgan serving as president of both.[23] In June 1992, the Drăgan-led League approached Drăgulin to initiate an extraordinary legal appeal and demanded that Parliament annul the sentences against the Marshal and his co-defendants and pass a law on "honoring the memory of the martyr-hero Ion Antonescu."[24]

The extremists appear to have some friends in the Prosecutor General's office who are sympathetic to the idea of Antonescu's rehabilitation. One of them is General Ioan Dan, a member of the military section of the office, who even wrote a book fully exonerating the Marshal.[25] Another politician pushing for the Marshal's rehabilitation is Petre Ţurlea, a member of the Chamber of Deputies,

[22] One of the leaders of this group is Major General Marin Popescu.

[23] At the November 23, 1996, Congress of the "Marshal Ion Antonescu League and Foundation," Drăgan was reelected Honorary President. Also elected were Nicolae Baciu as Honorary President of the League's National Council, Gheorghe Buzatu as Executive President of the League, and Radu Theodoru as Executive President of the Foundation. "Congresul Ligii şi Fundaţiei 'Mareşal Ion Antonescu'" (The Congress of the "Marshal Ion Antonescu League and Foundation"), *Naţiunea* (The Nation), December 6–12, 1996.

After the collapse of the Communist regime, Theodoru had emerged as a vicious, Holocaust-denying anti-Semite. A Ceauşescu hagiographer with ties to the *Securitate*, he was for a while the editor in chief of *Socialistul* (The Socialist), the organ of the Left-Fascist Socialist Party of Labor. Shafir, "Anti-Semitism Without Jews in Romania," p. 24. For further details on Theodoru's anti-Semitic activities, see below.

[24] For some details, see Shafir, "Marshal Antonescu's Postcommunist Rehabilitation."

[25] See his *"Procesul" Mareşalului Ion Antonescu* (The "Trial" of Marshal Ion Antonescu) (Bucharest: Editura Tempus, 1993). For some additional details on General Dan, see Shafir, "Marshal Antonescu's Postcommunist Rehabilitation."

who had initiated the Parliament's tribute to Antonescu in May 1991.[26]

As former President Ion Iliescu of Romania was reminded on July 18, 1995, by Senator Alfonse D'Amato and Congressman Christopher H. Smith, the leaders of the Commission on Security and Cooperation in Europe, "no other European nation has erected statues of a war criminal since the end of World War II." Protesting "the lack of official condemnation and vigorous investigation of the desecration of the main Jewish cemetery in Bucharest,"[27] the American officials also asked the Romanian President "for a public statement denouncing Antonescu as a war criminal and Nazi ally," warning that by "the continuing efforts to honor Antonescu as a national hero ... the foundation is being laid in Romania for a resurgence of fascism, anti-Semitism, and crude ethnically-based nationalism."

The American officials also expressed their disappointment over the crass expediency that appeared to guide the government's cooperation with the extremist parties. Their anger was clearly reflected in their letter:

> We were startled to learn that there are periodic programs on government-controlled television that support the rehabilitation of Antonescu and other Romanian war criminals. *The production and broadcast of these programs implies government sponsorship of this effort.* (Italics supplied.)

As President, Iliescu consistently condemned the manifestations of anti-Semitism and opposed any official moves toward the rehabilitation of Marshal Antonescu. He also participated in several Holocaust memorials and spoke out vigorously against all

[26] For some additional details on Ţurlea's activities and the American reaction to the drive for Antonescu's rehabilitation, see ibid.

[27] Jewish cemeteries and synagogues were also desecrated in several provincial cities, including Alba Iulia, Braşov, Fălticeni, Galaţi, Oradea, and Târgu Mureş.

manifestations of anti-Semitism. Political expediency, however, appear to have prevented the President from matching his rhetoric with concrete action against the xenophobic nationalists. While he distanced himself from the extremist press, President Iliescu had accepted the endorsement of Right radical parties, including the PUNR and the PRM, in his election campaigns and collaborated with them in governing the nation.[28] This ambivalent position is also reflected in his August 18, 1995, response to Senator D'Amato and Congressman Smith, in which he assured the American statesmen that Romania was practicing no anti-Semitism and that the anti-Jewish acts were minor incidents committed by juveniles. Overlooking the two pro-Antonescu leagues' appeal to the Prosecutor General, the President declared that "no attempt was ever made in Romania to rehabilitate him legally." As to the honors bestowed on Antonescu, President Iliescu reminded the Americans about the ceremonies that surrounded the return of the remains of Miklós Horthy, the Regent of Hungary (together with those of his wife and son) and their reinterment in Kenderes, Hungary, in July–September 1993.[29] In comparing the

---

[28] The collaboration with the PRM came to an end in the fall of 1995. The political divorce was followed by mutually vicious *ad hominem* attacks based on leaked *Securitate*-file secrets. Corneliu Vadim Tudor, who planned to oppose Iliescu in the presidential race of 1996, accused the President of having been a KGB agent and a tool of the Jews. With the apparent support of Măgureanu, the SRI head, the President, in turn, revealed Tudor's past *Securitate* link and likened him to Vladimir Zhirinovsky, the Russian chauvinistic nationalist. For details on this bizarre political infighting, see Shafir, "Marshal Antonescu's Postcommunist Rehabilitation."

[29] "România nu practică antisemitismul" (Romania Does Not Practice Anti-Semitism), *Vocea României* (The Voice of Romania), September 8, 1995.

Adrian Riza, the Ceauşescu propagandist, took it upon himself to respond to the D'Amato-Smith note at greater length. In his response, focusing on the wartime record of Romania, he relied primarily on the accounts by Rabbi Alexander Şafran, Rabbi Moshe Carmilly-Weinberger, and Raoul Şorban to defend Antonescu's wartime policies on the Jews. See his "Răspuns deschis la o scrisoare deschisă" (An Open Response to an Open Letter) *Timpul* (Time), August 21–28 and August 28–31, 1995. For details on Riza and his references, see chapters 4–6.

two pro-German leaders, the President most probably was thinking primarily of Horthy's anti-Romanian policies and not of the differences in their treatment of the Jewish question.

Ironically, the extremists dedicated to the judicial rehabilitation of the Antonescu regime have won a major victory after the defeat of President Iliescu in the elections of November 1996 by the "liberal" Emil Constantinescu. On October 22, 1997, Sorin Moisescu, the Prosecutor General appointed by President Constantinescu, recommended to the Supreme Court of Romania that it approve the posthumous rehabilitation of six members of the Antonescu government: General Radu Rosetti, Minister of Education; General Gheorghe Potopeanu, Minister of the Economy; Petre Nemoianu, Minister of Agriculture; Ion Petrovici, Minister of Culture; Constantin Atta Constantinescu, Minister of Public Works; and Gheorghe Dogan, Acting Minister of Justice.[30] Ignoring the overwhelming evidence presented during the 1948–1949 trials, demonstrating beyond challenge that these ministers had to various degrees been involved in the persecution, expropriation, and destruction of Romanian and Ukrainian Jews, the Prosecutor General based his recommendation on "lack of evidence." While realizing that the judicial procedures for the rehabilitation of these Fascist ministers were fraught with "delicate international implications," President Constantinescu asserted that the six ministers had been "outstanding Romanian cultural figures who were not associated with any of the negative aspects of Antonescu's rule."[31]

[30] *Cronica Română* (Romanian Chronicle), Bucharest, October 23, 1997. Convicted in 1949 for "crimes against peace," these anti-Semitic figures of the Antonescu regime had been sentenced to prison terms ranging from two to ten years and the confiscation of their property. As it turned out later, the Prosecutor General also included in the list two other members of the Antonescu government: Aurelia Pan and Toma Petre Ghilulescu, an Under Secretary in the Ministry of National Economy.

[31] Overlooking the anti-Semitic activities of the six ministers, the President made these comments during an interview with a correspondent of Radio Free Europe/Radio Liberty in Berlin on November 7, 1997. Reacting to a protest note addressed to President Emil Constantinescu by Senator D'Amato and Congressman

The international reaction was swift and resolute. As in the case of President Iliescu's failure to act against the anti-Semitic incidents and pro-Antonescu manifestations, Senator D'Amato and Congressman Smith approached President Constantinescu on November 10, 1997. In a stern warning, the American legislators stated:

> We write to bring to your attention a matter of serious concern to us, as Chairman and Co-Chairman of the Commission on Security and Cooperation in Europe, and that should be of equally serious concern to you, your government, and your country in view of Romania's aspirations for eventual integration into the economic and security systems of the West.... Posthumous rehabilitation of these six officials who were convicted of participation as leaders in the implementation of the Nazis' "Final Solution" (on the grounds of lack of evidence) would shock us and others in the West who have come to Romania's support. It would call into question the sincerity of Romania's commitment to the West's most fundamental shared values and is likely to trigger a reassessment of support for Romania's candidacy for membership in our common economic and security institutions.

A similarly stern letter was addressed to President Constantinescu on November 6, 1997, by Miles Lerman, the

---

Smith, Moisescu defended his position by arguing that since ultimate power in wartime Romania was held by Antonescu, neither the principle of collective governmental responsibility nor that of personal responsibility applied to the ministers. *Adevărul* (The Truth), Bucharest, November 21, 1997.

In the wake of the American pressure, the Prosecutor General decided to proceed with the rehabilitation of Ghilulescu only, arguing that he had resigned his position before Romania joined the war against the Soviet Union. The Supreme Court of Justice was scheduled to review the issue relating to the rehabilitation of all the eight Antonescu cabinet members on March 9, 1998.

Chairman of the United States Holocaust Memorial Council. Mr. Lerman emphasized that "Romania is the only European country that has erected monuments that glorify World War II war criminals" and reminded the President that the "Romanian attempts to rehabilitate Antonescu and his regime are contrary to the most welcome trend in most European countries to acknowledge and atone for their past."

It is impossible to determine whether President Constantinescu's reference to the convicted criminals as "outstanding Romanian cultural figures" was due to political expediency or personal conviction. Fortunately, the domestic and, above all, foreign reactions to the rehabilitation drive, including allusions to its possible negative impact on Romania's aspirations to join NATO and the European Union, had a swift result. In a remarkable turnabout, on November 22, Moisescu announced his decision to annul the judicial procedure for the rehabilitation of the Antonescu cabinet members.

It is safe to assume, however, that the chauvinistic nationalists will view this reversal as a mere temporary setback. They will undoubtedly continue their drive for the rehabilitation of the Antonescu regime, a drive envisioned to be crowned by the rehabilitation of the Marshal himself.

THE MINORITIES ISSUE

Another issue that continues to plague the Romanian government relates to the treatment of the ethnic and national minorities. While all manifestations of anti-Semitism are officially condemned by the responsible leaders of the country, the age-old scourge still permeates considerable segments of Romanian society. The phenomenon of anti-Semitism without Jews is nourished by the relentless propaganda campaign of xenophobic nationalists who continue, in the Fascist tradition, to blame the Jews for all the ills of Romania. Like the Nazis before them, these extremists portray the Jews as members of a conspiracy aimed to dominate the world. One of the most vicious proponents of this propaganda is Paul

Everac, one of Ceauşescu's cherished writers, who for a while served as the head of Romanian TV under President Ion Iliescu. He claimed the few thousand surviving Jews of Romania, who are mostly elderly and destitute, form part of a world conspiratorial network able to influence and dominate the country's economic, political, and cultural life. Everac expressed his obscenely anti-Semitic views in a book published while in office. He stated, among other things:

> The Jews are no longer a small minority, but a great world power—in our view the greatest power. This power is diffuse and occult.... The international Jewish network is today indestructible. It dominates world politics [and] decisively influences the balance of power.... They advanced generous ideas without ever forgetting their interest, the need to dominate.... The Jews succeeded in the material transformation of the world and in identifying money as the highest criterion the moment they acquired most of the money themselves.[32]

Everac and his ideological colleagues are no more charitable with Romania's two largest ethnic-national minorities: the Gypsies and the Hungarians. The Gypsies are subjected to discrimination and occasional violence.[33] A nomadic group, they are usually depicted in highly negative terms,[34] and are believed to represent an intractable problem. But despite the seriousness of the Gypsy problem in the nationalists' preoccupations, the issues that virtually obsess them have a different focus: they relate to the large minority of ethnic Hungarians living mostly in Transylvania, and are interwo-

[32] See his *Reacţionarul. Eseu moral-politic* (The Reactionary. Moral-Political Essay) (Bucharest: Editura Românul, 1992), pp. 110–124.

[33] According to the census of 1992, there were 427,000 Gypsies in Romania. Roma spokesmen claim that their number is much higher.

[34] In a chapter titled "A Threatening Minority," Everac describes the Gypsies in the standard stereotypical terms, identifying them as dirty and dishonest and, above all, a potential demographic threat. Ibid., pp. 111–115.

ven with the problems due to the historical Hungarian-Romanian conflict over the region.[35]

Subdued during the Communist era, the animosities that characterized Hungarian-Romanian relations during the prewar period resurfaced soon after the collapse of the Soviet bloc. Romanian nationalists view the Hungarian minority as disloyal to the Romanian state, seeking cultural separation, political autonomy, and ultimately the reunification of Transylvania with Hungary. The Hungarians, in turn, insist that they are treated in a discriminatory fashion, especially in the area of education and culture.[36]

Inter-ethnic relations worsened in the immediate post-Ceauşescu era, when several clashes took place in many parts of Transylvania. Some of these appear to have been provoked by Hungarian nationalists, both indigenous and foreign. Thousands of Hungarians crossed into Romania from Hungary to "help celebrate March 15"—Hungary's national holiday commemorating the day in which serfdom was abolished and the union of Transylvania with Hungary was proclaimed. By far the bloodiest encounter took place in Târgu Mureş (Marosvásárhely), a center of Hungarian culture, late in March 1990. The inter-ethnic fighting claimed three lives and 300 wounded, including András Sütő, the well-known Hungarian writer and playwright. These events helped spark the appearance of *Vatra Românească* (see above) and the "reorganization" of the *Securitate*.[37]

[35] The number of ethnic Hungarians living in Romania is close to two million. According to the Romanian census of 1991, there were 1,620,199 Hungarians at the time. For some additional details on the treatment of minorities in post-Communist Romania, see *Human Rights and Democratization in Romania* (Washington, DC: Commission on Security and Cooperation in Europe, June 1994).

[36] The interests of the Hungarians in Romania are represented by *Uniunea Democrată Maghiară din România*—UDMR (Hungarian Democratic Union of Romania)—a frequent target of xenophobic nationalists.

[37] Shortly after the violent inter-ethnic clashes in Târgu Mureş in March 1990, the *Securitate* was reorganized as the Romanian Information Service (*Serviciul Român de Informaţii*—SRI) under the leadership of Colonel Victor Măgureanu. According to some observers of Romanian affairs, the SRI is in fact the old *Securitate* under a new name. For some details on Măgureanu, see Shafir, "Marshal Antonescu's Postcommunist Rehabilitation."

The anti-Hungarian diatribes are often coupled with the crudest forms of anti-Semitic expressions. Xenophobic nationalists, including former *Securitate* agents, tend to link Jews and Hungarians by portraying them as joint enemies of Romania.[38] One of them addressed an open letter (May 1991) to then Prime Minister Petre Roman, requesting "clarification concerning 'the Hungarian-Jewish alliance,' an alliance said to have become 'extremely aggressive and even very dangerous for the Romanian state.'" The theme is a constant in such publications as *Europa* and *România Mare* as well those financed by Drăgan.[39]

Responding to domestic and especially foreign pressures, the government consented in April 1993 to the establishment of a Council for National Minorities (*Consiliu pentru Minorităţile Naţionale*). Brokered by the Project on Ethnic Relations, a New Jersey-based American organization, the Council is theoretically designed to help resolve inter-ethnic disputes. It is mandated, among other things, to monitor the specific problems of persons belonging to ethnic minorities and to investigate complaints. Viewed by its critics, including some minority group representatives, as merely window-dressing to impress the West, the Council has yet to demonstrate its effectiveness in carrying out its mandate in the multinational state.[40]

Tensions over the treatment of the Hungarian minority in Romania and the Romanians' fear of irredentism eased consider-

---

[38] One of the best known former *Securitate* agents in this category is Pavel Corut. His best-selling six novels in the series titled *Octogonul în acţiune* (The Octagon in Action) dwell on the danger represented by the Jewish-Hungarian conspiracy. See "Former *Securitate* Agent Takes Up a Poisoned Pen." *Research Bulletin* (Radio Free Europe), December 7, 1993.

[39] Shafir, "Anti-Semitism Without Jews in Romania," pp. 27, 29.

[40] *Human Rights and Democratization in Romania*, op. cit., pp. 24–25. Chief Rabbi Moses Rosen expressed his frustrations over the failure of the Council to act on the issue of anti-Semitism and Holocaust denial during its meeting of January 26, 1994. *Revista Cultului Mozaic*, February 8, 1994. Judging by a report in the December 26, 1997 issue of *The New York Times* ("Hungarians and Romanians at Odds in Transylvania"), the prospects of inter-ethnic peace in the region are not very encouraging.

ably in the fall of 1996. Motivated by the desire to join NATO and the European Union, Hungary and Romania signed a treaty on September 16, 1996, under which the Hungarians dropped their long-standing demand for autonomy in Transylvania and renounced any claims on Romanian territory. The Romanians, in turn, undertook to respect the individual rights of the close to two million Hungarians. Only the future will tell whether this treaty will be implemented in good faith and lay the foundation for a possible historical reconciliation between the two countries or serve merely as a temporary vehicle for the attainment of specific political objectives.

Another encouraging development has been the appointment of György Tokay, an ethnic Hungarian, to serve as head of the Department for the Protection of the National Minorities (*Departamentul pentru Protecția Minorităților Naționale*), a new agency that was established following the election of Emil Constaninescu as President of Romania in November 1996.

THE DRIVE AGAINST CHIEF RABBI MOZES ROSEN

During the first few years of the post-Ceaușescu era, the nationalists directed their venomous ire primarily against Dr. Mozes Rosen, the Chief Rabbi of Romania since 1948.[41] The Chief Rabbi has been subjected to a constant barrage of viciously anti-Semitic attacks by sundry xenophobic nationalists, ranging from Corneliu Vadim Tudor of the PMR to Raoul Șorban, a Righteous Gentile associated with the Left-Fascist PSM. A controversial figure, Chief Rabbi Rosen had served his country loyally, representing the interests of the Ceaușescu regime during his frequent trips abroad. He was particularly helpful in serving as a liaison between the Romanian government and Israel, the United

---

[41] Chief Rabbi Rosen was born on July 9, 1912, in Moinești, a small town near Bacău. He died of heart failure in Bucharest on May 6, 1994.

States, and the many major Jewish international organizations, giving the dictator a figleaf of respectability in the eyes of much of the West. While serving the national interests of Romania, Chief Rabbi Rosen was also helpful to the country's ever dwindling Jewish community. Among other things, during his tenure he made possible the emigration of more than 300,000 Jews to Israel and was instrumental in providing adequate social welfare services for needy Jews remaining in the country.[42]

Given the repressive political climate in Communist Romania, Chief Rabbi Rosen's attitude toward the Holocaust in general and the tragedy of Romanian Jewry in particular was quite equivocating. Throughout the Ceauşescu era he remained basically silent on this issue. The first Holocaust-related pamphlet published during his tenure, in tune with Ceauşescu's nationalist-socialist policies, was an anti-Hungarian overview of the destruction of the Jews of Northern Transylvania.[43] He began to test the level of political tolerance in this sensitive field in June 1986, when he first organized a commemoration of the Jassy pogrom—an event that was repeated every year thereafter.

After the fall of the Ceauşescu regime, up to his death in May 1994, Chief Rabbi Rosen devoted much of his energy to counteracting the vicious campaign the neo-Fascists and chauvinistic nationalists were waging to distort or deny the tragedy that befell Romanian Jewry during the Nazi era. He courageously brought the issue of Antonescu's crimes against the Jews onto the front burner of Romanian politics. In his drive to defend the historical record against the manipulations of the nationalists, Rabbi Rosen often referred to Antonescu as a hangman (*călău*), pinpointing the

---

[42] Of the 760,000 Jews or 4.3 percent of the total in 1930, only about 14,000 remained by the mid-1990s. Over 60 percent of these are well over 65 and they are mostly concentrated in Bucharest and a few other larger cities.

[43] *Remember. 40 de ani de la masacrarea evreilor din Ardealul de Nord sub ocupaţia Horthistă* (Remember. Forty Years Since the Massacre of Jews in Northern Transylvania Under Horthyite Occupation) (Bucharest: Federaţia Comunităţilor Evreieşti din Republica Socialistă România, 1985).

Marshal's personal responsibility for the murder of close to 270,000 Romanian and Ukrainian Jews.[44] The Rabbi was then subjected to vicious and relentless personal attacks by chauvinistic nationalist elements, including many former Ceauşescu hagiographers. The neo-Fascist anti-Semitic press, financed largely by foreign and domestic Iron Guard and Antonescu sympathizers, persistently identified him as an enemy of the Romanian people. Notwithstanding Chief Rabbi Rosen's services to Romania throughout the Communist and post-Communist periods, the media campaign continued to identify him as a Zionist agent bent on distorting Romania's wartime humanitarian record.

In addition to challenging Antonescu's positive portrayal by the Right extremists, the Chief Rabbi took on the struggle against the anti-Semitic press and some of its main collaborators. Late in May 1991 he sued *Europa* and Captain Nicolae Radu, a leading anti-Semite, for publishing defamatory conspiratorial theories about the Jews.[45] In an interview, Radu accused the Jews of trying to transform Romania into "a colony of a Mediterranean state"—a clear reference to Israel—and claimed that the International Monetary Fund, like the government, was an instrument of "the international Jewish conspiracy." He also maintained that the uprising against Ceauşescu in December 1989 had actually been

---

[44] Şorban facetiously refers to those who identify themselves with the views of Chief Rabbi Rosen as "mosesrosenists." In tune with the practices followed by the Ceauşescu regime's propaganda organs, Şorban and like-minded Romanian nationalist intellectuals tend to engage in *ad hominem* accusations, identifying all those who disagree with their interpretation of Romania's role during the Holocaust as "enemies of the Romanian people," "agents in the service of Hungarian revisionism," or "Bolsheviks." See, for example, Şorban's reaction to those who criticized his views on the Holocaust in *Timpul* (Time), June 27–July 2, 1995 ("Incapacitatea de a accepta istoria"; The Incapacity to Accept History). The three-part salvo is directed especially against this writer.

[45] The Romanian press followed up a hint expressed by Chief Rabbi Rosen during his press conference of May 16, 1991, and discovered the linkage between Captain Radu and Lybia. Shafir, "Anti-semitism Without Jews in Romania," pp. 27–28.

masterminded by the CIA, which he identified as an annex of the Mossad, the Israeli Secret Service. Captain Radu even appealed "to the army to act against the Jewish population"—an incitement that induced Chief Rabbi Rosen to also lodge a complaint with Constantin Spiroiu, then Minister of National Defense.[46]

Rabbi Rosen took his struggle against the xenophobic nationalists to the Romanian Parliament as well. In his June 3, 1991, testimony before the Senate Committee on the new draft constitution, he expressed his outrage over the many physical and propagandistic manifestations of anti-Semitism. He declared, among other things:

> The Jews were entitled to demand the elementary right that our democratic state no longer delay the protection we are entitled to and put an end to such criminal instigations to pogrom.... The year 1991 is not 1941 ... and it should not be forgotten that anti-Semitism had brought Hitler to Romania, causing ... not only the death of 300,000 Jews but also that of 600,000 Romanians.[47]

The Right radicals, undeterred, actually intensified their venomous campaign against the Chief Rabbi. Their assault became particularly vicious after the June 1991 commemoration of the fiftieth anniversary of the Jassy pogrom, which the Chief Rabbi organized with the participation of many foreign dignitaries, including Nobel Laureate Elie Wiesel.[48] The commemoration in the Choral Synagogue of Bucharest offered an occasion to acquaint Romanians with the realities of the Holocaust. During the Communist era, the Romanians were merely given to believe

---

[46] Ibid., pp. 27, 29.

[47] Ibid., p. 28.

[48] Among those present from the United States were also Israel Singer of the World Jewish Congress and Rabbi Arthur Schneier of the Appeal for Conscience Foundation.

that "hundreds of thousands of Romanians, including Jews, were killed by the Germans and the Hungarians and a few misguided Romanian Fascists." The Chief Rabbi spoke boldly in the presence of several cabinet members[49] and, referring to the nationalists' history-cleansing campaign, he paraphrased Elie Wiesel by emphasizing that the Romanian Jews had been murdered twice: "They were murdered in the Holocaust of the Jewish people, and we were forbidden to weep for our dead." Elie Wiesel warned the Romanian leaders about the negative consequences and poor image the anti-Semites were creating for their country abroad:

> I address the leaders of this country; I hope you know that
> your representatives have great difficulties in the world to
> mobilize sympathy, political and economic support for your
> country. Your image is not the best. You must know that.
> You must know that unless these anti-Semites are shamed
> in society you will suffer. You will be isolated. The world
> is following with astonishment, dismay and outrage.[50]

Elie Wiesel repeated his warning at a Jassy commemoration of the pogrom a day later, only to be taunted by a Fascist provocateur.[51] The reaction of anti-Semitic nationalists to the commemorative events in Bucharest and Jassy was predictably virulent. They attacked the Chief Rabbi and his foreign guests as opponents of Romania and enemies of the Romanian people. Outraged by the anti-Jewish outbursts following the commemoration, the U.S.

---

[49] President Ion Iliescu and Prime Minister Petre Roman were in Prague for the final meeting of the Warsaw Pact leaders.

[50] Ioanid, "Romania," p. 248.

[51] A woman, reportedly a close relative of one of the war criminals condemned for the massacres, interrupted Wiesel's speech by shouting: "It's a lie! The Jews didn't die. We won't allow Romanians to be insulted by foreigners in their own country." Emil Alexandrescu, the city's mayor, assured Wiesel that the woman did not represent the "real sentiments of Romanians." For some details on the incident, see Henry Kamm, "Anti-Semitic Taunt at Wiesel Talk in Romania," *The New York Times*, July 3, 1991.

House of Representatives and the Senate issued a Concurrent Resolution on July 29, 1991, expressing the will of the Congress:

1. Condemning the resurgence of organized anti-Semitism, and ethnic animosity in Romania, including the existence of extremist organizations and publications dedicated to such repugnant ideas;

2. Urging the Romanian government to continue to speak out against anti-Semitism and to work actively to promote harmony among Romania's ethnic and religious groups;

3. Calling on the people of Romania to resist the negative appeal of these repugnant organizations and their activities and to strengthen the forces of tolerance and pluralism existing in Romanian society;

4. Calling on the Government of Romania to continue to take steps toward greater respect for internationally recognized human rights, including the rights of minorities; and

5. Calling on the President of the United States to ensure that progress by the Government of Romania in combating anti-Semitism and in protecting the rights and safety of ethnic minorities shall be a significant factor in determining levels of assistance to Romania.

The response of President Iliescu was subdued and diplomatic, placing the blame for the anti-Semitic manifestations in Romania on both the extremist press and Chief Rabbi Rosen. He reproached the Chief Rabbi "for his attempt to promote the idea that the Holocaust started in Romania."[52]

Chief Rabbi Rosen was also taken to task by Adrian Păunescu, the Ceaușescu hagiographer who assumed a leading role in the campaign for the rehabilitation of Antonescu. Reacting to the Chief Rabbi's comments during a 1992 TV debate with Buzatu,

---

[52] Ioanid, "Romania," pp. 249–250.

Neacşu, and Theodoru, Păunescu accused Rosen of whitewashing the crimes perpetrated by Jews against the Romanian army and defended Antonescu's wartime record. He emphasized that the Marshal saved the Jews not only by opposing Hitler's demand for the implementation of the Final Solution in Romania, but also by transferring many of them to Transnistria "to save them from starvation and the illnesses prevailing under the conditions of war— an attempt that unfortunately failed."[53]

Paul Everac, the former head of Romanian TV, identified Chief Rabbi Rosen as a link in the Jewish conspiracy to dominate the world. He referred to him not as a Rabbi but as an "ambassador" with far-reaching political powers. As a consequence, he argued, "Romania's policy toward the Jews is subordinated to its policies toward the Great Powers."[54]

On January 24, 1994, Romanian TV broadcast a three-hour program in which the panelists glorified Marshal Antonescu, calling for his rehabilitation. They blamed the Jews for the "military actions" that had been taken against them "in self-defense" during the withdrawal of Romanian forces from Northern Bukovina and Bessarabia in June–July, 1940. The Chief Rabbi's reaction was swift and resolute. At a press conference held at his headquarters in the Choral Synagogue (January 27, 1994), he expressed his outrage over the rehabilitation drive, emphasizing the danger it represented not only for the Jews but also for the Romanian people in general. He expanded on the theme in a speech televised on February 3. The Chief Rabbi methodically refuted the assertions of the panelists, demonstrating that their intention was to distort and deny the Holocaust and bring about the rehabilitation of the Marshal. The Chief Rabbi unmasked the propagandistic nature of their arguments and presented a succinct but graphic description of the

---

[53] On this and additional details on Păunescu, see Shafir, "Marshal Antonescu's Postcommunist Rehabilitation."
[54] Everac, *Reacţionarul*, p. 123.

Holocaust in Romania. He offered documentary evidence about the antecedents and realities of the anti-Jewish drive, including the pogroms of Dorohoi and Jassy and the mass murders in Odessa and Transnistria.[55]

The Rosen Antidote. In their relentless campaign against Chief Rabbi Rosen, the Romanian nationalists took full advantage of the additional ammunition provided by his ecclesiastic rivals, Carmilly-Weinberger and Alexander Şafran,[56] as well as Şorban. Indeed, one of the common denominators that linked these "rescuers" to the nationalists was their opposition, if not hatred, of the Chief Rabbi. The rivalry between the rabbis can be traced back to the early postwar years. The opposition of Şorban and of the other nationalists is linked to the Chief Rabbi's steadfast refusal to accept their interpretation of Romania's and especially Antonescu's role during the war. The Romanian nationalists were naturally eager to exploit the "rescue" accounts propagated in the lectures, interviews and publications of the three antagonists to blast Rabbi Rosen's alleged anti-Romanianism.[57]

In his introduction to Radu Lecca's memoirs, Dan Zamfirescu, an anti-Semitic nationalist, blamed Chief Rabbi Rosen and his supporters abroad for the failure to accept the "fact" that Romania had a "humanitarian" record during the war.[58] He wrote:

---

[55] The speech is reproduced in both Romanian and English in *Revista Cultului Mozaic*, February 8, 1994.

[56] For some details on Rabbi Şafran's unwitting collaboration with the Romanian nationalists, see chapter 6.

[57] For some details on Rabbi Carmilly-Weinberger's lectures and interviews, see footnote 21 of chapter 2 and chapter 7.

[58] A former Ceauşescu hagiographer, Zamfirescu is one of the few intellectuals to openly admit that he had worked for the *Securitate*. As a literary critic during the Ceauşescu era, he contributed articles to such subtly anti-Semitic journals as Eugen Barbu's *Săptămâna* (The Week) and Adrian Păunescu's *Flacăra* (The Flame). After Ceauşescu's ouster, he founded the *Roza Vânturilor* (Wind Rose) publishing house, specializing in pro-Iron Guard works. See also chapter 1.

...We were woken up suddenly and unexpectedly after the revolution of 1989 by an intensive domestic and international campaign that was initiated by the masterly hands of His Eminence Dr. Moses Rosen, the Chief Rabbi of the Jewish Community of Romania—a campaign supported without reservations by the State Department of the United States, the Council of Europe, and an international press with maximum distribution and authority.[59]

Zamfirescu's views were shared by Şorban. During his January 1996 pro-Antonescu dialogue-interview with Adrian Păunescu, the nationalist-socialist Ceauşescu hagiographer, Şorban recollected Chief Rabbi Rosen's alleged reactions to Rabbi Carmilly-Weinberger's positive comments about Romania's wartime role in his customary slanted way. Claiming that he had met Chief Rabbi Rosen for the first and only time in 1987 in the company of Professor Nicolae Cajal, the President of the Jewish Community of Romania since the spring of 1994, Şorban quoted the Chief Rabbi as having said:

What? The Chief Rabbi of Cluj made declarations that Romania had helped the Jews, when it is known that all Romanians are anti-Semites?... The Romanians are the assassins of kikes.[60]

Şorban boasted about his alleged response:

Doctor Rosen, for four years I lived in a border town that was Cluj and I have seen Jews and non-Jews cross the border from Hungary to Romania to save themselves, to

---

[59] Radu Lecca, *Eu i-am salvat pe evreii din România* (I Saved the Jews of Romania) (Bucharest: Roza Vânturilor, 1994), p. 6.
[60] "Mareşalul Antonescu i-a salvat pe evreii din România" (Marshal Antonescu Saved the Jews of Romania), *Totuşi Iubirea*, Bucharest, no. 3, January 1996, p. 2.

save their lives. However, I did not see a single Jew or German or Frenchman crossing the border from Romania to Hungary to save their lives.[61]

Typical of his use of selective memory, Şorban appears to have forgotten the large number of Jews and non-Jews who crossed the border from Romania to Hungary soon after the Hungarian annexation of Northern Transylvania in September 1940, and especially in the wake of the Iron Guard massacres that began in December 1940.

THE PERSISTENCE OF HOLOCAUST DENIAL

Given the political climate in post-Communist Romania, the attempts of Chief Rabbi Rosen to enlighten Romanian public opinion about the realities of the Antonescu era were not very successful. The tragedy that befell the Jews of Romania during the war continues to be generally distorted. The belief that Romania's wartime record was almost exclusively "humanitarian" and that the Antonescu regime protected its Jews and offered asylum to many tens of thousands of refugees is held not only by xenophobic nationalists but also by "moderate" political figures, including current and former parliamentarians and governmental leaders. The belief is based upon the contention that the anti-Jewish operations in Bukovina, Bessarabia, and Transnistria had been actions of self-defense against pro-Soviet "saboteurs" and that the only Holocaust that took place on Romanian soil was the one perpetrated by the Hungarians in Northern Transylvania.

The "Moderates." A classic example of the "moderate" view is represented by Petre Roman, the former Prime Minister and

---

[61] Ibid. He repeated the same argument in a dialogue with Gabriel Ţepelea, a leading figure of the National Peasant Party. See Ţepelea's *Însemnări de taină* (Secret Notes) (Bucharest: Editura Fundaţiei Culturale Române, 1997), p. 357.

leader of the Front of National Salvation. Roman's views on the tragedy that befell the Jews of Romania during the war may have subconsciously been induced by a desire to conceal his background. Of Jewish origin (the grandson of a Rabbi and the son of a former high Communist official under Ceauşescu), Roman spent considerable time after his dismissal in September 1991 attempting to "prove" his Christianity by reference to his mother, a Spanish Roman Catholic, and arranging for publication of a photocopy of his certificate of baptism issued by the Romanian Orthodox Church. Despite these efforts, his political opponents continue to remind him—and the public at large—about his Jewish origins.[62]

Roman, a young and charismatic academic, has consistently condemned manifestations of anti-Semitism. During the worldwide Holocaust remembrance period, he even expressed his sorrow over the tragedy that befell European Jewry during the Nazi era—expressions that may have been motivated by both genuine feelings of sorrow and political considerations. His personal views on the Romanian Holocaust were revealed during a visit to the U.S. Holocaust Memorial Museum on April 16, 1991. They were fundamentally not very different from those advanced by the ultra-nationalists.[63] The prime minister unmasked his insensitivity to the tragedy of Romanian Jewry in his response to a reminder by Mark Talisman, one of the officials of the Museum, that Romania

[62] A candidate for the presidency in the November 1996 elections, Roman was once again a target of anti-Semitic attacks. Leaflets distributed by his opponents called on the voters to prevent the country from being led by a "kike." *OMRI Daily Digest*, Prague, no. 201, part 2, October 16, 1996.

Roman received 20.54 percent of the vote. His party, the third largest, obtained 13.16 percent of the vote in the race for the Senate, gaining 23 seats, and 12.93 percent in the race for the Chamber of Deputies, gaining 53 seats. *Curierul Românesc* and *Cronica Română*, op. cit.

[63] The Prime Minister's entourage included Virgil Constantinescu, Romania's Ambassador to Washington, Andrei Busuioceanu, the Cultural Attaché, and Neagu, deputy director of the USA desk in the Romanian Ministry of Foreign Affairs.

and Albania were the only countries in Europe that had failed to respond to the Museum's appeal for artifacts and archival materials. Like other nationalists, Roman attempted to generalize the destruction of Romanian Jewry with the suffering of ethnic Romanians at the hands of the Hungarians. He also tried to deemphasize the tragedy of the Jews in Transnistria and in Jassy, claiming that only a few hundred Jews were killed during the pogrom. He attempted to "balance" the suffering of the Jews with the massacre of Romanians in the villages of Trăsnea and Ip during the Hungarian occupation of Northern Transylvania in September 1940. When this writer attempted to enlighten him about the fundamental difference between the regrettable killing of a few hundred Romanians with the Holocaust, emphasizing that the Jews had been killed in "all the Trăsneas and the Ips" in Northern Transylvania, Hungary, and elsewhere, he snapped back, asserting that I had tried to differentiate between the Jewish and Romanian victims of the Hungarian occupation.[64]

A more recent example of a "moderate" politician's anti-Semitism is that of Senator Vasile Dumitru, a member of President Iliescu's then ruling Party of Social Democracy of Romania. Borrowing a page from the Nazis' propaganda handbook, Senator Dumitru used the remnant of Romanian Jewry as scapegoats for all the economic and social problems engendered by the government's ill-conceived policies, rampant mismanagement, and widescale corruption. During a plenary session of the Senate (June 18, 1996), Senator Dumitru, pleading for the reintroduction of the death penalty, declared among other things in language reminiscent of the Nazi era:

Hundreds of aliens who cheat, kill, deplete the country of its wealth, in which an Itzik lays his hands on the money bag of a great Romanian merchant killed by a bullet vac-

[64] See reports prepared by Radu Ioanid and this writer on the meeting with Prime Minister Roman, dated April 16 and April 17, 1991, submitted to Michael Berenbaum, then Project Director of the U.S. Holocaust Memorial Museum.

cine, buries industry, brings agriculture to its knees,
indebits the country, and gorges himself.[65]

In response to an open letter published by the leaders of
Romanian Jewry protesting the Senator's anti-Semitic statements,
Adrian Năstase, the President of the Chamber of Deputies, assured
the heads of the Jewish community that the Senator's views did
not represent those of his party, the Romanian Parliament, or the
majority of the Romanian people.[66] The moderates, especially
those in positions of power, are clearly worried about Romania's
image abroad. They are relatively sensitive to world public opinion and tend to publicly condemn all manifestations of anti-
Semitism. However, many among them share the xenophobic
nationalists's views on the Holocaust in Romania although they
express them in a more sophisticated manner.

The Xenophobic Nationalists. The anti-Semitism of the neo-
Fascist nationalist extremists includes the denigration and denial
of the Holocaust. One of their standard positions is that the mass
murder of Jews during the withdrawal of the Romanian forces
from Northern Bukovina and Bessarabia in June-July 1940, were,
in fact, acts of self-defense against pro-Soviet collaborators. A
major vehicle for the propagation of these views is the prestigious
Revista de Istorie Militară (Review of Military History). One of
the most influential among the proponents of this view is Major
Constantin Hlihor.[67]

---

[65] "Ce știți cu adevărat despre Ițic, domnule senator?" (What Do You Really Know
About Itzig, Mr. Senator?) *Realitatea Evreiască* (Jewish Reality), Bucharest, July
16–August 15, 1996. See also János Szász, "Egy fasiszta a Szenátusban" (A Fascist
in the Senate), *Romániai Magyar Szó* (Hungarian Word of Romania), Bucharest, June
24, 1996.
[66] *Realitatea Evreiască*, Bucharest, July 15–August 15, 1996, p. 13.
[67] See his "Calvarul retragerii armatei române din Basarabia și Bukovina de Nord"
(The Calvary of the Romanian Army's Retreat from Bessarabia and Northern
Bukovina), *Revista de Istorie Militară* (Review of Military History), Bucharest, no. 1
(12), 1992, pp. 13–17.

A second major thesis involves the denial of the Holocaust in Romania by "overlooking" the liquidation of close to 270,000 Romanian and Ukrainian Jews during the euphoric, pre-Stalingrad phase of the war, and focusing on the survival of most of the Jews in Old Romania and Southern Transylvania. The only chapter of the Holocaust they admit as having taken place on Romanian soil is the one perpetrated by the Hungarians in Northern Transylvania, the region that was part of Hungary between 1940 and 1944. Their "historical" technique involves the twisting of statistical data and out-of-context quoting from the writings of leading Holocaust scholars and pro-Romanian sympathizers.[68] The group of Romanian "historical revisionists" includes both former and neo-Fascists associated with the Iron Guard.

One of the most influential Holocaust deniers with academic credentials is Gheorghe Buzatu, a well-known historian associated with the Center of European History and Civilization of the Jassy Branch of the Romanian Academy—an institution reportedly supported by Iosif Constantin Drăgan,[69] who even expropriated the term "Holocaust" to depict the suffering of Romanians at the hands of the Hungarians and the Soviets.[70] Buzatu collectively portrays the Jews as having sympathized or collaborated with the Communists. A leading figure of the Marshal Antonescu League and other Right extremist causes,[71] Buzatu claims that the idea

[68] See, for example, Constantin Botoran, "1940–1944. Holocaustul evreilor din România?" (1940–1944. The Holocaust of Jews of Romania?), Ibid., vol. 4 (10), pp. 20–22.

[69] Drăgan reportedly also supports the Center's publishing house, the European Institute for Scientific Cooperation. Victor Eskenasy, "Historiographers Against the Antonescu Myth," in Braham, *Destruction*, pp. 271–302.

[70] See his *Aşa a început holocaustul împotriva poporului român* (This Is How the Holocaust Against the Romanian People Began) (Bucharest: Editura Magadahonda, 1995).

[71] His extreme Rightist ultra-nationalist orientation is reflected, among other things, in a book he edited in cooperation with Corneliu Ciucanu and Cristian Sandache: *Radiografia dreptei româneşti, 1927–1941* (The Radiography of the Romanian Right, 1927–1941) (Bucharest: FF Press, 1996).

that there was a Holocaust in Romania was invented by the Jews, "who had been in the first lines of the Communist movement." A pro-Iron Guard revisionist historian, he exploits every opportunity to warn against the dangers to contemporary Romania presented by "Russian imperialism, the Magyars, and Jewish propaganda." Buzatu attempts to "balance" the "alleged" crimes committed by the Iron Guard with those inflicted by the Communists (read Jews) against the Romanians. He wrote: "One cannot and should not forget the [assassinations] committed by the Communists in the pay of Moscow, for the genuine Holocaust has been that launched and implemented against the Romanian people."[72] Buzatu believes that the same linkage between the Jews and Moscow is responsible for the drive against Antonescu. He claims that "the portrayal of the Marshal as Hitler's servant and as a war criminal was due to the Kremlin's propaganda, which is largely directed by Jews." Buzatu was quick to add a "benevolent warning" that the preoccupation with the Jewish problem of the Antonescu era and, especially, its "exaggerations ... risked the provocation of—and have actually provoked—manifestations of anti-Semitism."[73]

One of the most obscenely anti-Semitic Holocaust-denying nationalists is Radu Theodoru, the executive president of the Marshal Antonescu Foundation. He synthesized his anti-Jewish diatribes in a "scholarly monograph," which incorporates standard anti-Semitic views about the Jewish conspiracy to rule the world, the lies of the charlatans who call themselves "historical revisionists," and a number of specifically Romanian elements of contemporary anti-Semitism.[74] Theodoru aims to convince his

---

[72] For some details on Buzatu's background and activities, see Eskenasy, "Historiography," and Michael Shafir, "Marshal Antonescu's Postcommunist Rehabilitation."

[73] Gheorghe Buzatu, "Mareşalul Antonescu şi problema evreiască" (Marshal Antonescu and the Jewish Problem), *Revista de Istorie Militară*, no. 6 (28), 1994, pp. 23, 26.

[74] See his *România ca o pradă* (Romania as a Prey) (Bucharest: Editura ALMA, 1996).

readers that the Jews, pursuing the establishment of a "Universal Republic under the leadership of Judaistic plutocracy," have already succeeded in dominating and exploiting the United States, England, and France. Like his counterparts elsewhere, he identifies the Jews with both capitalism and Communism, "proving" that the leaders of world Communism, including "Lenin-Ziderblum," were Jewish. As to the Holocaust in Romania, Theodoru denies any responsibility on the part of any Romanians and claims, like Buzatu and others, that all the military measures taken against the Jews during the Antonescu era were exclusively in self-defense against pro-Soviet collaborators. He attempts to "prove" that Romania was an oasis for Jewish refugees during the war.[75] Theodoru contrasts Romania's wartime "humanitarianism" with the "great harm" the Jews caused the country throughout the ages, and especially after World War II. He blames the Jews for all the "sufferings" Romanians had to endure both before and after the Ceaușescu era and, following Buzatu's thesis, claims that the real Holocaust was that experienced by the Romanians. He stated:

> I affirm with all responsibility that the Judaic minority of Romania constituted and continues to constitute one of the long-term noxious factors responsible for a long series of crimes against the Romanian people beginning with the Holocaust in the extermination camps and ending with the cultural Holocaust.[76]

The idea that it was the Romanian people rather than the Jews who suffered the "real Holocaust" was also conveyed in a daily of the National Peasant Party: "The Jewish Holocaust with its loss of 6,000,000 lives, paled against the 'Holocaust of the Romanian

---

[75] To support his thesis on wartime Romanian humanitarianism, Theodoru cites the writing of Rabbi Carmilly-Weinberger (p. 284).
[76] Ibid., pp. 316–317.

people' with the 20,000,000 'psychic victims of Communism' ... and these 20,000,000 were all the victims of a doctrine brought to Romania by the Jews."[77] Şerban Şuru, a neo-Fascist Legionary leader, was just as blunt: "There was neither a Holocaust against the Jews nor a Fascist regime in Romania."[78] Ovidiu Gules, the editor-in-chief of *Gazeta de Vest* (Western Gazette), a viciously anti-Semitic paper published in Timişoara, provided an old "Christian" explanation: "Jewish suffering, including the Holocaust, was nothing but the outcome of the earlier Jewish 'original sin,' that of having refused to recognize Christ as the Messiah."[79]

Besides whitewashing the Romanian involvement in the mass murder of Jews,[80] Buzatu and his colleagues also aim to keep alive the nationalists' territorial ambitions relating to Northern Bukovina and Bessarabia, which are currently parts of the republics of Ukraine and Moldova, respectively.[81]

The Nationalists v. the U.S. Holocaust Memorial Museum. The Holocaust-denying nationalists are particularly upset over the depiction of the Romanian chapter of the Holocaust at the U.S. Holocaust Memorial Museum in Washington, D.C.—one of the most popular museums in the American capital. They are clearly concerned about the image millions of people from all over the world are acquiring about Romania's murderous role during the

---

[77] *Dreptatea* (Justice), February 16, 1990 as cited by Shafir, "Anti-Semitism Without Jews in Romania," p. 24.

[78] See his "Mişcarea legionară şi noua putere din România" (The Legionary Movement and the New Power in Romania), *Cronica Română* (Romanian Chronicle), November 29, 1996, as cited in *Realitatea Evreiască*, no. 39 (839), November 1996. Şuru is the head of the "Liberty" Center for Legionary Documentation (*Centrul de Documentare Legionară "Libertatea"*) of Bucharest and is also actively involved in spreading the Legionary message on the internet.

[79] *Gazeta de Vest*, Timişoara, no. 52, 1991, as cited by Shafir, "Anti-Semitism Without Jews in Romania," p. 25.

[80] See, for example, his "Mareşalul Antonescu şi problema evreiască."

[81] See, for example, Buzatu's *Românii în arhivele Kremlinului* (The Romanians in the Kremlin's Archives) (Bucharest: Univers Enciclopedic, 1996).

Holocaust era. Identifying the Romanian section of the exhibit as "false" and "anti-Romanian," they were particularly upset over the attendance of President Ion Iliescu at the inauguration of the Museum on April 23, 1993. Theodoru, for example, identified Iliescu's presence at the festivities as "one of his capital mistakes."[82] By far the most viciously anti-Semitic views about the Museum in general and President Iliescu's attendance in particular were expressed in an open letter addressed to the President by Corneliu Vadim Tudor, Eugen Barbu, and Mircea Muşat, the founders and leaders of the neo-Fascist Greater Romania Party. Dated April 23, 1993, the letter stated, *inter alia*:

> Your participation at the festivities occasioned by the inauguration of the Holocaust Museum in Washington confirms once again the regrettable lack of dignity you manifest toward the tendencies of world Zionism to hold countries and nations culpable in order to lead mankind without any opposition. During the three and a half years since you're serving as President of Romania you have granted numerous concessions and favors to your Jewish protegees, but this time you have exceeded your mandate and brought the country to a dangerous slope, to the falsification of history.... Do not mortgage the future of Romania, do not participate in the attempts to falsify history, and do not allow that, after the Communist dictatorship brought by the Jews on Soviet tanks, Romania should fall under a Zionist dictatorship![83]

One of the people accompanying President Iliescu as part of the Romanian delegation to the opening of the Holocaust Museum

---

[82] Theodoru, *România ca o pradă*, p. 10.

[83] "Scrisoare deschisă adresată preşedintelui Ion Iliescu" (Open Letter Addressed to President Ion Iliescu), *România Mare*, April 30, 1993.

was Raoul Şorban, presumably because of his status as a
Righteous Among the Nations. When questioned by Adrian
Păunescu, Şorban responded that he had attended the opening
only because he had been invited by the President. He was quick
to assure Păunescu that he had told Iliescu that the Museum's
depiction of the Holocaust in Romania contradicted his own
views.[84]

President Iliescu's attendance at the U.S. Holocaust Memorial
Museum's inauguration was but one of many sources of discontent about his "pro-Jewish" behavior for the xenophobic nationalists. While in office, the former President was consistently condemned for his involvement in the annual Holocaust remembrance ceremonies organized by the Jewish community in
Bucharest.[85] The nationalists' resentment over these "pro-Jewish
and anti-Romanian" activities was exacerbated by the former
President's consistent and resolute opposition to the rehabilitation
of Marshal Antonescu. Engaging in *ad hominem* attacks, the
nationalists "explained" the President's position as having been
motivated by his and his father's Communist activities.

Ion Coja, a former Senator from Constanţa, is among the most
vocal activists agitating against the depiction of the Holocaust in
Romania at the U.S. Holocaust Memorial Museum. He expressed
his unhappiness over the failure to depict the wartime "humanitarian" record of the Romanians and the "emphasis" on the crimes
that were "allegedly" committed against Jews by the Antonescu
regime in an open letter to Alfred Moses, the American Ambassador

---

[84] "Confuzia şi neştiinţa sunt mai dăunătoare decât nedreptatea" (Confusion and Lack
of Knowledge Are More Harmful Than the Untruth), *Totuşi Iubirea*, no. 4 (281),
January 1996, p. 10.

[85] In their messages or talks at such memorial gatherings, President Iliescu and the
other leading members of the government usually expressed their sorrow over the
tragedy of European Jewry during the Nazi era, but usually avoided any specific reference to the Romanian chapter of the Holocaust. For the text of some of President's
addresses, see *Revista Cultului Mozaic*, no. 757, April (II), 1993, and no. 778, April
(I), April 1994.

in Bucharest, requesting his intervention to bring about the appropriate changes.[86] A request for the "toning down" of the depiction of Marshal Antonescu as a war criminal at the Museum was reportedly also advanced by Rabbi Carmilly-Weinberger.[87]

The campaign against the U.S. Holocaust Memorial Museum is clearly part of the multifaceted drive by Romanian xenophobic nationalists to refurbish the historical past. By distorting and denying the Holocaust, these nationalists have reinforced the traditional characteristics of Romanian anti-Semitism by new virulent strains.

---

[86] "Ion Coja redeschide bătălia pentru adevărul despre atitudinea românilor față de evrei" (Ion Coja Reopens the Battle for the Truth About the Romanians' Attitude Toward the Jews), *Vremea* (Time), Bucharest, January 22, 1997. Coja originally approached Ambassador Moses on October 17, 1995. A complaint against the Museum's protrayal of the Romanian chapter of the Holocaust was also lodged by Bujor Nedelcovici in standard nationalist tones in the November–December 1997 issue of *Curierul Românesc* (Romanian Courier), the organ of the Romanian Cultural Foundation (*Fundația Culturală Română*).

[87] Personal communication by Radu Ioanid of the U.S. Holocaust Memorial Museum.

CHAPTER 4

Forging a Rescue Legend

THE MAIN PROTAGONISTS

The campaign to sanitize Romania's wartime historical record on the Jews became intensified in the mid-1980s, when Romanian nationalists took advantage of the largely unfounded accounts of rescue across the Hungarian-Romanian border. These accounts were given and advanced by two elderly individuals who developed a commonality of personal interests: Dr. Moses Carmilly-Weinberger,[1] the former Chief Rabbi of the small Neolog Jewish community of Cluj (Kolozsvár in Hungarian), and Dr. Raoul Şorban, a painter and professor of art history at the University of Bucharest. The former was eager to find solid support against the accusations that were—and have continued to be—directed against him since the end of the war. It is said that although aware of the realities of Auschwitz, he essentially abandoned his flock by escaping to Romania with his wife on the eve of the ghettoization of the Jews of Northern Transylvania (May 2, 1944), leaving his congregation to fend for itself without the support of their Rabbi's spiritual guidance, and uninformed about the

---

[1] His original name was Weinberger. He changed it to Carmilly-Weinberger, the name used throughout this text, shortly after his arrival in Palestine in 1944.

horrible fate awaiting them.[2]   In his joint efforts with Şorban, Rabbi Carmilly-Weinberger was presumably bent on finding corroboration for his claim that his escape was in fact an important "mission of rescue." Şorban, a basically self-righteous, opportunistic, and vehemently anti-Hungarian Romanian, was presumably eager to obtain recognition for his oft-asserted wartime pro-Jewish, anti-Hungarian and anti-Nazi activities.

Rabbi Carmilly-Weinberger and Şorban pursued their differing careers in different parts of the world and were not in direct contact for more than forty years.[3]   However, after Rabbi Carmilly-Weinberger took the initiative in 1985, the two developed an apparent *Interessengemeinschaft* that soon led to the joint advancement of their respective objectives. They developed and propagated accounts of wartime rescue of Jews across the Hungarian-Romanian border that scholars have not been able to corroborate either in standard Holocaust literature or through archival records.[4]   With the passage of time, these accounts

[2] See, for example, the July 13, 1991, letter addressed to Rabbi Carmilly-Weinberger by László Erős, one of the survivors of Kolozsvár. Copy of the letter is in this author's archives. See also Erős's "Dr. Moshe Carmilly interjújának margójára" (On the Margin of Dr. Moshe Carmilly's Interview, *Szabadság* (Freedom), Cluj, May 16, 1991. Rabbi Carmilly-Weinberger's escape and so-called rescue activities were also denounced by some of his former students, including Aliz Kaye (née Hirsch) and Alice Kandel (née Gulkovski), both of Australia, and Ladislaus Deutsch of Hamburg. Their statements are in this author's file.

[3] Rabbi Carmilly-Weinberger was aware of Şorban's whereabouts early in 1973, when he appeared rather unenthusiastic in his support of an initiative by Professor A. Ronen of Tel Aviv University to have Şorban recognized as a Righteous Gentile by Yad Vashem. For details, see chapter 6.

[4] With the exception of what one might characterize as an equivocally supportive letter by Éva Pamfil (née Semlyén), Şorban's former fiancée, the Şorban file at Yad Vashem contains no letter by any of the thousands of Jews Şorban and Rabbi Carmilly-Weinberger claim to have rescued during the war. Şorban File, no. 3499, Department of the Righteous Among the Nations, Yad Vashem. (Cited hereafter as Şorban File.) The failed attempt to rescue Éva Semlyén in which Şorban was also involved is discussed in chapter 5.

became ever more grandiose and, one may perceive, self-serving, making available ammunition to Romanian nationalists involved in history-cleansing. These accounts received a great deal of media coverage, especially in Romanian nationalist and neo-Fascist newspapers, and were aired on both Romanian radio and TV. Interestingly, virtually none of the details of the sensational rescue accounts advanced after 1985 appear in either the 1970 or the *1988* edition of Rabbi Carmilly-Weinberger's memoirs.[5] They are also absent from the long statement Şorban wrote in prison on June 14, 1945,[6] at a time when his recollections were still fresh and his personal interests would appear to have required him to emphasize them. The rationale for the largely unfounded accounts of rescue is reflected in the background of these *dramatis personae.*

RABBI CARMILLY-WEINBERGER

Awareness of the Final Solution. According to the currently available evidence, by March 19, 1944, when the Germans occupied Hungary and sealed the fate of Hungarian Jewry, the members of the Jewish Council of Kolozsvár, including Rabbi Carmilly-Weinberger, were as fully aware of the realities of Auschwitz as were the members of the Central Jewish Council of

[5] See "Versenyfutás a halállal" (Race With Death) in *A Kolozsvári zsidóság emlékkönyve* (The Memorial Book of Kolozsvár's Jewry), ed. Mózes Carmilly-Weinberger (New York: The Editor, 1970), pp. 213–235. For the slightly different English version, titled "The Tragedy of Transylvanian Jewry," see pp. 286–304. It also contains a Hebrew version. The book is cited hereafter as Carmilly-Weinberger, *A Kolozsvári zsidóság.*

[6] Arrested a few months after the liberation of Transylvania by newly-allied Romanian and Soviet troops, Şorban wrote a lengthy statement in his defense. Dated June 14, 1945, the statement is in File 59/1946 (formerly File 181/1945) of the People's Tribunal of Cluj. *Ministerul Afacerilor Interne* (Ministry of the Interior), Bucharest, dos. no. 40030, vol. 17. For further details, see chapter 5.

Budapest. Their sources of information were many and reliable.[7] It is precisely this factor that makes the Hungarian chapter of the Holocaust so controversial.

The leaders of the Jewish community of Kolozsvár enjoyed a great advantage over those of the other provincial Jewish communities of Hungary. The head of the Jewish community and later chairman of the Jewish Council of Kolozsvár was József Fischer, the father-in-law of Rudolph (Rezső) Kasztner, the controversial Zionist leader then involved in negotiations with the SS for the possible rescue of Hungarian Jews. Fischer was also among the few provincial Jewish Council leaders who attended the March 21, 1944, meeting with the SS in Budapest. He and the other members of the local Jewish Council, including Rabbi Carmilly-Weinberger, were consequently in possession of information that was shared neither with the Jewish masses in the local brickyard ghetto nor with the leaders of the neighboring Jewish communities.[8] The more than 18,000 Jews concentrated in the ghetto of Kolozsvár during the fateful months of May–June 1944, were

---

[7] For details, see Randolph L. Braham, *The Politics of Genocide. The Holocaust in Hungary* (New York: The Rosenthal Institute for Holocaust Studies of the City University of New York, 1994), pp. 806–849. (Cited hereafter as Braham, *Politics*.)

[8] When cross-examined during the so-called Grünwald-Kasztner case in Israel in 1954, Kasztner admitted that he had informed the leaders of Kolozsvár's Jewish community about the impending disaster. Ibid., p. 1108. Another indication of these leaders' awareness of Auschwitz was given by Lajos Marton, one of the "prominent" figures in the Kasztner transport. He asserted that Fischer and several other leaders who were aware of the murder processes in Auschwitz had been reluctant or refused to take a shower during the trip. Ibid., p. 1155 (footnote 102). Hansi Brand, one of Kasztner's closest associates, provided additional corroboration. She insisted that the Jewish leaders of Kolozsvár had been informed exactly about what was happening to the Jews in Poland.... Ibid., p. 1159 (footnote 155). For a thoroughly documented overview of the tragedy that befell the Jewish community of Kolozsvár, see Dániel Löwy, *A téglagyártól a tehervonatig. Kolozsvár zsidó lakossága a második világ-háború idején* (From the Brickyard to the Freight Train. The Jewish Inhabitants of Kolozsvár During the Second World War) (Kolozsvár: Erdélyi Szépmíves Céh, 1998).

"informed and reassured" that they would be taken to "Kenyérmező" in Western Hungary for the duration of the war.[9]

That Rabbi Carmilly-Weinberger was familiar with the danger awaiting the Jews is also implicit in a passage from Yehuda Bauer's *Jews for Sale?*, discussing the rescue opportunities across the Hungarian-Romanian border:

> When Rabbi Moshe Weinberger (Gefen) tried to organize a group of like-minded individuals in Cluj and explained to the local leaders that they were facing death and should run for their lives, he was overwhelmingly rejected. Only about 150 people joined him, and they left Cluj and crossed the border illegally, helped by Romanian peasants for money. [10]

Rabbi Carmilly-Weinberger also appears to have been informed about the ultimate tragic fate awaiting the Jews by Şorban himself. In a letter dated April 24, 1986, Şorban reminded the Rabbi:

> When the Gestapo and the SD set up office in Cluj, after March 20, 1944, more exactly early in April, Dr. Aurel Socol, a lawyer, and myself were given a sure piece of information by two German NCO's, namely, that the

[9] See, for example, the statements of Andor Feuerlich and Sámuel Sámuel in Carmilly-Weinberger, *A Kolozsvári zsidóság*, pp. 238 and 241.

After the war, several Jewish leaders of Kolozsvár who had escaped before the deportations began late in May 1944, claimed that they shared the masses' belief about the relocations to Kenyérmező. However, they failed to explain why, in light of that belief, they decided to escape instead of providing continued leadership for the masses in Kenyérmező *where the Jews "were expected to be engaged in agricultural labor for the duration of the war."*

[10] Yehuda Bauer, *Jews for Sale?* (New Haven: Yale University Press, 1995), pp. 160–161.

rumour about the concentration of Jews in ghettos in the cities of Hungary-occupied Transylvania had no truth in it and that the Jews were to be deported to some unknown place *they will never return from*! I, for one, told you and through you, the Cluj "Judenrat," to send the information to Oradea, Dej, Satu Mare, Sighetul Marmației, etc., which you did.[11]

But apparently he did not. Like most other Jewish leaders of Kolozsvár who were privy to the great secret, Rabbi Carmilly-Weinberger escaped. He and the other leaders exploited the available opportunities to rescue themselves. Many of them decided to save themselves and their families by taking advantage of a controversial deal Kasztner had struck with the SS. They were among the 388 Jews taken out of the ghetto of Kolozsvár and escorted to Budapest early in June 1944.[12] Shortly thereafter they were included in the so-called Kasztner transport and, after a relatively brief stay in Bergen-Belsen's *Bevorzugten* camp, were taken to Switzerland.

Rabbi Carmilly-Weinberger's Escape. Rabbi Carmilly-Weinberger had decided to escape by another route even before the Kasztner deal. His intentions were revealed by Şorban in an interview published in 1986. Supplementing his April 24, 1986, personal letter in which he reminded the Rabbi about how he had warned him about the realities of the ghettoization, Şorban provided additional information about that warning. He identified the source of that ominous information as Müller, an *SD-Scharführer* originally from the Transylvanian town of Beszterce (Bistrița). He quotes the *Scharführer* as having said on April 23, 1944:

---

[11] Şorban File.

[12] The list was put together by József Fischer and his and Kasztner's associates in Kolozsvár. Braham, *Politics*, pp. 1154–1155 (footnote 97).

It's good for you to know that things won't stop with
ghettos. Jews will be deported. I swear on my mother's
head this is true. None of those who will enter the ghettos will survive.[13]

Tudor Bugnariu, one of the Romanian anti-Nazis who worked
closely with Şorban, recalls that the *SD-Scharführer*, who was also
referred to as Petri, came to Kolozsvár as part of the Eichmann-
Sonderkommando.[14]

According to Şorban, a few hours after the *Scharführer*'s revelations, he warned Rabbi Carmilly-Weinberger: "You're in mortal danger." The Rabbi, Şorban intimates, was already aware of
this because on April 16, 1944, when the news about the ghettoization was reportedly first leaked, the Rabbi had told him that
"the only way out is to cross to Romania."[15] In his June 14, 1945,

---

[13] Adrian Riza, "România pămînt al speranţei. Fascism şi antifascism pe meleaguri
Transilvane. Reţeaua omeniei" (Romania, Land of Hope. Fascism and Anti-Fascism
in Transylvanian Regions. The Network of Humanity," in *Almanahul "Luceafărul"
1986* ("Luceafărul" Almanac 1986) (Bucharest, 1986), pp. 63–92.

[14] Tudor Bugnariu, "Pe marginea problemei deportării evreilor din Nordul Transilvaniei"
(On the Question of the Deportation of Jews from Northern Transylvania"), *Societate şi
Cultură* (Society and Culture), Bucharest (forthcoming). That the *Scharführer*'s name
was Petri and a friend of Şorban was also confirmed by Gheorghe Dâncuş (see footnote
53). Interestingly, in the Riza interview, Şorban talked about *SD-Scharführer* Müller; in
an interview with Pál Benedek, an Israeli journalist, he identified the *Scharführer* as
Reiner (*Új Kelet*, April 7, 1987). In his April 24, 1986, letter to Rabbi Carmilly-
Weinberger, Şorban referred to "two German NCOs." In a dialogue-interview with
Adrian Păunescu, Şorban claims that he collaborated in Kolozsvár with two members of
Himmler's *Sicherheitsdienst* "who helped in the rescuing of Jews across the Hungarian-
Romanian border. See "Totuşi unde sunt românii?" (Yet, Where Are the Romanians?),
Totuşi Iubirea (Love Nevertheless), Bucharest, no. 5, January 1996.

[15] Adrian Riza, "România pămînt al speranţei," p. 82. Fragments of Riza's interview
with Şorban were also published in English after Şorban had been recognized as a
Righteous Among the Nations on November 6, 1986. See his "The Network of
Humanity" in *Romania Today*, Bucharest, no. 5 (390), 1987, pp. 26–28. A copy of
this issue of the journal was also placed in the Şorban File at Yad Vashem and at the
New York-based Jewish Foundation for Christian Rescuers, an organization affiliated
for a while with the Anti-Defamation League.

statement cited above, Șorban, in fact, claimed credit for having helped in the rescue of Rabbi Carmilly-Weinberger and his wife— a claim that is corroborated neither in the Rabbi's own memoir nor in any other contemporary account.[16]

The currently available evidence reveals that the former Chief Rabbi of the relatively small Neolog community of Kolozsvár and his wife[17] were smuggled across the border into Romania on May 2, 1944, on the eve of the ghettoization in Kolozsvár, with the aid—and at the expense—of an underground Zionist group headed by Hannah Ganz (Grünfeld). Mrs. Ganz summarized the rescue arrangement as follows:

> I used to go to Kolozsvár with groups of refugees on the way to Romania.... I would go to the Jewish Council to inquire whether they had any candidates to be taken across the border. One day Dr. Weinberger slipped a note in my hand, asking me to come to a particular address at 3:00 p.m.... The address was Dr. Weinberger's home. There he asked me to take him and his wife to Romania. I asked him to cover the fees I had to pay the smugglers.... According to his explanations he could not pay and so I had to cover the expenses from the money I had from the Budapest Relief and Rescue Committee. At that time, there was no mention of any local (rescue)

---

[16] Interestingly, when Rabbi Carmilly-Weinberger approached the New York-based Foundation to Sustain Righteous Christians shortly after it was established in September 1987, requesting financial aid for Șorban, he stated that Șorban had "saved hundreds of Jews among them himself." Communication by Eva Fogelman, one of the leading figures of the Foundation, dated April 11, 1993.

[17] In his book he identified himself as "formerly, Chief Rabbi of Kolozsvár" whereas he was only the Chief Rabbi of the Neolog congregation, which was much smaller than the traditional Orthodox one. The accounts relating to his "rescue" activities published in Romania after 1985 consistently identify him by this inflated title.

committee; it was simply the rescue of the Weinberger people.[18]

The Weinbergers' first stop in Romania was Turda (Torda), a border town, where they were reportedly treated like other escapees and refugees by a local relief and rescue team that included Arnold Finkelstein, a leading official of the Jewish community, and Arieh Hirsch (later Eldar), one of the heroic figures of the rescue effort. A prominent role in the rescue work was also played by Carol (Majsi) Moskovits and Eszter Goro (Fränkel), whose widowed mother sheltered Arieh Hirsch, who was then both very ill (he suffered from tuberculosis) and an illegal resident in Turda.[19] During the few days in Turda, Hirsch supplied the Weinbergers with false identification and travel documents. Mrs. Weinberger was provided with papers identifying her as the wife of an ailing Romanian officer in Bucharest. Rabbi Weinberger's documents identified him as a Protestant minister with the rank of captain being called to Bucharest to clarify his status.[20]

[18] Archives of the Center for Historical Documentation, University of Haifa. See also Asher Cohen, *The Halutz Resistance in Hungary, 1942–1944* (New York: Institute for Holocaust Studies of the City University of New York, 1986), pp. 91–92. Presumably confronted with this statement in a collection prepared by this author, Rabbi Carmilly-Weinberger acknowledged Hannah Ganz's role in his and his wife's escape in a book published in 1994. For details, see chapter 7.

[19] Arieh (Ernest) Hirsch, who changed his name to Eldar after his arrival in Israel in 1951, came from Erzsébetváros (Dubrăveni). For details on his background and activities, see Arnold David Finkelstein, *Fénysugár a borzalmak éjszakájában* (A Ray of Light in the Night of Horrors) (Tel Aviv: P. Solar and J. Nadiv, 1958), pp. 249–252, 282–289. See also Eszter (Fränkel) Goro's statement of June 3, 1992 at the Institute for Holocaust Studies at the Graduate Center of the City University of New York. Goro's statement is also available in several other major Holocaust-related archives, including those of the U.S. Holocaust Memorial Museum in Washington, Yad Vashem, and the Strochlitz Institute for Holocaust Studies at Haifa University.

[20] Statement of Arieh (Hirsch) Eldar, dated March 7, 1977, pp. 15–16. Center for Historical Documentation, University of Haifa, Archives, Doc. R3c7.

Arnold D. Finkelstein, the highly regarded secretary of the Jewish community and one of the leading figures of the rescue committee of Turda, provided some additional details about the Weinbergers' Aryan identification:

> On the basis of its Order No. X, the *Cerc* (the local military recruitment center) sent Dr. Mózes Weinberger, the Chief Rabbi of the Neolog Congregation, as Dr. Ákos Szabados, Reformed minister of Sármás, directly to the appropriate section of the Ministry of War to clarify his status as a field minister. The "minister" fitted perfectly into his role; he did not even have to hang a cross on his chest. But this was not the case with his wife, the reverend lady, who traveled separately from her husband as a Christian woman. She, to be sure (I beg her pardon for this small gossip), hung a sizable golden cross around her neck.[21]

After a few days in Turda, the Weinbergers were taken by train to Bucharest, from where they managed, after a short while, to leave for Palestine via Constanţa and Istanbul. They reached Haifa on July 12, 1944.

Controversy over the wartime behavior of the Jewish leaders of Kolozsvár arose almost immediately after the liberation of Transylvania by newly allied Soviet and Romanian forces in October 1944.[22] It gained momentum after the end of the war. Survivors of concentration and labor service camps began to wonder how it was possible that some "prominent" Jews had survived with their families and friends almost intact, while they had lost most of theirs. As in several other countries during the immediate

---

[21] Finkelstein, *Fénysugár a borzalmak éjszakájában*, p. 276.
[22] Romania extricated itself from the Axis Alliance on August 23, 1944, and shortly thereafter joined the Soviets, fighting against the Germans and the Hungarians.

postwar period, the Hungarian authorities considered emulating the Romanian authorities.[23] by initiating plans to indict the top leaders of the Budapest Jewish Council and of the Zionist-dominated Relief and Rescue Committee "for collaboration with the enemy."[24]

A similar plan was under way in Transylvania, where there was considerable bitterness, especially in Kolozsvár, against the local wartime Jewish leaders. The controversial role the Jewish leaders of Kolozsvár played during the German occupation was revealed during the 1953–1955 Grünwald-Kasztner trial in Israel.[25] The controversy also engulfed the Weinbergers.[26] A number of his former parishioners and students expressed their anger over the Rabbi's failure to share the "big secret" with them. Some even claimed that the Rabbi actually misled them by urging them to obey and carry out all the orders of the authorities while he himself was already preparing to flee the country. Ladislaus (László) Deutsch, a former student and parishioner of the Rabbi stated:

[23] During the immediate postwar period, the Romanian authorities initiated criminal proceedings against the top leaders of the Center of the Jews in Romania (*Centrala Evreilor din Român̂ia*), including Dr. Nandor Ghingold, A. Willman, and Adolf Grossman-Grozea. Convicted of collaboration, Ghingold was sentenced to life imprisonment, Willman to twenty years, and Grossman-Grozea to ten years. They were released by the Communist authorities after serving part of their terms. For details, see Bela Vago, "The Ambiguity of Collaborationism. The Center of the Jews in Romania, 1942–1944" in *Patterns of Jewish Leadership in Nazi Europe, 1933–1945* (Jerusalem: Yad Vashem, 1979), pp. 287–316.

[24] Only one member of the Budapest Jewish Council was actually tried. Identified by several of bis Council colleagues as an informer in the service of the Hungarian Nazis, Rabbi Béla Berend of Szigetvár was convicted by a people's tribunal in Budapest and condemned to ten years' imprisonment in 1946. A year later, however, the National Council of People's Tribunals reversed the lower court decision and Rabbi Berend was allowed to leave Hungary for the United States. For details on this controversial case and its aftermath, see Braham, *Politics*, pp. 480–489.

[25] For details on the trial, see ibid., pp. 1104–1112.

[26] The controversy over the wartime behavior of the Jewish leaders of Kolozsvár came to a climax during the Grünwald-Kasztner trial in Israel in 1953–1954. For details see ibid., pp. 1104–1112.

In the last day before the Hungarians transported the Jews of Cluj-Kolozsvár to the brickyard outside of the town, designed as a ghetto [which was] the last station before the deportation to Auschwitz-Birkenau, Rabbi Weinberger held his last speech in our synagogue, telling us to remain together whatever would happen, to obey the Hungarian authorities, and to execute correctly their orders. He was shocking. And what he recommended for us to do was the worst proposal one could ever make. The second shock came later when I learned that the Rabbi fled to Romania probably the same night.... Regarding his rescue actions, I never heard anything about a single real case, about a single name of somebody saved by him.[27]

The same sentiment was expressed in a 1948 article published in a Hungarian-Jewish paper of Kolozsvár:

In the evening of the same day he told his "parishioners" that they had no reason to escape to Romania, Rabbi Weinberger himself escaped across [the border].[28]

The Rabbi's rescue accounts since the mid-1980s have aroused the ire of other former students and parishioners as well.[29]

Uncorroborated Explanations.   Rabbi Carmilly-Weinberger offered his explanation for his escape from Kolozsvár in an account many would call self-serving.[30]   Here he states that the Jewish

---

[27] Personal communication dated October 21, 1996.
[28] F. E., "Fischer József, Balázs Endre és a többiek..." (József Fischer, Endre Balázs and the others...), *Egység* (Unity), Cluj, December 24, 1948, p. 7. See also Löwy, *A téglagyártól a tehervonatig.*
[29] Communications by Alice Kaye of Sydney, Australia, dated December 15, 1995, and Mrs. Alice Kandel of Melbourne, Australia, dated May 15, 1996.
[30] See Carmilly-Weinberger, *A Kolozsvári zsidóság*, pp. 213–239.

Council of Kolozsvár had a plan soon after the occupation to send a three-man rescue mission to Romania, but that it was abandoned because of fear that the Council members and many other Jews would be exposed to mortal danger if it were revealed. However, he claims that on May 2, when announcements about the ghettoization of the Jews of Kolozsvár were posted all over the city, Fischer called on him—one of the three men in the envisioned first rescue plan—to undertake the mission alone.[31] Although Fischer did not approach him until 4:00 P.M., i.e., only two hours before the official curfew time, Rabbi Weinberger and his wife were apparently already packed and ready to leave! While referring parenthetically to Hannah Ganz and paying tribute to the heroism of Arieh Hirsch,[32] in this account the Rabbi fails to acknowledge the *real* role these individuals played in his and his wife's escape. He also fails to note any role Şorban and his Romanian associates may have had.

As to his "mission," there is no independent source to corroborate it. József Fischer, who allegedly entrusted him with the task, apparently never "shared the secret" with anyone, orally or in writing. If Fischer had done so, is it conceivable, as Dezső (David) Schön, the editor-in-chief of the *Új Kelet* (New East), put it in a December 10, 1970, letter to Rabbi Carmilly-Weinberger: would Fischer not have included the parents of the person he sent on an important and dangerous mission in the Kasztner group?[33] Furthermore, is it possible that Fischer never revealed Rabbi Weinberger's "important rescue mission" to Kasztner, his son-in-law, who was in the forefront of the national rescue operations?

---

[31] Rabbi Carmilly-Weinberger does not explain why Fischer, and presumably the other leaders of Kolozsvár's Jewry, suddenly lost their fear of retribution.

[32] Carmilly-Weinberger, *A Kolozsvári zsidóság*, pp. 227, 238.

[33] A copy of the letter is available in this author's archives. Rabbi Carmilly-Weinberger's parents were deported together with the other Jews of Kolozsvár to Auschwitz, where they perished.

Kasztner does not even refer to Rabbi Carmilly-Weinberger in his many postwar reports and statements.

On the other hand, those who did write about the Weinbergers' escape, i.e., the individuals in charge of the rescue campaign in Turda, are unanimous in their recollections. All of them state that the Weinbergers were merely escapees whom they helped across the border like other refugees; none of them showed any awareness of any "mission" by the Rabbi. Arnold Finkelstein, for example, had this to say:

> From among the members of the so-called Rescue Committee of Kolozsvár, with whom Ari [Arieh Hirsch] maintained close contact so that they had a well designed escape route—and were also well endowed materially— only the members of the Committee and perhaps two to three individuals with close ties to them were saved, namely Ernő Hátszegi, Dr. Mór [sic] Weinberger, the Neolog Chief Rabbi and his wife, Dr. Ernő Marton, the editor-in-chief of the *Új Kelet*, and Jancsi [János] Guttfried....
>
> The Rescue Committee of Kolozsvár, thus, exploited the rescue route and material means at their disposal exclusively for their own rescue. And that they selected this route not as an end, but as the safest possible means of escape is also proven by the fact that precisely the most prominent personalities, Dr. Ernő Marton, Chief Rabbi Dr. Weinberger, and Ernő Hátszegi, selected this route as more advantageous and secure for themselves than the Bergen-Belsen [Kasztner] transport into which they would undoubtedly have been included.[34]

---

[34] Finkelstein, *Fénysugár a borzalmak éjszakájában*, pp. 292 and 294. The father of five children, Finkelstein was highly regarded by Arieh Hirsch and the others involved in the rescue effort in Turda. Appreciation for Finkelstein's rescue activities is often also expressed by Şorban.

Among those who were particularly chagrined over what many have described as the "cowardly" and "irresponsible" behavior of the Jewish leaders of Kolozsvár was reportedly Arieh Hirsch. He and the other individuals involved in the rescue effort in Turda were upset that relatively few refugees were coming from Kolozsvár, and even these were coming on their own without organized assistance, relying only on sheer luck.[35] Eszter (Fränkel) Goro, who worked closely with Hirsch, concurred. In her view, "Rabbi Weinberger and his wife used the Turda route as an escape, and like everybody else left for Bucharest after a day or two. I never heard that Weinberger had any role in the rescuing of Jews from Kolozsvár."[36]

Rabbi Carmilly-Weinberger claims that the very night he and his wife arrived in Bucharest (May 7), he went to see Dr. Alexander Şafran, the Chief Rabbi of Romania, and "informed him about the situation in Hungary." In response to his alleged request, Rabbi Carmilly-Weinberger states, on the next day Chief Rabbi Şafran "contacted the Swedish and the Swiss legations and the Nunciature which informed the Pope in a telegram about the situation in Hungary."[37] Is it possible that the Chief Rabbi of Romania would have forgotten such an important international rescue effort if he had been involved in it? In his memoirs, Chief Rabbi Şafran had only the following to write about the Weinbergers: "Among the refugees were Rabbi Moshe Weinberger of Cluj and his wife. They came to Bucharest, to my home, in a terrible state, both bleeding and covered with wounds, their clothes torn."[38] Not a word or even a hint about a rescue mission or about contacts with foreign legations! The book also fails

---

[35] Ibid., p. 292.
[36] See statement by Eszter (Fränkel) Goro cited above.
[37] Carmilly-Weinberger, *A Kolozsvári zsidóság*, p. 231.
[38] Alexander Şafran, *Resisting the Storm. Romania, 1940–1947* (Jerusalem: Yad Vashem, 1987), p. 114. Reportedly, in the French version (*Un tison attaché aux flammes*, Paris: Stock, 1989) even this reference is left out.

to make any reference to Raoul Şorban.[39]

In addition to Chief Rabbi Şafran, Rabbi Carmilly-Weinberger claims that he also contacted Dr. W. Filderman, the leader of Romania's Jewry, who, two days after the meeting, allegedly sent a shattering letter to Prince Barbu Ştirbey, then in Cairo conducting secret negotiations with the Allies, and arranged for him (Weinberger) to meet the Bucharest representative of the International Red Cross as well as Zissu, the person in charge of Palestine emigration matters.[40] Again, no corroboration of these assertions has been found or brought forward.[41]

Having crossed Romania on a "mission of rescue," Rabbi Carmilly-Weinberger felt compelled to "explain" his decision to continue on "to Istanbul." In the Hungarian version of his account, he claims that shortly after Ernő Marton's arrival in Bucharest they agreed on a division of labor: Marton would remain in the Romanian capital and he would go on to Istanbul, where the *Va'ad Hatzala* (Rescue Committee) of Palestine had a main office. This account goes counter to the explanation provid-

---

[39] Rabbi Şafran "updated" the story in the 1996 Romanian edition: *Un tăciune smuls flacărilor* (Bucharest: Editura Hasefer, 1996). The updating followed the uproar over his pro-nationalist speech in the Romanian Senate on March 28, 1995. In the Romanian edition, Rabbi Şafran notes the "rescue" activities of Rabbi Carmilly-Weinberger and Şorban in a footnote (p. 211). For details on the uproar and the "updated" Romanian edition, see chapter 6.

[40] Carmilly-Weinberger, *A Kolozsvári zsidóság*, pp. 231–232. In a book dealing with Zissu's postwar ordeal there is no reference to Rabbi Carmilly-Weinberger. See *Sionişti sub anchetă. A. L. Zissu. Declaraţii. confruntări, interogatorii* (Zionists on Trial. A. L. Zissu. Declarations, Confrontations, Interrogations) (Bucharest: Edart-FFP, 1993).

[41] The Filderman archives contain no reference to Rabbi Carmilly-Weinberger. See *The Dr. W. Filderman Archives (Record Group P-6)*, Jean Ancel, comp. (Jerusalem: Yad Vashem Central Archives, 1974), 156 p. The absence of reference to Rabbi Weinberger in the Filderman Archives was corroborated in a March 10, 1993, communication by Ancel, a leading authority on the tragedy of Romanian Jewry. In connection with Zissu, Ancel wrote: "I can ... confirm that Weinberger's name was not mentioned between September 1944-December 1947 in the Zionist Press (*Renaşterea Noastră* [Our Rebirth] or *Mântuirea* [Rescue]) as having fulfilled a great role or any role in rescue matters."

ed in the English version of the same memoir.⁴² Be that as it may, while in Bucharest Marton developed a vast rescue and relief network with the aid of the local Jewish organizations and the International Red Cross.⁴³

Rabbi Carmilly-Weinberger and his wife boarded a Turkish ship—the *Kazbek*—in Constanța on July 7, 1944, "en route to Palestine." Two days later the Rabbi allegedly managed with the aid of the Turks to meet Chaim Barlas, the head of the Istanbul Vaadah.⁴⁴ After allegedly informing him about the events in Hungary and asking him to establish contact with Marton, the Rabbi reboarded the *Kazbek* for Palestine. However, just as Marton makes no reference to Rabbi Carmilly-Weinberger, let alone to any division of labor with him,⁴⁵ Chaim Barlas also

---

⁴² In the English-language version ("The Tragedy of Transylvanian Jewry") Rabbi Carmilly-Weinberger does not refer to any division of labor with Marton. He simply states that after learning that the Transylvanian deportation trains "had left in the direction of the town of Csap....I saw no reason for remaining in Romania and continued my journey to Turkey, then the centre of the Rescue Committee." Cf. p. 233 of the Hungarian version with p. 304 of the English version of the account in his *A Kolozsvári zsidóság*.

⁴³ For some details on Marton's activities in Romania, see Bela Vago, "Political and Diplomatic Activities for the Rescue of the Jews of Northern Transylvania" in *Yad Vashem Studies*, vol. 6 (Jerusalem: Yad Vashem, 1967), pp. 155–173. This well-documented study has no reference to either Rabbi Carmilly-Weinberger or Şorban. See also Braham, *Politics*, pp. 1042–1048.

⁴⁴ Rabbi Carmilly-Weinberger fails to explain how the Turks were persuaded to provide him a motor boat to get to Istanbul. According to most accounts, the Turks were very strict in enforcing their role as neutrals in the war and were quite reluctant to permit Jewish refugees to set foot on Turkish soil.

⁴⁵ Ernő Marton's archives were deposited at the Center for Historical Documentation at the University of Haifa. A thorough search of the archives revealed no reference to Rabbi Carmilly-Weinberger. No reference to Rabbi Carmilly-Weinberger was found in the Marton microfilms received from Yad Vashem either. In his lengthy November 28, 1944, memorandum on the Jews of Northern Transylvania, including a section on the rescuing of Jews across the Hungarian-Romanian border, Marton mentions neither the Rabbi nor Şorban. The memorandum is among the documents received from the Center for Historical Documentation at the University of Haifa through the courtesy of Zeev Rotics. For some details on Şorban's dealings with Marton, see chapter 5.

appears to have forgotten the important encounter—he makes no mention of it in his memoirs either.[46] Shortly after his arrival in Palestine, Rabbi Carmilly-Weinberger allegedly also briefed Yitzhak Gruenbaum, the head of the *Va'ad Hatzala* and Chief Rabbi I. Herzog about the events in Hungary. But, again, no corroboration of these encounters has been found or brought forward.[47]

Some Controversial Allegations. After the end of the war, the wartime behavior of the lay and ecclesiastical Jewish leaders of Kolozsvár aroused considerable anger among the survivors in Palestine/Israel as well as in Transylvania.[48] Rabbi Carmilly-Weinberger' escape was also subjected to scrutiny. Among those reported to have questioned the Rabbi's postwar rescue claims were, interestingly enough, Dr. József Fischer, the very man who allegedly sent him on the "mission," and Dr. Ernő Marton, his "alibi" for leaving Bucharest shortly after having arrived there.[49] Following his immigration to Palestine, Marton resumed the publication of *Új Kelet*, the Hungarian-Jewish newspaper of Kolozsvár that had been suppressed by the Hungarian authorities in the early 1940s. It was primarily in this paper that the contro-

---

[46] Chaim Barlas, *Hatzala bimei Shoa* (Rescue in the Days of the Holocaust) (Beit Lohamei Hagetaot, 1975), 371 p. The book contains many document reproductions, including some relating to the Hungarian chapter of the Holocaust, with no reference to Rabbi Carmilly-Weinberger.

[47] Yitzhak Gruenbaum, *Bimei churban v'Shoa* (From the Years of the Catastrophe and the Holocaust) (Jerusalem-Tel Aviv: Chaverim, 1946), 222 p. According to a communication by Asher Cohen, Professor of History at the University of Haifa, no reference to any wartime memoirs by Rabbi I. Herzog could be found. This was confirmed by a communication from Moshe Ayalon dated February 10, 1996.

[48] According to László Erős, one of the Holocaust survivors of Kolozsvár, Rabbi Carmilly-Weinberger "failed to return to Kolozsvár in 1945 because he did not wish to look into the eyes of the few Auschwitz survivors." See his "Dr. Moshe Carmilly interjújának margójára," op. cit.

[49] Communication by Dezső (David) Schön, former editor-in-chief of *Új Kelet*, dated June 27, 1991.

versy revolving around Rabbi Carmilly-Weinberger was brought into the limelight, especially through the articles of Sándor (Mihájlovits) Sauber. According to Dezső Schön, Marton's successor as editor-in-chief of the paper, "Rabbi Carmilly-Weinberger practically fled Israel in the wake of Sauber's revelations."[50]

Rabbi Carmilly-Weinberger's explanations in "Race with Death" failed to put the controversy to rest. In contrast to many among the survivors of Kolozsvár, who admit only privately that "the good Rabbi abandoned his flock during the time of peril," others, including a number of his students, and scholars of the Holocaust in Hungary, Israel, and elsewhere continued to challenge—and resist—what continues to appear to many to be his attempts to distort the historical record.[51] Indeed, some of the survivors have expressed their resentment not so much over the Rabbi's secret decision to save himself and his wife, as over his post-1985 activities, inadvertently advancing the interests of "the most chauvinistic Romanian nationalists," including Şorban.[52]

RAOUL ŞORBAN

Şorban was born in 1912 in Dés (Dej in Romanian), the seat of Szolnok-Doboka County in the then Hungarian-ruled Transylvania. A painter and art historian, he had a small art studio in Cluj. In 1939–1940, he had worked as secretary to Coriolan Tătaru, the royal representative in Cluj—a position he reportedly acquired through the support of Alexandru Vaida-Voevod, a noto-

---

[50] Letter by Dezső Schön dated September 14, 1992.

[51] In the first edition of this writer's *The Politics of Genocide*, for example, Rabbi Carmilly-Weinberger's escape to Romania is charitably noted only in one sentence and in a footnote. See Braham, *Politics* (1st ed.), p. 972 and footnote 15 on p. 919. The Weinbergers' reported displeasure over these two relatively minor references in a work of 1269 pages was communicated to this author by some of their friends; the latter pleaded for the deletion of these references in forthcoming editions.

[52] See, for example, the undated [November 1996] letter by Agnes Neufeld, one of the former students of the Rabbi. A copy of the letter is in possession of this author.

rious anti-Semite.[53]   After the death of Şorban's father, Vaida-Voevod, a neighbor of the family, became Raoul's guardian—a man he "loved and venerated."[54] His mother, whose maiden name was Elena (Ilona) Bogdánffy, came from a Magyarized Armenian family and spoke only Hungarian. Şorban was first married to Olga Kaba, a woman who reportedly sympathized with the Iron Guard.[55] Şorban himself was by all accounts an anti-Nazi democrat, who associated with many Jews even after they were compelled to wear the Yellow Star.   After the Hungarian annexation of Northern Transylvania early in September 1940, Şorban fled to Romania but returned to Kolozsvár at the end of the same year, presumably because he became a thorn in the sides of Romanian Iron Guard Legionnaires. It was at this time that he met Éva Semlyén, who soon became one of his art students and fiancée. Şorban also emerged as a good and trusted friend of the Semlyén family (see chapter 5). Perplexed by Şorban's virulently anti-Hungarian positions after the war, Tudor Bugnariu, his close friend at the time, claimed that Şorban had in fact been quite well off under the Hungarians. He was, among other things, allowed to work as an assistant of Zoltán Felvinczy Takács at the Hungarian university, served as the editorial secretary of *Tribuna Ardealului* (The Tribune of Transylvania), the only Romanian-language paper allowed by the Hungarians, organized exhibitions, and played a role in both Hungarian and Romanian public life.[56]

[53] Şorban's resume at Yad Vashem and at the Jewish Foundation for Christian Rescuers, a branch of the Anti-Defamation League in New York, does not include this detail. See Gheorghe Dăncuş, "Despre Raoul Şorban şi alţi 'democraţi'" (About Raoul Şorban and Other "Democrats") in his *În contra ticăloşilor* (Against the Scoundrels) (Cluj, 1945), pp. 12–17.

[54] See "Totuşi, unde sunt românii?" (Yet, Where Are the Romanians?), *Totuşi Iubirea* (Love Nevertheless), Bucharest, February 8–15, 1996. This is part three of a three-part Şorban-Păunescu dialogue.

[55] Statement by Éva Semlyén (Pamfil) taped and transcribed by Zoltán Tibori Szabó in Cluj-Napoca (Kolozsvár) on May 5, 1997. (Cited hereafter as Semlyén, *Testimony*.)

[56] Tudor Bugnariu, "Pe marginea problemei," op. cit. See also Semlyén, *Testimony*.

For some reasons not clearly identified, Şorban was arrested by the Hungarian authorities in March 1942 and taken to Miskolc. There, together with two or three other Romanians, including Aurel (Bubi) Socol, the lawyer and local National Peasant Party leader, he was assigned to a punitive labor service company consisting of 100 Jews. But unlike the Jews, who were sent to the Ukraine, where most of them perished, these Romanians were freed and allowed to return to Kolozsvár a few months later. They were freed, among other things, thanks to the efforts of Éva Semlyén, who intervened in their behalf in both Miskolc and Kolozsvár.[57] Upon his return to Kolozsvár, Şorban was reportedly held for a while for psychiatric observation.[58] Şorban makes no reference either to Éva's role in his release or to his psychiatric difficulties in any of his many post-1985 rescue-related comments or interviews.

Additional details about Şorban's release were provided by Count Béla Bethlen, the wartime prefect of Szolnok-Doboka County. In his memoirs, Bethlen reveals that he personally intervened with Minister of Defense Lajos Csatay to have Şorban released following a plea by his mother.[59] In a controversial interview designed, among other things, to help bring about the rehabilitation of Marshal Ion Antonescu, Şorban not only denies Count Bethlen's account, but also provides an unverified story about his arrest and freedom. He dramatizes his ordeal by transmogrifying the suffering endured by the Jews as his own, and asserts that he was freed only after a threat by Marshal Ion Antonescu about "arresting and punishing four Hungarian intellectuals the same way as were the four Romanians in Hungary."[60']

---

[57] Semlyén, *Testimony*. See also Éva's letter of September 22, 1986, addressed to Yad Vashem, in the Şorban File at Yad Vashem.

[58] Semlyén, *Testimony*.

[59] See his *Észak-Erdély kormánybiztosa voltam* (I Was the Government Commissioner for Northern Transylvania) (Budapest: Zrínyi, 1989), pp. 95–96.

[60] "Mareşalul Antonescu i-a salvat pe evreii din România. Un dialog Raoul Şorban-Adrian Păunescu. Bucureşti, 17 ianuarie 1996" (Marshal Antonescu Saved the Jews of Romania. A Raoul Şorban-Adrian Păunescu Dialogue. Bucharest, January 17, 1996), *Totuşi Iubirea*, January 28–February 2, 1996.

In an apparent lack of gratitude, Şorban also asserts that "even though [Count Bethlen] knew that he was condemned to death [*sic*] in 1942 he refused to intervene in his behalf."[61]

The exaggeration of his suffering at the hands of the Hungarians and the distorted assessment of Count Bethlen's attitude are reflective of Şorban's virulent anti-Hungarianism. He appears to have become obsessed with the danger represented by "Hungarian revisionism" and the irredentist threat allegedly inherent in the struggle of the large Hungarian minority for cultural autonomy in Romania. During the Ceauşescu era, Şorban published several virulently anti-Hungarian "studies." One of them appeared in *Lupta întregului popor* (The Struggle of the Whole Nation), published under the auspices of the Center for Military History and Theory, a bastion of "historical revisionism" headed by General Ilie Ceauşescu, the dictator's brother.[62]

Şorban's animosity to both Hungary and the Hungarians of Transylvania has also been reflected in a booklet he completed in March 1989 and supplemented, after the fall of Ceauşescu, in April 1990.[63] The English-language version of the anti-Hungarian diatribe was brought out in Italy with the support of Iosif Constantin Drăgan, the main supporter of neo-Fascist activities in post-Ceauşescu Romania.[64] In July 1996, Şorban went as far as to assert that the Final Solution in Hungary was not the consequence

---

[61] "Totuşi unde sunt românii," op. cit.

[62] Michael Shafir, "Marshal Antonescu's Postcommunist Rehabilitation. *Cui bono?*," in *The Destruction of Romanian and Ukrainian Jews During the Antonescu Era*, Randolph L Braham, ed. (New York: The Rosenthal Institute for Holocaust Studies of the City University of New York, 1997), pp. 349–410. See also his "'Revisionism' Under Romanian General's Fire: Ceauşescu's Brother Attacks Hungarian Positions," *Radio Free Europe Research. Background Report No. 86*, May 17, 1989.

[63] See his *Fantasma imperiului ungar şi casa Europei. "Maghiaromania" în doctrina ungarismului* (The Fantasy of the Hungarian Empire and the Home of Europe. "Magyarmania" in the Doctrine of Hungarism) (Bucharest: Globus, 1990), 94 p.

[64] See *România şi Europa* (Romania and Europe) (Rome: Revista Fundaţiei Drăgan, December 1991). For some details on Drăgan and his activities in post-Ceauşescu Romania, see chapter 3.

of the German occupation but of an initiative taken by Prime Minister Miklós Kállay—the very man who consistently rejected the German pressures for such a "solution" while in office.[65]

Şorban's anti-Hungarianism is also reflected in his political activities. Şorban has for a while played an active role in the Left-Fascist Socialist Labor Party (*Partidul Socialist al Muncii*—PSM), the remnant of the Ceauşescu-type Communist Party led by Ilie Verdeţ, a former Prime Minister and top Politburo member.[66] (As a candidate of this nationalist-socialist party in the September 1992 elections, Şorban unsuccessfully ran for a Senate seat.) At a county meeting of *Vatra Românească* (Romanian Hearth), Şorban warned the followers of this chauvinistic "cultural" organization about the dangers represented by the Hungarians, claiming that they were "confronting not only a clique, but an entire people."[67] At a later date, he castigated President Árpád Göncz of Hungary for his translation of a wartime book by Endre Bajcsy-Zsilinszky, the fiercely anti-Nazi Hungarian parliamentarian, about his vision of Transylvania.[68]

Şorban clearly has had no problem in reconciling his militant anti-Hungarianism with his status as a Righteous Among the Nations—a controversial status he largely acquired through Yad Vashem's acceptance of his account relating to the ultimately unsuccessful attempt to save Éva Semlyén, his Jewish fiancée.[69]

---

[65] Raoul Şorban, " 'Rezolvarea' problemei evreieşti" (The "Solution" of the Jewish Question), *Curierul Naţional* (The National Courier), Bucharest, July 13, 1996.

[66] Following the elections, the PSM formed a parliamentary coalition in the Senate with the viciously anti-Semitic Greater Romania Party (*Partidul România Mare*—PRM), both led by former Ceauşescu hagiographers.

[67] "Vátra konferencia. A pánikkeltés nagymesterei" (Vatra Conference. The Grand Masters of Panic), *Szabadság* (Freedom), Cluj-Napoca, June 3, 1993. For some details on *Vatra Românească*, see chapter 3.

[68] "Raoul Şorban, "Un indemn la luciditate" (An Inducement to Lucidity) *Curierul Românesc* (Romanian Courier), Bucharest, vol. 7, no. 8, August 1995, p. 20. One can only speculate as to what subconscious role his mother's Hungarian background may have had in his virulently anti-Hungarian outbursts.

[69] For some details on Yad Vashem's decision in connection with the Semlyén case, see chapter 6.

CHAPTER 5

The Semlyén-Şorban Issue

THE ORDEAL OF ÉVA SEMLYÉN

Background. Éva Semlyén was born in Szamosújvár (Gherla in Romanian) on August 28, 1918, into a well-to-do assimilated secular Jewish family of Hungarian culture and language. She dropped out of high school because she could not cope with the Romanian language and, having an aptitude for drawing and sketching, she studied and for a while practiced high-fashion dressmaking. Her father, Hugó Semlyén, was a bank director in Kolozsvár (Cluj-Napoca in Romanian) until the 1930s, when the Great Depression brought about the collapse of the banking business. He later bought and operated a distillery in Szamosújvár that had been founded by his father. Her mother, Irén Klärmann, came from a merchant family in Dés (Dej in Romanian), where she learned to play the piano under Guilelm (Willy) Şorban, Raoul's father. The family lived in a luxury apartment in one of the fashionable Péter-Pál villas in Kolozsvár.

Éva got to know Raoul Şorban in the winter of 1940 in Kolozsvár, where he had an art studio on Király Street. She soon became one of his art students. Though engaged shortly thereafter, they could not marry because of the racial laws then in effect. But despite these laws, Éva—like most other Jews—continued to have a relatively normal personal and social life until the

German occupation of Hungary on March 19, 1944.[1]

DISTORTIONS AND REALITY

Almost immediately after the entry of the Germans into Kolozsvár in late March 1944, the *Sicherheitsdienst* selected the Péter-Pál villas as their headquarters and ordered the Semlyéns and the other Jews to vacate their apartments within 10 minutes. The Semlyéns tried to save as much of their belongings as possible with the aid of Raoul Şorban, who was then a close family friend. In light of her interventions to save Şorban from a punitive labor service camp in 1942,[2] Éva found it natural to move into the studio of her fiancée and family friend, together with her older sister, Judit. At that time this involved no risk for Şorban since as yet there were no residence restrictions in effect. According to Sari Reuveni, Yad Vashem's expert adviser on Hungarian righteous cases, Şorban was not hiding the Semlyéns at the time but merely let them stay in his apartment, which was then not a punishable act. It only became a crime, she emphasized, after the establishment of the ghetto on May 3.[3] Éva's parents found refuge in their own two-room furnished summer cottage in the Török-vágás section of the city.

As conditions became ever worse and the news and rumors about the impending disaster ever more persistent, Éva and her Christian friends began to think seriously about her possible escape to Romania. Among the chief organizers of such illegal escapes was Aurel (Bubi) Socol, a lawyer and prominent member

---

[1] Data based on Éva Semlyén's testimony which was recorded by Zoltán Tibori Szabó, the former editor-in-chief of *Szabadság* (Freedom), the Hungarian daily in Kolozsvár. The recording took place on May 5, 1997, in her apartment at Argeş Street, 20 (the former Péter-Pál villa). (See Appendix B., cited hereafter as Semlyén, *Testimony*.)

[2] See chapter 4.

[3] Personal communication dated February 20, 1996.

of the Romanian National Peasant Party in Kolozsvár, who was one of the three Romanians Éva had helped in 1942. One of Socol's "trusted" smugglers was Vasile Crişan, a Romanian peasant, who charged 1,000 pengő for each Jew taken across the Hungarian-Romanian border. This was quite a lot of money. The official value of the pengő in the early 1940s was $0.20. Under the conditions of the anti-Jewish laws, especially after the German occupation of March 19, 1944, when the Jews had to surrender their valuables, very few Jews had that much money. That the Romanian and the other smugglers were paid relatively large sums of money was also confirmed by Arie Hirsch (Eldar).[4] He recollects that each of the smugglers was paid 60,000 lei, the equivalent of $30.00, per Jew smuggled across the border.[5] (In a 1992 TV-documentary on their rescue activities, Rabbi Carmilly-Weinberger and Şorban falsely claimed that the Romanians had performed their border-crossing rescue activities for free and that no groups were ever apprehended.)[6]

Éva's escape was first discussed by her Romanian Christian friends, including Şorban, Socol, Tudor Bugnariu, and Vasile (Vaszi) Moldovan, around the middle of April 1944. Not well organized, the escape attempt failed as did several others, including the one in which Éva's family members were involved. The postwar rescue accounts by Socol, Bugnariu, and Şorban are self-serving and contradictory. The true story behind the failed

---

[4] For some details on Eldar, see chapter 4.

[5] See his testimony in the archives of the Center for Historical Documentation at the Strochlitz Institute for Holocaust Studies, University of Haifa, Doc. T3C3, p. 8.

Socol's and Crişan's involvement in the attempt to rescue Éva Semlyén was acknowledged by Şorban in the statement he gave to the police authorities of Cluj on June 14, 1945. The statement is in File 59/1946 (formerly File 181/1945) of the People's Tribunal of Cluj. *Ministerul Afacerilor Interne* (Ministry of the Interior), Bucharest, dos. no. 40030, vol. 17. (Cited hereafter as *People's Tribunal File 59/1946.*)

[6] For details on the documentary, see chapter 7.

rescue was revealed by Éva Semlyén in May 1997, when she finally agreed to record it for posterity.[7]

With respect to his own and Şorban's involvement in Éva's escape, Socol provides the following succinct account:

> I sent smaller groups across the border. One group, when Raoul Şorban quietly came into my office and told me: We have to save Éva, Éva Semlyén, today Mrs. Gabriel Pamfil. At that time she was Şorban's fiancée. I told him that she would be transferred across the border that same evening and made an appointment in his house at 8 P.M. There I also found Estera Salamon, today the wife of Teodoru, and the young journalist for the *Tribuna*, Vasile Moldovan (later director of the National Theater of Cluj). I sent both to Crişan.... They crossed the border without difficulty but there, mistakenly heading in the wrong direction, they walked into the arms of Craioveanu's gendarmes and these extradited them to the Kolozsvár police.[8]

Bugnariu provides a more detailed and in some respects also inaccurate account of the escapees' ordeal. He was apparently motivated by the desire to counteract the distortions and omissions in Şorban's account of rescue as recorded by Adrian Riza in 1986 — a propaganda account Yad Vashem had apparently accepted at face value in identifying Şorban as a Righteous Among the Nations that year.[9] Bugnariu stated:

[7] See footnote 1.

[8] Aurel Socol, *Furtună deasupra Ardealului* (Storm Over Transylvania) (Cluj-Napoca: Biblioteca Tribuna, 1991), pp. 62–64.

[9] See Adrian Riza, "România pămînt al speranţei. Fascism şi antifascism pe meleaguri Transilvane. Reţeaua omeniei" (Romania, Land of Hope. Fascism and Anti-Fascism in

I was present when Éva Semlyén and her family prepared
to cross the border illegally. The group of Jews composed
of the Semlyén family and their friends crossed the border
alright, and Vasile Moldovan led them into Turda [Torda
in Hungarian]. Having carried out his mission, [Moldovan]
returned to Kolozsvár. Although I warned the Semlyén
family not to stay in Turda for a second, and for them to
spread out and to go deep into the country by train or bus
because in following the population movements caused
by the bombings in the country's interior there were no
more controls, the group stayed in the city, failed to spread
out, attracted the attention of the police and was arrested.
Gendarmerie Colonel Crainiceanu [*sic*] handed the group
over to the Gestapo, which returned it to Kolozsvár,
where, after some investigations, it was placed into the
ghetto.

Bugnariu reveals that it was a feeling of "national solidarity"
that prevented Riza and Şorban from admitting that it was in fact
Antonescu's agents who were responsible for the apprehension
and return of the Semlyén group to Hungary. He also provides
details about the background of Éva Semlyén's appeal for help to
Şorban, who was then in Turda. Writing in the third person,
Bugnariu provides the following account about his own predica-
ment after the group's return to Kolozsvár:

As the organizer of the crossing, he had to disappear from
Kolozsvár. Had he been caught, the Gestapo could easily discover who was behind the operation. This is what
happened: It was the same Müller (or Petri), who had free

Transylvanian Regions. The Network of Humanity) in *Almanahul "Luceafărul" 1986*
("Luceafărul" Almanac 1986) (Bucharest, 1986), pp. 63–92. For details on the Riza
account and its impact on Yad Vashem, see chapter 6.

border crossing privileges, who took them in his car to
Turda. (It was also he who took along the Semlyén family's jewelry, which he handed over to Şorban.)[10]

[Riza's piece] reproduces a letter by Éva Semlyén
addressed to Raoul Şorban: "I am hiding in Kolozsvár.
Bugnariu will put you in contact with me." A careful
reader will ask himself: How did Şorban's fiancée manage to be hidden in Kolozsvár? The explanation is as follows: The Jewish hospital continued to function in the
city and the sick persons from the ghetto were brought
there by guards for treatment. Éva Semlyén managed to
register herself on the list of patients and was brought to
the hospital. Then my wife, in search of those ready to
escape from the ghetto, picked her up and took her home
to us. After a few days, an employee of Éva's father
found a more secure shelter. (This employee was Hungarian, which proves that even among the Hungarians
there were people who took risks saving Jews. This
writer knows of a number of such cases.)

I remained continually in contact with Şorban, waiting for
a suitable opportunity for Éva Semlyén's crossing into
Romania. In the meantime the Jews had been deported.
With the exception of Şorban's fiancée, her whole family
was deported. Her mother and sister never returned.

---

[10] For some details on Şorban's alleged contacts with Müller (Petri), see below and
chapter 4.

The issue of jewelry was also raised by Eszter Goro and Gheorghe Dâncuş (see
below). Éva Semlyén states, however, that "a few fairly valuable pieces of jewelry
were indeed taken to Turda...which survived the difficult times with Mrs. Erzsébet
Engel Gergely.... I gave Raoul a necklace and some other pieces so he would have
something to sell in case he needed money...but this was an absolutely personal and
normal thing because we had that kind of relationship." See Semlyén, *Testimony*.

Impatient in her desire to escape the unpleasant conditions of clandestineness, Éva Semlyén adopted a course from which neither I nor the devoted Hungarian woman could stop her. A friend of Éva—a member of the group arrested in Turda who escaped from the ghetto—had, together with the journalist István Gábor, established contact by some strange ways with Éva's relative in the Budapest ghetto and convinced her to come with them to the capital where the deportations had been cancelled. As a result, when I went with food to the apartment where Éva was hidden I no longer found her there. It later turned out that the whole story about Éva's relative was but a tale of the Horthyite police that was swallowed by Pista Gábor and Éva's friend, dragging Şorban's fiancée into deportation as well.[11]

Şorban provided a number of conflicting accounts of his involvement in the attempted rescue of Éva Semlyén. In his interview with Riza, Şorban recollects the comments by *Scharführer* Müller, the Nazi who had informed him—and through him Rabbi Carmilly-Weinberger—about the ultimate fate awaiting the Jews placed into ghettos. Şorban revealed that Müller had known a secret he (Şorban) purportedly did not. He cites the *Scharführer* as having said:

I know that three hiding Jews await you in your house....
I went home where I indeed found three Jews who had found shelter after having been thrown out from their

---

[11] Tudor Bugnariu, "Din Nordul Transilvaniei." Manuscript planned for publication by *Societate & Cultură* (Society and Culture), Bucharest. A copy of the manuscript is in possession of this author.

homes by the SD. Éva Pamfil, who is alive, her sister, and her father. Éva's mother was hidden elsewhere.[12]

Clearly, Şorban not only fails to note that Éva Pamfil's maiden name was Semlyén and she was his fiancée, but also exaggerates the number of those who had then found shelter in his studio by including Éva's father as well. The reader is led to believe that three Jews unknown to Şorban had sought shelter in his house.

It is fair to assume that when Éva was smuggled across the Hungarian-Romanian border toward the end of April, Şorban was motivated not only by a genuine concern for her safety, but also by the understandable desire to avoid any possible complications with the authorities.[13] But in light of his oft repeated claim that he and Rabbi Carmilly-Weinberger had been in the forefront of rescuing Jews since 1942, one wonders why he felt it necessary to seek the aid of Socol in rescuing his own fiancée. Be that as it may, the record shows that the one rescue attempt Şorban was clearly involved in ended in disaster.

Éva's Personal Account. Éva Semlyén revealed some aspects of her story in 1986. She was at the time clearly still fearful and reluctant to talk about all the details of her ordeal. In her September 22, 1986, letter addressed to Yad Vashem, responding to a request by Mina Iancu of the Department for the Righteous

---

[12] Riza, "România pămînt al speranţei," p. 82. In the English version of the abbreviated interview, the reference reads: "I know that you hide three Jews in your home.... I went home where indeed three Jews were hiding, driven out of their homes by the SD: Éva Pamfil, who is still alive, her sister and father. Éva's mother was hiding in a different place." Riza, "The Network of Humanity," p. 28.

[13] For some additional details relating to the Şorban-Semlyén relationship, see Eszter (Fränkel) Goro's statement of June 3, 1992, in the archives of the Rosenthal Institute for Holocaust Studies of the Graduate Center of the City University of New York, and several other major Holocaust-related archives. See also Appendix A.

Among the Nations in connection with the Şorban case, Éva provided the following summary: In April 1944, when her father's house was taken over by the Gestapo (i.e., before the ghettoization of the Jews), she and her sister found shelter and were hidden in Şorban's studio. Later that month, she and some other Jews from Kolozsvár crossed the Hungarian-Romanian border with the aid of Şorban, Socol, and a student named Vasile Moldovan. Captured by Romanian border guards, they were returned to Kolozsvár and eventually ended up in the local ghetto. She managed to escape, went into hiding, and requested Şorban's help via Tudor Bugnariu, a mutual friend. Şorban, who was then in Romania, informed her that a Romanian peasant woman would fetch her and help her across the border. However, her hiding place was discovered by Hungarian gendarmes and she ended up in Auschwitz.

Éva Semlyén revealed the detailed story of her ordeal only in 1997. It is, indeed, one of the more tragically bizarre stories of the Holocaust era. Around the middle of April 1944, Éva's plans to escape into Romania were discussed and worked out by Socol and Şorban, the two men she put her trust in, in the former's law office on Kossuth Lajos Street. Although the original plans involved only her escape, she ended up with a companion, Eszter (Estera) Salamon, a 47-year old woman who also had a Romanian Christian friend at the time (who later became her husband), Constantin Teodoru. At first Şorban wanted Teodor Harsia, a fellow painter, to accompany the women across the border and assume the role of Éva's husband in case of capture by the border guards. Declining the request, Harsia wondered aloud why Şorban was not himself taking them across. Şorban, Éva stated, "didn't have the courage," and asserted instead that "if something should happen to her," he would "come across the border officially and be of help." At the end it was Vasile Moldovan, the young journalist who later became the head of the State Theater of Kolozsvár, who agreed to accompany the two women. Éva Semlyén emphasized that this put him at great risk, for if he were caught he could be punished as a military deserter. Reminiscing about this crossing more than five decades later, she said:

> In retrospect, I in fact attributed [Şorban's failure to accompany me] to cowardice on his part. He had tried so hard to convince me that should my border crossing fail he would have to cross the border officially to free me that I believed it. He was not a hero. There are people who under certain circumstances become heroes; others, on the other hand.... I didn't tell him, because under certain circumstances I am quite uncommunicative and fearful, but there was great sorrow within me. I felt a certain repressed reproach which, however, I did not reveal. I felt this especially when he took me by taxi to Crişan at Monostor and then turned back.[14]

Accompanied by Şorban, the two women and Moldovan went by taxi to Monostor (Mănăştur in Romanian), a nearby village where Vasile Crişan, the guide, lived. Şorban took leave and went back to Kolozsvár. Then, shortly after they entered the woods, Crişan quietly disappeared under the cover of darkness, leaving the group to fend for itself. (Years later, Éva speculated that Crişan might in fact have been in the employ of the Hungarian counterintelligence service.) They were helped across the border by a Gypsy who was wandering in the area. Following Socol's instructions, they stopped at the house of a peasant named Gligor hoping he would take them to Turda. However, the peasant declined his services, arguing that his horse had been requisitioned by the authorities. They walked on and reached the village of Erdőfelek (Feleac in Romanian) on Romanian territory on their own. Moldovan went on to Turda to return for the two women

---

[14] Semlyén, *Testimony*.

with a car. Exhausted, Éva and Eszter went into a peasant's house, where their clothing and poor Romanian betrayed them as "foreigners." Instead of shelter, they soon found themselves in the hands of the Romanian border police.

The two Jewish women were taken to the police station in Turda, where they were at first threatened with jail in Jilava for illegal border-crossing—a fate they favored to being returned to Hungary. But they were handed over to the gendarmerie, where they came across another large group of detainees whose crossing had also been organized by Socol through Şorban. Among these were Éva's parents and sister, and many of her friends and acquaintances. This group, too, was caught at Felek, presumably after the authorities had been tipped off. In emphasizing the importance of the larger group's arrest, Éva concludes that "it was never cleared up where and how they were caught."[15] Bugnariu, on the other hand, is specific: "It was the same Müller (or Petri), who had free border crossing privileges, who took them in his car to Turda."[16]

As originally agreed upon, Şorban, in possession of a valid passport, came to Turda two or three days later and tried his best to free his fiancée through the intermediation of his contacts at city hall and the local Jewish community. It was hoped that all the detainees would be sent to Szeben (Sibiu in Romanian) to be tried by a military tribunal for illegal border crossing—as had been the case in such situations until that time. In those days, it was still better to be in a Romanian jail than be returned to German-occupied Hungary. They received these "assurances" from both the local Jewish leaders and gendarmerie and police authorities, including Colonel Gheorghe Craioveanu, the commander of the

---

[15] Ibid.
[16] See Bugnariu's statement quoted above. On Şorban's dealings with Müller, see chapter 4.

gendarmerie unit in Turda.[17] But despite what they were told, all of the detainees were in fact sent back to Felek, where the guards, apparently tipped off, also apprehended still another truckload of Jews, including András Semlyén, Éva's cousin. In Felek, they were all handed over to the SS, who promptly took them back to Kolozsvár. After a few days in the cellars of the Péter-Pál villas, where they were interrogated by the SS, they were taken into the brickyard ghetto. The horrors of ghetto life were occasionally balanced by the loyalty displayed by Emilia Wertlen (nicknamed Mici), a former employee of Hugó Semlyén, who would occasionally smuggle food for them into the ghetto.

A resourceful woman, Éva managed to get out of the ghetto by surreptitiously joining a group of ill people taken for examination or treatment to the Jewish Hospital, which was outside the ghetto walls. In the hospital she was recognized by Tudor Bugnariu's wife, Kata, who, though Jewish, was exempted by virtue of her Christian husband. At her urging, Éva stayed a few days at the Bugnarius and then she was hidden in a woodshed that belonged to a Reformed Church minister in the Török-vágás section of the city and supplied with food by Kata. After a few days, she moved into another area of Török-vágás, where Ilona Botár, the Semlyéns' former cook, lived. A few days later she was taken by Mici to the home of a Mrs. Rappaport, a Christian woman whose Jewish husband had been taken away. Éva continued to be supported by Mici, who also helped her friend Vera Simon and her fiancée, the journalist István (Pista) Gábor, who were in hiding nearby. The latter two came up with the idea of writing for help to László Devecseri in Budapest, one of Éva's cousins who did a lot of work for the Hungarian military and thus had many influential friends. In the letter, which Éva also signed, Devecseri was

---

[17] Craioveanu gave a statement in connection with Şorban's case before the Cluj People's Tribunal in 1945–1946. See *People's Tribunal File 59/1946.*

asked to send someone he trusted to take all three of them to Budapest. The letter, which was reportedly given by István to one of his "trusted" friends for delivery, never reached its destination. Whether this unidentified friend was captured or willingly denounced the Jews was never clarified. The Hungarian police authorities immediately arrested and interrogated Vera and Pista, who did not know where Éva was hiding but were tricked into revealing Mici's address. Mici, informed by a police agent that he was Devecseri's trusted man, happily took him to Éva's hiding place. Coincidentally, Éva had just been secretly informed by Şorban via Tudor Bugnariu that a peasant woman would soon contact her to smuggle her back to Romania. Confronted with the luxury of two "rescue" opportunities, Éva wondered out loud whether she should go with her cousin's "guide" to Budapest where the same anti-Jewish measures could be put in effect as in Kolozsvár, or whether she should return to Romania. The police agent, playing his game shrewdly, suggested that he would wait outside for a while until she made up her mind. Before leaving, however, he parenthetically inquired whether she had any valuables. By the time she realized the ominous nature of the question, the agent returned with a colleague; both had revolvers in their hands. Éva was placed under arrest and taken back to Monostor, from where, after a short interrogation, she was escorted by a gendarme to Nagyvárad (Oradea in Romanian), where the last provincial ghetto in Northern Transylvania was still in operation. It was from there that she and Vera and Pista were deported to Auschwitz.

Young and healthy looking, Éva was selected for labor, receiving soon thereafter a new identification—A9661—which was tattooed on her arm. Her suffering and survival in Auschwitz-Birkenau were quite typical of those of many other survivors of this Kingdom of Death. She was among those who were removed from the camp early in November 1944 in the wake of the Soviet advance. She was first taken to Bergen-Belsen and from there, about a month later, to Braunschweig, where the inmates were required to clear the rubble of the bombed city. A short while later, she was taken to Helmstedt, where she worked in an airplane parts plant in an underground salt mine, then to Beendorf, and finally to Oxenzoll, near Hamburg. Éva was quite fortunate, because the inmates in and around Hamburg were handed over to the Swedish Red Cross early in May. The emaciated survivors were taken to Malmö, Sweden, via Denmark. It was from there that she sent a telegram to Raoul Şorban on May 29, 1945, requesting news from back home.

Éva returned to Kolozsvár in 1946. Şorban, her fiancée at the start of the ordeal, had already married someone else by then. Éva herself married Gabriel Pamfil, a pharmacist, and the couple soon had two children.

ŞORBAN UNDER ARREST

About a half a year after the liberation of Northern Transylvania by newly allied Soviet and Romanian troops in October 1944, Raoul Şorban was arrested by the Kolozsvár police authorities. One of the major elements of the case against him involved the arrest of the two groups of Jews who had been taken across the Hungarian-Romanian border in late April 1944 and their deportation to Auschwitz.

The "Case" Against Şorban. Part of the case against Şorban was focused on the unsuccessful attempt to rescue Éva Semlyén. He was arrested on March 27, 1945, and held in solitary confinement for several months. According to his police dossier, Şorban was held on the basis of a decision by the regional "screening commission" (*Comisia de triere*), a unit of Romania's denazification system. The case against Şorban clearly had political undertones. The security police of Cluj, in possession of several accusatory statements, accused Şorban of having been "anti-Semitic, anti-democratic, and anti-Soviet."

With reference to the Semlyén case, the most damaging accusation was presented by Dr. Vasile (László) Glück, a physician and friend of the Semlyéns. In a declaration dated March 28, 1945, Dr. Glück accused Şorban of having in fact been involved in the apprehension of the escapees, among whom was his cousin Vera Simon, by the Romanian border guards. According to him, Şorban had alerted "the Gestapo and the Gendarmerie in Turda" in order to get rid of Éva and marry someone else. Glück claimed to have heard the details from Hugó Semlyén, Éva's father, with whom he spoke in Kassa while serving as a physician attached to a labor service company and Mr. Semlyén, along with his family, was on a deportation train heading toward Auschwitz. To "prove" Şorban's intentions to get rid of Éva, Dr. Glück asserted that Şorban had gotten married in Romania shortly after the deportations.[18] (Şorban, in fact, married another woman in November, 1944.)[19] One can only speculate about Dr. Glück's motivations, but his claim that he had heard the "story" from Éva's father while he was in a deportation train in Kassa is hard to believe. It is almost inconceivable that the SS who took control of the deportation trains in Kassa or the gendarmes who accompanied the trains to that city would allow anyone to come near the locked freight cars, let alone engage in a conversation with the deportees.[20]

Particularly serious were the accusations directed against Şorban by Professor Gheorghe Dâncuş, one of his former colleagues at the Cluj-based *Tribuna Ardealului*, the Romanian-language paper in Hungarian ruled Northern Transylvania. He had accused Şorban of having been in the service of King Carol II's dictatorship, and, during the war, of the security police of Romania, the Hungarian counterintelligence, and the Gestapo.

---

[18] Ibid. Dr. Glück reiterated his accusations in his deposition for the People's Court of Cluj, dated March 19, 1946.

[19] In her declaration of June 18, 1945, Mrs. Şorban (née Cenariu) claims that she had met her husband only in September 1944 and married him two months later. Ibid.

[20] Both Éva and her father denied the contentions of Dr. Glück. Semlyén, *Testimony*.

Dâncuş further claimed that Şorban and the other leaders of the paper brought about his arrest and incarceration by the Hungarians. In connection with the Jews and Éva Semlyén in particular, Dâncuş, like Bugnariu many years later, claimed that Şorban had the jewelry of the Semlyéns smuggled into Romania through Petri, the Gestapo agent.[21] Dâncuş also claimed that Şorban and others involved in the "rescue" first took the Jews' money and jewelry and then denounced them to the authorities.[22]

In contrast to the above, a number of individuals who had been involved in the 1944 rescue effort, including Eszter Goro, Ernest Hirsch, and Moritz Glancz of Turda, testified that Şorban had always manifested a democratic attitude and was helpful to the Jews. Similar statements were signed by Aurel Socol and Emil Haţieganu, Şorban's senior colleagues at the *Tribuna Ardealului*.[23]

In his statement of June 14, 1945, written a few months after his arrest and before his trial, Şorban defended himself against the accusations directed against him. In connection with Dr. Glück's accusations, he cited the telegram Éva Semlyén had sent him from Sweden on May 29, 1945, via the Romanian Legation in Stockholm,

---

[21] See footnote 10.

[22] *People's Tribunal File 59/1964.* The file also contains a printed version of the accusations entitled "Despre Raoul Şorban şi alţi 'democraţi'" (About Raoul Şorban and Other "Democrats"), in *În contra ticaloşilor* (Against the Scoundrels) (Cluj, 1945), pp. 12–17. Dâncuş's accusations were summarized in an open letter to Şorban published in 1991. There is no evidence that Şorban responded to it. See Valeriu Sabău, "Scrisoare deschisă domnului Raoul Şorban" (Open Letter to Mr. Raoul Şorban), *NU* (No), Cluj, October 14–20, 1991.

At the suggestion of Michael Berenbaum, then Project Director at the U.S. Holocaust Memorial Museum in Washington, D.C., Radu Ioanid, an official of the Museum, sent a copy of the open letter to Mordecai Paldiel, the head of the Department for the Righteous Among the Nations at Yad Vashem.

[23] Similar testimony was provided by Eszter Salamon and Constantin Teodoru. *People's Tribunal File 59/1946.*

The file does not contain any testimony by Ernő Marton even though he had been asked by Şorban in an "urgent" undated Hungarian-language letter to write a statement on his behalf. Şorban's letter is in the Ernő Marton Files at The Strochlitz Institute for Holocaust Studies at the University of Haifa.

as proof of his innocence. The message read: "We are well, awaiting news."[24] Of course, it was natural for Éva Semlyén, one of the many Hungarian Jews taken to Sweden for physical and psychological recuperation following her liberation from the Nazi concentration camps, completely unaware of the previous year's events back home, to contact her fiancée for news about her family that was engulfed in the catastrophe that befell the Jews. How could she have been aware of the details described by Dâncuş, Glück, Bugnariu, and others?

Şorban also described his version of how the two groups of Jews were apprehended by the Romanian gendarmes and returned to Kolozsvár. He provided some details about his own efforts to free the Jews with the aid of the Jewish leaders of Turda. He boasted that despite the tragic experience of these groups, he, Aurel Socol, and Tudor Bugnariu, the former mayor of Cluj, had succeeded in rescuing several groups of Jews across the Hungarian-Romanian border. "Among these," he wrote, "I remember the following: Ernest Hategy [sic] his wife and two children, Rabbi Veinbergher [sic] and his wife, Mrs. Lederer of Budapest, and others whose names I don't recall."[25]

The statement, which was written while the events were still relatively fresh in Şorban's mind, contains no other accounts of wartime rescue activities although these would have been very useful at the time, and even the statements referring to the rescuing of the Hátszegis and the Weinbergers are unsubstantiated.[26]

Later Assessments. Many years after Şorban's legal problem had ended, several leaders of the Turda-based rescue group pro-

---

[24] The telegram, part of the *People's Tribunal File 95/1946*, was handed to Şorban during his imprisonment.

[25] Ibid.

[26] There is not even a hint about Şorban's involvement in their rescue in either Rabbi Carmilly-Weinberger's memoir (see chapter 4) or Hátszegi's writings. See Ernő Hátszegi, I. *Kazbek. Riport regény. II. Újkori rabszolgaságban* (I. Kazbek. II. In Modern Slavery) (Haifa: The Author, 1944). Hebrew version: *Kazbek. Te'udat zmaneinu* (Tel Aviv: Am Oved, 1945).

vided their own accounts about Şorban's involvement in their wartime rescue activities. In his postwar testimony, Arieh (Eldar) Ernest Hirsch, whom Şorban often praised as his wartime collaborator, recollects only one incident in which Şorban was helpful. It involved the settling of a police court case concerning the baggage of Ernő Hátszegi, one of the "prominent" Jews of Kolozsvár who had escaped via Turda almost concurrently with the Weinbergers. Upon arriving in Palestine, Hátszegi noted that one of his suitcases was missing and asked his brother, named Zuckerman, to lodge a complaint in Turda, allegedly implicating Hirsch in the disappearance.[27] Şorban, who was identified to the Turda police official as a press attaché of the Ministry of Foreign Affairs—a position he had held during various periods of his career—helped settle the case.[28] According to Şorban, the suitcase was given by Hirsch to a refugee on the way to Bucharest, but presumably was never delivered to Hátszegi. In a letter addressed to Ernő Marton on September 14, 1944, i.e., three weeks after Romania had switched sides in the war, Şorban explained his involvement in the settlement of the case as follows:

> To prevent a scandal I signed a declaration in which I acknowledged that it was I who took these things from Ari and took them to Bucharest where I handed them over to Ernő Hátszegi in your and Martin Hirsch's presence.... Hátszegi's brother (a big idiot) will investigate. I beg you to confirm our statements; otherwise I will be in trouble.[29]

[27] For some background information on Hátszegi, see Arnold Finkelstein, *Fénysugár a borzalmak éjszakájában* (A Ray of Light in the Night of Horrors) (Tel Aviv: P. Solar and J. Nadiv, 1958), pp. 261–262. Rabbi Carmilly-Weinberger identified Hátszegi as a member of the Kolozsvár Rescue Committee. However, Hátszegi made no reference to Rabbi Carmilly-Weinberger (or Şorban) in his *Kazbek*, the autobiographical account he published after his arrival in Palestine.

[28] See Eldar's testimony of March 1977 (parts 2 and 3, pp. 6–7) at the Center for Historical Documentation, University of Haifa, Archives, Doc. R3c7.

[29] Ibid, Ernő Marton Files.

Şorban had several other communications with Marton, detailing his work with Arieh Hirsch and requesting urgent monetary assistance.[30]

Arnold Finkelstein, another leading figure of the Turda Jewish rescue group often praised by Şorban, noted only his (Şorban's) efforts to free Éva Semlyén after her arrest by the Romanians.[31] Finally, Eszter Goro, also favorably mentioned by Şorban, expressed mixed feelings about him. While recollecting that Şorban, who had "enjoyed considerable influence in the police circles of Turda," helped free a young Jewish Communist involved in the rescue operations, she emphasized that, in his 1986 interview with Riza, Şorban had portrayed his alleged involvement in the saving of Jews in an "exaggerated ... slanted, distorted, and false way." Goro also claims that while in Israel in 1989, when she asked Arieh Hirsch about Şorban's alleged role in the rescuing of Jews, his answer was: "None."[32]

THE SEMLYÉN FACTOR IN
ŞORBAN'S DRIVE FOR RECOGNITION

Şorban's linkage with Éva Semlyén also emerged as a source of many inconsistencies in his search for recognition as a Righteous Among the Nations in the mid–1980s.

In pursuing this objective, Şorban has been quite inconsistent about his 1942–1944 relationship with Éva Semlyén, at least in his public pronouncements. Although she was his fiancée, Şorban,

---

[30] In the letter cited above, Şorban asked Marton to send him 100,000 lei to Sibiu in care of Coriolan Tătaru, the interwar representative of the Romanian king in Transylvania for whom he had worked. He repeated the request for 100,000 lei on September 21, 1944. Ibid. The file does not contain any record of monetary transfers.

[31] Identifying Şorban as a journalist from Kolozsvár, Finkelstein wrote: "[Şorban was] Éva's fiancée, who tried everything in his power in Turda to free her, but was unsuccessful." See his *Fénysugár a borzalmak éjszakájában*, p. 23.

[32] See the Eszter Goro (Fränkel) statement cited above.

reflecting what would appear to be his changing interests, occasionally identified her as "his Jewish wife" or simply as "a friend of mine." In his letter of April 24, 1986, addressed to Rabbi Carmilly-Weinberger, for example, he referred to her as one "of the persons who crossed the frontier into Romania assisted by me...." In some of the interviews relating to his "rescue" activities, Șorban merely identified her as "one of the Jews" or "one of the persons" he tried to help. This is clearly the case in the Riza interview, which was exploited in the drive to grant him the coveted title as Righteous Among the Nations by Yad Vashem. In a 1996 article dealing with his "rescue" activities, he failed even to mention her.[33]

The confusion regarding Éva Semlyén's relationship to Șorban is compounded by others who accepted the Carmilly-Șorban rescue story at face value. In his January 8, 1974, letter addressed to Yad Vashem, Professor Avraham Ronen, who initiated the drive to have Șorban recognized as a Righteous Among the Nations in the early 1970s, remembers Șorban referring to Éva Semlyén as "his Jewish wife."[34] Oliver Lustig, who incorporated the unfounded details of the "rescue story" in his accounts on the tragedy of the Jews in Northern Transylvania, quotes Șorban's reference to her as "a friend of mine."[35] In his 1994 book, Rabbi Carmilly-Weinberger refers to her only once without identifying her relation to Șorban or describing her ordeal.[36] In his statement in support of Șorban's designation as a Righteous, Yitzhak Artzi

---

[33] Raoul Șorban, "Protecția Statului român" (The Protection of the Romanian State), *Curierul Național* (National Courier), Bucharest, June 8, 1996.

[34] Yad Vashem, Department for the Righteous Among the Nations, Șorban File, no. 3499. For further details on Professor Ronen's role, see chapter 6.

[35] See his *Blood-Bespotted Diary* (Bucharest: Editura Științifică și Enciclopedică, 1988), p. 245.

[36] See his vanity press publication *The Road to Life* (New York: Shengold Publishers, 1994), p. 113. The book attempts to justify his rescue story in light of the criticism directed against it. For a critical review of this book, see chapter 7.

stated: "Prof. Şorban also had a personal interest; he had a Jewish woman friend in Cluj which he wanted to spirit out of the city."[37] Other accounts on the rescue story are even less charitable to Éva Semlyén: she is ignored altogether.[38]

It is apparent that Yad Vashem failed to investigate the issues that revolved around the Semlyén rescue attempt and Şorban's incarceration in 1945–1946. It is also evident that it was lackadaisical in identifying the commonality of interests that motivated Şorban and Rabbi Carmilly-Weinberger in advancing their ever more grandiose rescue accounts.

---

[37] For details on Artzi's role in the designation of Şorban as a Righteous Among the Nations, see chapter 6.

[38] See, for example, Vasile T. Ciubăncan, Maria I. Ganea, and Ion V. Ranca, *Drumul holocaustului* (The Road to the Holocaust) (Cluj-Napoca: Editura Ciubăncan, 1995).

CHAPTER 6

The Drive for Şorban's Recognition as a Righteous Among the Nations

THE FIRST INITIATIVES

Raoul Şorban's story of rescue was first brought to the attention of Yad Vashem in January 1974 by Professor Avraham Ronen, then associated with Tel Aviv University. Professor Ronen apparently became interested in Şorban following a chance meeting with him during a brief visit to Bucharest in October 1972. A professor of archeology, Ronen, whose parents had emigrated from Romania to Palestine in 1924, visited the country "to see some prehistoric materials."[1] Upon his return to Israel, Ronen, excited about what he had heard from Şorban, got in touch with Rabbi Carmilly-Weinberger. In his letter of January 14, 1973, he wrote:

---

[1] See his letter of February 24, 1973, addressed to Rabbi Carmilly-Weinberger in the Rabbi's *The Road to Life* (New York: Shengold Publishers, 1994), p. 171. According to Şorban, Professor Ronen had been on a nostalgic visit to Surduc, Sălaj County, a small Transylvanian village from which his parents emigrated to Palestine in the early 1920s. See his dialogue with Adrian Păunescu entitled "Mareşalul Antonescu i-a salvat pe evreii din România" (Marshal Antonescu Saved the Jews of Romania), *Totuşi Iubirea* (Love, Nevertheless), Bucharest, no. 3 (280), January 1996. According to Ronen, his parents were born in Târgu Mureş (Marosvásárhely) and near Jibou (Zsibó), respectively.

[Şorban] told me about your book, and that he heard that
you mention there his role in saving Jews of Transylvania.... Based on your book I could only find that Mr.
Şorban arranged a meeting for you and informed you
about the fate of the Jews of Cluj. *There is no mention—
at least I did not find such—as to his having saved Jews.*
(Italics supplied.)[2]

And indeed, in his memoirs, Rabbi Carmilly-Weinberger
makes only two relatively minor references to Şorban, and even
these differ in the Hungarian- and English-language versions. In
the Hungarian version, which was presumably the first, Rabbi
Carmilly-Weinberger merely notes that Şorban was helpful in
introducing him to Iuliu Maniu, the leader of the Romanian
National Peasant Party, then under house arrest, and that Şorban
illegally went to and returned from Cluj with the news that there
were no more Jews in the city. The English version includes,
within parentheses, a more charitable reference to Şorban: "(Raoul
Şorban, it must be noted here, was one of the few non-Jews who
extended a helping hand to the Jews notwithstanding the dangers
involved.)" This version also includes a revealing comment about
Maniu's views, which dovetail with those later advanced by the
nationalist history-cleansers: "Maniu wished to prove to the world
that the Rumanians [*sic*] were a more humanitarian people than
the Hungarians."[3]

In his February 1, 1973, response to Professor Ronen, Rabbi
Carmilly-Weinberger, reflecting awareness of Yad Vashem's criteria for the Righteous Among the Nations award, informed

---

[2] Carmilly-Weinberger, *The Road to Life*, pp. 168–169.
[3] Mózes Carmilly-Weinberger, ed., *A kolozsvári zsidóság emlékkönyve* (The
Memorial Book of Kolozsvár's Jewry) (New York: The Editor, 1970), pp. 232–233
and 302.

Professor Ronen: "*I don't know if Prof. Raoul Şorban really saved the life of one Jew in reality.* I can only testify that he was the only non-Jew who was ready to help in those days" [italics supplied].[4]

Undaunted, Professor Ronen persisted in his quest and on February 24, 1973, provided the following amplification of his meeting with Şorban:

> He told me about that tragic time, and that he saved, or helped save about 500 Transylvanian Jews (he mentioned the name of Dr. Marton as one of them). Furthermore, after the war he was seven years in prison under the Communist regime. One of the "crimes" they accused him for was that he helped Zionists during the war!... He also said that, at a given moment during the war, he received a certificate to come to Palestine from the Joint, but in the last moment, did not leave because his wife in that time, who called him to come back and save her from Auschwitz, if I am correct.[5]

Apparently Professor Ronen was told only a part of the unfounded story in 1972. According to Şorban's 1996 version of the "story," A. L. Zissu, a Romanian Zionist leader, alerted him in July 1944 that he was in danger "because he worked and risked a lot" and suggested that he go to Palestine until the end of the war. Although provided with a passport bearing the name Robert Smilovici, to match the monogram on his shirt, he refused to leave because in the meantime had received an urgent call from his "life

---

[4] Sorban File, no. 3499 at Yad Vashem. (Cited hereafter as Şorban File.) In a self-serving "updated" account of his wartime "rescue activities," Rabbi Carmilly-Weinberger left out these sentences in describing his cooperation with Ronen on behalf of Şorban. See his *The Road to Life*, p. 115. For a critical review of this book, see chapter 7.

[5] Ibid, p. 171.

companion (a Jewess, lives in Cluj, Mrs. Pamfil)": "I've succeeded in escaping from the ghetto. If you know a God, save me."
Instead of going to Palestine, he returned to Turda to arrange for
her escape, but she was in the meantime arrested by the
Hungarians.[6] As is the case of several other of his basically
unfounded accounts, Şorban apparently "forgot" that by July,
when Zissu had allegedly warned him, Éva Semlyén had already
been in Auschwitz for two months!

Professor Ronen apparently failed to doublecheck Şorban's
unfounded assertions, including the lies about his alleged Jewish
wife and having saved Marton, and clearly unaware of the realities behind Şorban's rescue stories, he repeated them in his
January 8, 1974, letter addressed to Ms. D. Rosen of Yad Vashem
in support of Şorban. He emphasized Şorban's account of having
rescued Polish Jewish refugees across the Hungarian-Romanian
border. He was cautious enough to add, however, that "the activity of rescuing refugees from Poland is not known even to him
[Rabbi Carmilly-Weinberger]." He also repeated the story of
Şorban's decision not to go to Palestine "because his Jewish wife
was taken to concentration camp." Obviously unaware of the
background of Şorban's imprisonment in March 1945 and the
accusations directed against him, Professor Ronen wrote:

> I will add another detail that I heard from Professor
> Şorban: when the Communist regime was established he
> was arrested and spent a few years in prison. One of the
> accusations referred to his helping and rescuing of Jews.[7]

Apparently undisturbed by Rabbi Carmilly-Weinberger's own
assertions that he was not aware of Şorban's saving "the life of

---

[6] See his dialogue with Adrian Păunescu, "Mareşalul Antonescu i-a salvat pe evreii
din România," p. 10.

[7] Şorban File.

one Jew in reality" or helping Polish refugees, Professor Ronen suggested to Rosen that Şorban deserved recognition. He append- ed the Hebrew section of Rabbi Carmilly-Weinberger's book deal- ing with Şorban and a letter the Rabbi had written to him.[8]

Yitzhak Artzi, who eventually recommended the designation of Şorban as a Righteous Among the Nations at Yad Vashem,[9] also accepted the "story" of Şorban's Jewish wife and incarceration for saving Jews as fact. In his support statement of November 6, 1986, Artzi asserted, among other things:

> Şorban remained in Romania, where he was arrested by the Communist authorities. The aid to Jews ... which was viewed as anti-Socialist and anti-patriotic, constituted a charge in his trial.[10]

Needless to say—and this ought to have been obvious to both Ronen and Artzi—nobody in liberated territory in March 1945 would have been imprisoned for helping Jews. If anything, such individuals were generally hailed as heroes. Moreover, the Communist regime was established only after the ouster of King Michael at the end of 1947, and, according to a source, Şorban himself had been a member of the Communist Party in 1945.[11]

Professor Ronen apparently became a bit uneasy when Yad Vashem was well on its way to acting on his and Rabbi Carmilly-

---

[8] Ibid.

[9] See below.

[10] Artzi's comments are included in a communication by Mordecai Paldiel dated May 2, 1993.

[11] See, for example, Şorban's interview with Mihai Pelin in *Flacăra* (The Flame), Bucharest, vol. 29, no. 42, October 16, 1980, p. 25. In a dialogue interview with Adrian Păunescu, Şorban claimed that he joined the Communist Party in 1947 at the urging of Bugnariu and was expelled after three months. "Confuzia şi neştiinţa sunt mai dăunătoare decât nedreptatea" (Confusion and Ignorance Are More Harmful Than Injustice), *Totuşi Iubirea*, Bucharest, no. 4, January 1996.

Weinberger's recommendation in the mid-1980s. On July 7, 1986, he contacted the Israeli Legation in Bucharest, requesting that it verify the account by Şorban by contacting his references.[12] The Şorban file at Yad Vashem contains no evidence of whether the Legation actually followed up on his request or whether the Department for the Righteous Among the Nations, which had a copy of the letter, ever pursued the matter itself. There is no evidence that Professor Ronen pursued the matter any further.

FORGING AN INTERESSENGEMEINSCHAFT: THE PLANNING AND IMPLEMENTATION OF A STRATEGY

A decade later Rabbi Carmilly-Weinberger's "mission of rescue" was once again depicted as the flight of a Rabbi who had left his flock. Having received the address from Professor Ronen, Rabbi Carmilly-Weinberger contacted Şorban on August 18, 1985. Ignoring his earlier essentially non-committal, if not negative, 1973 letter to Professor Ronen, the Rabbi informed Şorban about his effort to have him recognized as a Righteous Among the Nations by Yad Vashem.[13] In the letter he virtually coached Şorban on what to do to advance the cause. He mentioned, among other things, a reference to Şorban in *Remember*, a pamphlet issued by the Federation of Jewish Communities earlier that year.[14] He wrote:

---

[12] Şorban File. A copy of the letter was sent to Mina Iancu of the Department for the Righteous Among the Nations.

[13] Ibid.

[14] Rabbi Carmilly-Weinberger sent Şorban a photocopy of the page in which the latter's name appeared, adding some notes and hints that might be useful to Şorban. The pamphlet, in tune with Ceauşescu's policies at the time, was devoted to the destruction of the Jews in Hungarian-ruled Northern Transylvania. It makes no reference to the mass murder of Jews in Northern Bukovina, Bessarabia, and Transnistria by the Romanians. For some details on the pamphlet, see chapter 2.

Would you be able to secure from the Federaţia Comunităţilor [the Federation of the Communities] an affidavit reaffirming [*sic*] the facts stated in that pamphlet?[15] As I remember you once returned to Kolozsvár from Bucureşti with 1,200 blank forms received from Iuliu Maniu, after I visited with him, to distribute among the Jews of Kolozsvár, to facilitate their movement after escaping Hungary into Romania. It would be helpful if that would be incorporated in the affidavit.

Rabbi Carmilly-Weinberger assured Şorban that he too would submit an affidavit on his behalf to Yad Vashem.[16] The detail about the so-called 1,200 blank forms emerged for the first time here: it is found neither in the Rabbi's memoirs (including the *1988* edition) nor in Şorban's statement, but is used consistently from this time on as part of the "joint rescue story."

The Rabbi and Şorban fail to note that such National Peasant Party identification blanks could easily have been obtained from the Cluj branch of the party. Moreover, even if 1,200 Hungarian Jews had actually escaped from Kolozsvár and other places in Northern Transylvania, the value of such party identification cards would have been of questionable value since the Jews of the region spoke mostly Hungarian and were poorly educated in Romanian history and politics.[17] Above all, the possession of such National Peasant Party affiliation cards was itself "dangerous" in Antonescu's Romania, which had kept Iuliu Maniu and other opposition leaders of the party under house arrest. In the absence

---

[15] Apparently either Şorban failed to follow up on this advice or the Federation for some reason neglected to respond for there is no reference to it in the Şorban file at Yad Vashem.

[16] Şorban File. The letter is partially reproduced on p. 92 in Riza's article. See below.

[17] Some of these points were also highlighted by Sari Reuveni, Yad Vashem's expert on Hungarian Righteous matters, in a letter dated February 20, 1996.

of other identification documents they were actually useless, if not outright dangerous.

The process of introducing new data in support of gradually more impressive accounts of rescue had begun. The correspondence, public lectures, newspaper accounts, and various interviews give details that most objective observers conclude did not jibe with the Rabbi's memoirs and Şorban's June 1945 statements to the police. Eventually, the names of Romanians involved in various rescue operations were supplied; various estimates relating to the number of people saved, ranging from 1,200 to 30,000, were provided; the humanitarianism of the Romanians versus the barbarism of the Hungarians was demonstrated; the symbiosis of Romanian-Jewish suffering during the Hungarian occupation of Northern Transylvania was documented; the proof that the Romanians involved in the rescue operation received no compensation was presented; and the fact that no groups of refugees were ever apprehended was ascertained. In the course of years, Şorban found many opportunities to provide variations of the above accounts in the Romanian press.[18]

Raoul Şorban's response to Rabbi Carmilly-Weinberger's contact-establishing letter of 1985 came eight months later. In Ceauşescu's Romania one could not respond to a foreigner's letter involving a taboo subject like the Holocaust without the approval of the appropriate authorities, especially in cases involving well-known people. An artist and presumably still a member of the Communist Party,[19] Şorban was also a professor of art history at the Academy of Arts and the University of Bucharest, both state-supported institutions. The approval for the establishment of contact must have been given—and this is, of

---

[18] See, for example, his three-part "dialogue" with Andrei Păunescu in *Totuşi Iubirea*, January–February 1996; and his series of articles in the May–July, 1996 issues of *Curierul Naţional* (National Courier) of Bucharest.

[19] See footnote 11.

course, only a conjecture—because the Ceauşescu regime at the time was pursuing an increasingly chauvinistic nationalist-socialist policy, which also included a cleansing of Romania's wartime history.[20]

The interests of the Romanian state in this matter apparently coincided with the personal interests of Raoul Şorban. In his April 24, 1986, response to Rabbi Carmilly-Weinberger's letter of August 18, 1985, Şorban (conveniently, some have wondered) repeats some of the details in Rabbi Carmilly-Weinberger's book, with which he was obviously familiar.[21] But Şorban also gives some details that Rabbi Carmilly-Weinberger did not include in his memoirs, among them the rescue activities of Aurel Socol, Mendi Lehrman (identified as "one of our connections"), and Gh. Giurgiu, the editor-in-chief of the only Romanian newspaper published in Northern Transylvania, or that Şorban had himself informed the Rabbi about the realities of the Final Solution. On the other hand, Şorban did not mention the one important—but uncorroborated—rescue activity he had emphasized in his June 14, 1945, statement—namely, that the Weinbergers themselves had been rescued in 1944 thanks to his involvement.

THE ADRIAN RIZA "STUDY"

The Weinberger-Şorban "rescue" story was publicized for the first time in the 1986 issue of *Almanahul "Luceafărul"* ("Luceafărul" Almanac), the yearly publication of *Luceafărul* (Morning Star), the

---

[20] See chapter 2.

[21] In his April 24, 1986 letter to Rabbi Carmilly-Weinberger Şorban wrote that he got the book "in the seventies." Şorban File. Interestingly, in the same letter, he expressed ignorance about Yad Vashem: "As to Yad Vashem—I do not know what kind of institution is that exactly?"

extreme nationalist weekly of Bucharest.[22] The story was revealed by Adrian Riza,[23] whom Şorban identified as "one of our great writers."[24] Riza may have been more accurately perceived by Radu Ioanid, an expert on the tragedy of Romanian Jewry who is associated with the U.S. Holocaust Memorial Museum in Washington, D.C., as "one of Ceauşescu's propagandists."[25] Michael Shafir, a renowned authority on Romania, claims that Riza's personal record was similar to that of Corneliu Vadim Tudor, the notorious anti-Semitic leader of the neo-Fascist Greater Romania Party (*Partidul România Mare*—PRM).[26] Victor Eskenasy, a highly regarded scholar of Romanian affairs, identified Riza as "one of the ideologists and promoters of protocronism, an anti-Semite in his writings."[27]

[22] Radu Ioanid, "Romania," in *The World Reacts to the Holocaust*, David S. Wyman, ed. (Baltimore: The Johns Hopkins University Press, 1996), p. 245. (Cited hereafter as Ioanid, "Romania.")

[23] See his "România pămînt al speranţei. Fascism şi antifascism pe meleaguri Transilvane. Reţeaua omeniei" (Romania, Land of Hope. Fascism and Anti-Fascism in Transylvanian Regions. The Network of Humanity), in *Almanahul "Luceafărul" 1986* ("Luceafărul" Almanac 1986) (Bucharest, 1986), pp. 63–92. For some critical comments about Riza's pro-Antonescu piece, see Tudor Bugnariu, "Pe margimea articolului "aproximaţiile unui reporter frenetic" de Mihai Pelin din Almanahul 'Săptămâna,' 1986" (Concerning the Article "Approximations of a Frenetic Reporter" by Mihai Pelin in the 1986 Săptămâna [Week] Almanac), *Societate şi Cultură* (Society and Culture), Bucharest, no. 33, 1996, pp. 33–38.

[24] See his letter of April 24, 1986, addressed to Rabbi Carmilly-Weinberger. Şorban File.

[25] Ioanid, "Romania," p. 245.

[26] Michael Shafir, "Marshal Antonescu's Postcommunist Rehabilitation. *Cui bono?*," in *The Destruction of Romanian and Ukrainian Jews During the Antonescu Era*, Randolph L. Braham, ed. (New York: The Rosenthal Institute for Holocaust Studies of the City University of New York, 1997), pp. 349–410. (The volume is cited hereafter as Braham, *Destruction*.)

[27] As a staff writer for *Luceafărul*, Riza has also published attacks on Zigu Ornea and other Jewish intellectuals. After 1989, he assumed the publication of *Timpul* (Time), a weekly "probably financed by Drăgan," on which Şorban serves as honorary director. Communication by Victor Eskenasy dated July 6, 1994.

In tune with Ceauşescu's directives, Riza's article was designed to serve an important political purpose. Exculpatory in nature, it aimed, among other things, to contrast Romania's "humanitarian" historical record with Hungary's "barbarism" and to contribute to the drive initiated by the Ceauşescu regime to bring about the gradual rehabilitation of Marshal Ion Antonescu. Selectively quoting from this writer's publications,[28] Riza provided a "comparative" historical overview of the Jews' status in Hungary and Romania before and after World War I. Reflecting the title of the "study," Riza portrays the Hungarians as a whole as "Fascist" while describing the attitude of the Romanians as "anti-Fascist" and humane. He focuses on the crimes committed by the Hungarian counterrevolutionary regime of Miklós Horthy, including the excesses of the White Forces in the early 1920s, the anti-Jewish and anti-Romanian revisionist policies of the successive conservative-aristocratic governments, the massacres of Kamenets-Podolsk and Újvidék and, above all, the persecution of the Jews and Romanians in Hungarian-annexed Northern Transylvania. He conveniently overlooks the anti-Semitic record of Romania, whitewashes the anti-Jewish policies of the Romanian governments during the interwar and wartime periods, and ignores the mass murders committed during the Antonescu era.

Overlooking the involvement of the Romanian army and gendarmerie in the murder of close to 270,000 Romanian and Ukrainian Jews, the Riza piece focuses almost exclusively on the tragedy of the Jews in Northern Transylvania. Exploiting the Holocaust of Hungarian Jewry for nationalist political ends, Riza claims that during the four years of Hungarian rule in Northern

---

[28] Riza selected and used out of context segments from this author's *The Politics of Genocide. The Holocaust in Hungary* (New York: Columbia University Press, 1981), and *Genocide and Retribution* (Boston: Kluwer-Nijhoff Publishing, 1984).

Transylvania the Romanians and the Jews were united in a veritable symbiosis of suffering. Relying on Carmilly-Weinberger's memoirs and on an extensive interview with Şorban, Riza amplified the story of the Romanians' involvement in the "mass rescuing" of Jews across the Hungarian-Romanian border during the Nazi era, highlighting once again their "humanitarianism" against the Hungarians' "barbarism."

The article is clearly part and parcel of a nationalist history-cleansing campaign which is at once both pro-Antonescu and anti-Hungarian. His pro-Antonescu bias even leads him to misquote Rabbi Carmilly-Weinberger's recollection about one of the many rumors that allegedly sustained the optimism of the North Transylvanian Jews prior to their ghettoization early in May 1944. The Rabbi identified the rumor as follows: "The Nazis have threatened the Hungarians that if they do not collaborate North Transylvania will be returned to Romania."[29] Riza "supplemented" the quote by adding: "and, consequently, they will soon be freed by ... Antonescu."[30]

Upon reading Riza's piece, Tudor Bugnariu, who was the mayor of Cluj during the immediate post-liberation period and a close friend of Şorban, concluded that "the depiction of the Holocaust in Northern Transylvania and the condemnation of Horthyism are but a pretext for participating in the campaign ... against the Hungarians and Hungary in general." An eyewitness to the tragedy of the Jews in Northern Transylvania, Bugnariu unmasks Riza's politically motivated distortions, identifying the "legends" and "exaggerations" relating to Şorban's alleged involvement in the rescuing of Jews as part of the anti-Hungarian political campaign.[31]

---

[29] Carmilly-Weinberger, *A kolozsvári zsidóság*, p. 294.

[30] Riza, "România pămînt al speranţei," p. 82.

[31] Tudor Bugnariu, "Pe marginea problemei deportării evreilor din Nordul Transilvaniei" (On the Question of the Deportation of Jews from Northern Transylvania), *Societate şi Cultură* (Society and Culture), Bucharest (forthcoming). A copy of the manuscript is in this writer's archives.

Riza's piece turned out to be one of the most important "evidentiary documents" used by the champions of Şorban's designation as a Righteous Among the Nations.[32] One can only wonder about the reasons why the officials at Yad Vashem accepted Riza's article as an important, if not the decisive, piece of evidence submitted by Rabbi Carmilly-Weinberger on Şorban's behalf! Was it because they relied on its interpretation by Mina Iancu and Yitzhak Artzi, the Romanian-speaking associates of the Department for the Righteous? An expert historian, if contacted, would clearly have been able to identify the fundamentally anti-Hungarian and pro-Antonescu objective of the unfounded account of the Weinberger-Şorban rescue story. Moreover, if the Israeli authorities had followed up on Professor Ronen's suggestion that Şorban's references be checked in Romania, perhaps Yad Vashem might even have had Bugnariu's statement as a basis for its deliberations.[33]

THE NEW DRIVE FOR
ŞORBAN'S RECOGNITION AS RIGHTEOUS

Almost immediately after he received Şorban's delayed response to his contact-initiating letter of August 18, 1985, Rabbi Carmilly-Weinberger approached Yad Vashem's Department for the Righteous Among the Nations on Şorban's behalf. Writing on April 27, 1986, presumably while on a visit to Israel—he used the stationery of the Dan Carmel Hotel in Haifa—the Rabbi reiterated the story of his "mission," combining the accounts given in his memoir and his August 18, 1985, letter to Şorban. But he also added a few details the veracity and meaning of which the people at Yad Vashem presumably were not acquainted with and regret-

[32] See Şorban File.
[33] For Ronen's appeal, see above.

fully neglected to doublecheck. For example, he continued to misidentify himself as the Chief Rabbi of Kolozsvár and, in accordance with the requirements of Yad Vashem and as distinct from his earlier accounts, stated that Şorban had endangered his life by returning to Kolozsvár. (Şorban traveled with a valid passport.) As major sources "substantiating the rescue effort," he identified his own book, an article he published in *Yad Vashem Bulletin*, and a "comprehensive article" published in Bucharest "about the rescue operations in which Professor Raoul Şorban played an important and dangerous role." The "comprehensive article" was the propaganda piece written by the pro-Ceauşescu Adrian Riza!

In his letter, Rabbi Carmilly-Weinberger failed to point out that the *Yad Vashem Bulletin* article was not a supplementary documentary item but the verbatim text of the English version of his memoirs in which there is no reference to an "important and dangerous role" played by Raoul Şorban.[34] Again, Rabbi Carmilly-Weinberger stated that he and Şorban had just reestablished contact after many years of searching. Of course it seems that he could as easily have gotten Şorban's address from Professor Ronen in the early 1970s as he in fact did in 1985 — but at that time one interpretation may be that he was not yet interested in establishing an *Interessengemeinschaft* with him.[35]

Presumably on Şorban's initiative, a copy of Rabbi Carmilly-Weinberger's letter of August 18, 1985, was given to the Israeli Legation in Bucharest.[36] It was forwarded to Mordecai Paldiel, the Director of Yad Vashem's Department for the Righteous Among

---

[34] In his book, Rabbi Carmilly-Weinberger fails to inform his readers that the English-language version of his memoirs—"The Tragedy of Transylvanian Jewry" (pp. 286–304)—was originally published in *Yad Vashem Bulletin*, Jerusalem, no. 15, August 1964, pp. 12–27.

[35] For Rabbi Carmilly-Weinberger's letter of April 27, 1986, see Şorban File.

[36] The letter was handed to the Legation by an Israeli student in Bucharest and forwarded to the Israel Ministry of Foreign Affairs with a cover letter dated April 18, 1986. Şorban File.

the Nations, by the Ministry of Foreign Affairs with a cover letter
dated May 22, 1986. Eight days later, Paldiel requested Rabbi
Carmilly-Weinberger to submit additional specific details about
Şorban's rescue activities, especially in connection with the 1,200
blank forms he allegedly took back to Kolozsvár. The Şorban file
at Yad Vashem contains no record of a reply or of a follow-up letter.[37] It does include, however, the reference pages from *Remember*
and Riza's piece in *Almanahul "Luceafărul" 1986*, two of the
many Ceauşescu-inspired distorted versions of the rescue of Jews
by Romanians and their massacre in Hungarian-controlled
Northern Transylvania.

Ms. Mina Iancu, Paldiel's deputy, wrote to Rabbi Carmilly-
Weinberger, asking him, among other things, to fill out a questionnaire. This is normally one of the most important documents
in the recognition process. The data requested by Yad Vashem
include specifics about the dates and places of rescue, the rescuer's motivations, the risks involved, and names and addresses of
those helped by the rescuer. In his reply of August 25, 1986, the
Rabbi indicated that he could not fill it out because he "had no
details," but expressed considerable impatience over Yad
Vashem's failure to act swiftly in the Şorban case. He wrote, in
part:

> I ask you whether it is not high time for us to act on this
> issue immediately, and Yad Vashem should be satisfied
> with my detailed testimony that I gave Dr. Paldiel orally
> and in writing, not to speak of the big article printed in
> *Luceafărul*. After all, my testimony is not a testimony of
> a man on the street.[38]

---

[37] The absence from the file of any reply by Rabbi Carmilly-Weinberger was recon-
firmed by Paldiel in a letter dated April 4, 1993.
[38] Şorban File.

For whatever reason, perhaps intimidation or simple neglect among them, it appears that Iancu and Paldiel did not follow up: they seem to have accepted the veracity of Riza's "big article" without further research, and failed to insist on getting the completed questionnaire from the Rabbi or his detailed account about Șorban's rescue activities. Had they pursued the investigation more thoroughly, they likely would have discovered that, unlike the "testimony of a man on the street," Rabbi Carmilly-Weinberger's testimony might be suspect of an ulterior motive.

On May 21, 1986, Iancu, who appears to have been disposed toward positive action, also approached Șorban for additional clarification concerning his involvement in the rescuing of Jews. In his response of July 1986,[39] Șorban basically repeats the story of rescue as told in his 1986 interview with Riza, but with some additional interesting nuances. He repeats, among other things, the Ceaușescu regime's language of the time concerning the destruction of the Jews of Northern Transylvania, presumably to highlight the rescue efforts of Romania:

> First of all I would like to confirm that I indeed participated in, and even organized, operations for the saving of Jews during (approximately) the April 10–September 30, 1944 period, a period in which the fury of the state authorities in Hungary—and even of a majority of the Hungarian population—was involved in the crime of the organized extermination of the Jews who were in those parts of Transylvania which came under Hungarian occupation by virtue of the Hitlerite-Fascist dictate of Vienna."[40]

[39] The date is missing or illegible on Șorban's response letter in his file. In a letter dated December 23, 1992, Mordecai Paldiel informed this writer that Șorban's response arrived "in early July 1986."

[40] Reference is to the Vienna Award of August 30, 1940 under which the leading Axis partners assigned Northern Transylvania to Hungary. For some details on this Award, see Braham, *Politics*, pp. 167–171.

Şorban repeats the version outlined in Rabbi Carmilly-Weinberger's memoirs and letter of August 18, 1985, stating that he helped several groups of Jews he "generally did not know personally" across the Hungarian-Romanian border. Differing from his 1973 statement to Professor Ronen, Şorban here does not refer to Polish refugees and, as opposed to what he said in his interview with Riza, he fails to refer even indirectly to the Semlyén family—let alone its tragic fate. He claims that he had to leave Hungary because he was being pursued by the police and the SD owing to his Jewish rescue operations, failing to mention what seems likely to have been a more pressing brush with the Hungarian authorities.[41] While in Turda, Şorban claims, he participated in rescue operations together with Finkelstein, Hirsch, and Eszter Goro. Presumably unaware of these rescue figures' *real* view of his wartime activities, Şorban identified the latter two[42] together with Rabbi Carmilly-Weinberger and Éva Pamfil (Semlyén), among his references. Finally, he asserted that he had no file on the rescue activity "because everything that I have done was the spontaneous reaction to a terrible tragedy and crime."[43]

Of the several references identified by Şorban in his letter to Iancu, the Şorban file at Yad Vashem contains only Éva Pamfil's response of September 22, 1986.[44] The letter by Pamfil is quite revealing, for it not only provides some positive comments about Şorban, but also details her and her family's tragedy. It identifies Şorban—her former fiancée—as a man who reflected "in those

---

[41] Şorban makes no reference to it in any of his rescue-related letters or interviews. The details were revealed by Éva Pamfil (Semlyén) in her September 22, 1986, letter addressed to Mina Iancu. See Şorban File. Additional details are provided by Éva Semlyén in her testimony, which was recorded in Kolozsvár on May 5, 1997, by Zoltán Tibori Szabó, the former editor-in-chief of *Szabadság* (Freedom), the Hungarian-language daily of the city. A copy of the testimony is in this writer's possession.

[42] Finkelstein was already dead by that time.

[43] Şorban File.

[44] Mina Iancu contacted Éva Pamfil on July 22, 1986.

times a humanist thinking in all manifestations and did not hide his anti-Hitlerian attitude."[45]

THE CONTROVERSIAL DECISION BY YAD VASHEM

The Şorban File. File No. 3499—the Şorban file at Yad Vashem—contains no evidence that Şorban's other references, including Eszter Goro and Arieh Hirsch, were contacted. Nor does it contain any testimony of persons actually saved by Şorban or through the "rescue activities" of Rabbi Carmilly-Weinberger. In this case at least, Yad Vashem apparently waived the requirement of "evidence by direct survivors."[46] The file fails, moreover, to include the accounts by Finkelstein and Hirsch about the rescue operations across the Hungarian-Romanian border near Turda, which were then available. The file also fails to include any indication that experts on the Holocaust in Romania and Hungary had been contacted or consulted for evaluative statements relating to the case. The record shows, for example, that Jean Ancel, then an associate of Yad Vashem and a leading authority on the tragedy of Romanian Jewry, was neither contacted nor consulted.[47] Ancel stated:

---

[45] For additional details, see chapter 5. See also Dániel Löwy, *A téglagyártól a tehervonatig. Kolozsvár zsidó lakossága a második világháború idején* (From the Brickyard to the Freight Train. The Jewish Inhabitants of Kolozsvár during the Second World War) (Kolozsvár: Erdélyi Szépmíves Céh, 1998).

[46] In the case of this writer, for example, Yad Vashem rightly insisted that my affidavit in support of István Novák, a Christian peasant from the village of Nyíri, be corroborated by the four other labor servicemen who had been sheltered—and thereby saved—by Novák in December 1944-January 1945. It followed an even more rigorous approach in 1996 in connection with the affidavit filed by Dan Danieli (supported by 22 "direct survivors") in support of Captain László Ocskay, the commander of Labor Service Company No. 101/359—a man who was posthumously awarded the Gold Order of Merit by the President of the Republic of Hungary in recognition of his rescue activities.

[47] Jean Ancel is the author or editor of numerous works, including *Documents Concerning*

I was not involved in the decision to grant the title to Mr. Şorban. Nobody informed me of this case and I myself do not believe the greater part of the story. It simply does not fit the historical background as I know it. I have never seen or spoken with Rabbi Carmilly but I remember that in November 1987 during one of my visits to Romania and again in 1988 "the comrades" from the Party's Historical Institute of the Central Committee tried to transfer to the Yad Vashem Archives, through my intermediary, a file of over a hundred pages with the so-called documents on Şorban-Carmilly "rescue activities" in which each one reinforced the other's affirmations plus copies of a few authentic documents of the period. After a brief check I refused to take them on the spot, stating that I did not want to include all kinds of pulp literature (*maculatură* in Romanian) in the Y. V. Archives.[48]

Yad Vashem also failed to contact either the late Asher Cohen, a professor of history at Haifa University and a recognized authority on the Halutz rescue and resistance movements in Hungary, or Sari Reuveni, its own "official" expert on Hungarian Righteous Gentiles. Neither was this writer, who has written extensively about the Holocaust in Hungary including a separate book on the tragedy of the Jews of Northern Transylvania,[49] and who has worked with Yad Vashem on a number of Righteous Gentile cases.

---

the Fate of Romanian Jewry During the Holocaust (New York: The Beate Klarsfeld Foundation, 1986–1987), 12 vols.; "The Romanian Way of Solving 'the Jewish Problem' in Bessarabia and Bukovina, June–July 1941," in *Yad Vashem Studies*, vol. 19 (Jerusalem: Yad Vashem, 1988), pp. 187–232; and "Plans for Deportation of the Romanian Jews and Their Discontinuation in Light of Documentary Evidence (July–October 1942)," ibid., vol. 16, 1984, pp. 381–420.

[48] Personal communication dated February 11, 1993.

[49] See *Genocide and Retribution* cited in footnote 28.

In addition to the above, the Şorban file also indicates that Yad Vashem apparently failed to:

– Follow up on Professor Ronen's request addressed to the Israeli Legation in Bucharest on July 7, 1986.
– Insist that Rabbi Carmilly-Weinberger fill out the standard questionnaire.
– Follow up on its request to Rabbi Carmilly-Weinberger and insist on getting an answer to its request of May 30, 1986, that he provide additional details about Şorban's rescue activities, especially in connection with the 1,200 National Peasant Party membership blanks.

In the absence of input by experts, the Commission for the Designation of the Righteous obviously overrated the importance of the party membership blanks. For one thing, they could easily have been obtained in the Kolozsvár branch of the outlawed party. Moreover, these blanks were allegedly "smuggled" to the Transylvanian capital after the Jews had already been deported. But even they had been taken in time, they, as stated earlier, would have been useless, if not actually "dangerous." Last, but not least, the "story" of the 1,200 blanks was invented in 1985—absent from the protagonists' earlier "recollections."

Yad Vashem apparently accepted the 1985 "story" of the smuggled blanks as fact and, clearly unaware of their nature, over-rated their importance. Mordecai Paldiel, the head of the Department of the Righteous Among the Nations, stated:

Şorban's secret trip to Cluj-Kolozsvár in order to try to help with the blank certificates he acquired in Bucharest, is in itself a deed worthy of consideration to the Righteous title—even if the mission failed because of events beyond Şorban's control.[50]

[50] Letter dated August 8, 1993.

Again, in the absence of input by experts, the Commission also overrated Şorban's readiness to "hide" his fiancée Éva Semlyén and her sister in his studio. Had its members consulted Sari Reuveni, for example, they would have learned that Şorban did not risk his life by hiding the Semlyéns in April 1944. He only provided shelter for them after their house was confiscated by the Gestapo—an act of generosity which was not yet deemed punishable. It became so only after the establishment of the ghettos in Northern Transylvania on May 3, 1944. Yad Vashem's apparent reliance on Şorban's interview with Riza, which was part and parcel of the Ceauşescu regime's campaign against Hungary and the Hungarians, is reflected in a rather confusing communication by Paldiel:

> According to Scharführer Müller's account, he (Şorban) found three Jews hiding in Şorban's studio. Éva Semlyén was not among them [*sic*], but she confirms in her statement that in April 1944 (after Hungary's takeover by the Germans), she and her sister found shelter and were hidden for a while in Şorban's studio.[51]

The same sentiments were expressed by Judge Moshe Bejski, the head of the Commission:

> As I see it, no one disputes the fact that Şorban hid his Jewish fiancée, Éva Pamfil, in the studio. The other Jewish

---

[51] Communication of August 8, 1993. Paldiel's statement is rather bizarre. He appears to accept *Scharführer* Müller's account as an "authoritative" source about Şorban's "righteous activities." For one thing, the account itself was not Müller's, but one that was planted by Şorban in the Riza propaganda piece. Secondly, the same *Scharführer* was identified by Tudor Bugnariu, the postwar mayor of Cluj, as a shady character who most probably was in fact responsible for the betrayal of the Semlyén family. See the statements by Bugnariu and Éva Semlyén regarding Müller (Petri) and the tragedy of the Semlyén family in chapter 5.

women were apparently also hidden there. Thus, in the light of these facts alone—which are indisputable (and which are also confirmed by Rabbi Şafran [sic])—the Commission would inevitably have arrived at the conclusion which it reached, since "whoever saves one life..." merits recognition as one of the Righteous according to the criteria laid down by Yad Vashem.[52]

In the absence of input by experts, Paldiel also misjudged the nature and importance of the two factors that Judge Bejski and the members of the Commission had found so convincing. But in contrast to Judge Bejski's self-justifying position, Paldiel adopted a more cautious stance:

If Şorban indeed sheltered for a time several Jews in his home, and also made that trip to Cluj-Kolozsvár in May [sic] 1944 for the purpose of saving Jews, then he deserves the Righteous title. *If those two items prove to be untenable, that of course changes the whole picture* (emphasis added).[53]

Even though the evidence concerning the "two items," had been published,[54] Paldiel has so far refused to admit that the "picture has changed." If anything, he continues to rationalize the "wisdom" of the original decision.[55]

---

[52] Communication dated February 8, 1996.
[53] Letter dated September 23, 1993.
[54] See Randolph L. Braham, "Romanian Nationalists and the Holocaust: A Case Study in History Cleansing," *Holocaust and Genocide Studies*, Washington, D.C., vol. 10, no. 3, Winter 1996, pp. 211–251.
[55] This is reflected, among other things, in his delayed reaction to this author's article cited in the previous footnote. In his letter of August 18, 1997, Paldiel again justified Yad Vashem's decision by relying almost exclusively on the "evidence" Rabbi Carmilly-Weinberger and Raoul Şorban had submitted. He failed to comment on the documentation that the crucial elements of that "evidence" had been basically invented

The Decision. The Commission decided to award Şorban the title of Righteous Among the Nations at its meeting of November 6, 1986. Paldiel emphasized the following reasons for the Commission's decision in favor of Şorban:

– His concealment of Éva Semlyén and three other Jews in his studio;
– His clandestine trip to Cluj with the blank forms;
– Rabbi Carmilly-Weinberger's two favorable statements (of 1970 and 1973) praising Şorban as a person who tried to help.[56]

The Commission heard a report by Yitzhak Artzi, the Commission-member appointed referee for the Şorban file. An influential political figure and leader of the ex-Romanian Jewish community in Israel, Artzi submitted his positive recommendation on the basis of his "examination of the Şorban file as well as his conversations with Şorban, Arieh Eldar (Hirsch), and an especially long telephone conversation with Rabbi Carmilly-Weinberger."[57] Artzi appears to have based his report almost exclusively on the "documentation" provided by Rabbi Carmilly-Weinberger and Şorban, accepting and repeating, among other things, Şorban's version of helping "a Jewish woman friend" (a clear reference to his fiancée, Éva Semlyén), of his arrest by "the Communist

---

by the two protagonists since 1985 to advance their mutual interests. He simply overlooked the fact that neither the Rabbi nor Şorban ever mentioned those elements of the "evidence" in any of their pre-1985 writings. He also overlooked Yad Vashem's failure to consult historians and insist on corroborated evidence of actual rescue before making its crucial decision. Judging by his letter of October 5, 1997, commenting on these "oversights" summarized in my letter of September 7, Paldiel continues to rationalize Yad Vashem's decision. Şorban File.

[56]   Letter of August 8, 1993.
[57]   A summary of Mr. Artzi's statement was included in a communication by Paldiel dated May 2, 1993.

authorities..." in 1945 because "the aid to Jews...was viewed as anti-Socialist and anti-patriotic." Apparently this explanation by Şorban was accepted at face value even though it was clearly inconsistent with the historical realities of the post-liberation era.

One is led to the inevitable conclusion that the Commission appears to have:

> – Relied heavily on "the documentation of rescue" provided by Şorban and Rabbi Carmilly-Weinberger in an interview with Andrei Riza, a pro-Ceauşescu propagandist, published in a nationalist-socialist journal.
> – Succumbed to the "pressures" by Rabbi Carmilly-Weinberger, a man who himself on February 1, 1973, expressed considerable skepticism about Şorban's rescue activities.
> – Accepted at face value all the stories of rescue invented since 1985—stories that could be found neither in Rabbi Carmilly-Weinberger's memoirs nor in Şorban's statement of June 14, 1945, when they clearly would have been in his interest to reveal them.

Paldiel himself concluded that "it would have been better for us to have waited a little longer and have before us the additional revelations ... before making the decision on Şorban's qualification to the Righteous title."[58] He once confided orally that the determination to award the title of Righteous to Şorban was made almost exclusively in response to relentless pressure by Rabbi Carmilly-Weinberger.[59] This is quite disturbing, even though some members of the Commission reportedly had considerable

[58] Letter of August 8, 1993.
[59] The same official, who asked not to be identified, told this writer that had the Commission been aware of what its members found out later, Rabbi Carmilly-Weinberger's pressures would have been resisted and Şorban would not have received the recognition as a Righteous Among the Nations.

misgivings about the nominee. Presumably, none of them had an inkling of Rabbi Carmilly-Weinberger's "interests" in the case. Nevertheless, the decision appears to have gone counter to the standard procedures followed in other cases, as well as the spirit and provisions of the 1953 law concerning the scope of Yad Vashem.[60]

Şorban's Reaction to the Award. In a letter dated December 9, 1986, Şorban expressed his gratitude for the honor Yad Vashem had bestowed upon him.[61] But he also provided a generalization of the Holocaust in line with the historical climate then prevailing in Ceauşescu's Romania. He wrote:

> I accept this title with humility in memory of the martyrdom of those who knew anxiety, prison, deportation, and even death as political phenomena; but also in the memory of those who were subjected to the moral, social, and intellectual degradations of Nazism and the horrible combination of crimes and cowardice that was planned and carried out against Slovaks, Jews, Romanians, Serbs, and Gypsies—united by a common suffering—during the time of Horthyite tyranny in 1939–1945.

Şorban apparently did not dare at the time to differentiate between the mass murder of the Jews—the Holocaust—and the political persecution of the other ethnic-national minorities in

[60] As a cosponsor of István Novák (see footnote 46) and an "expert advisor" in several other cases, I am aware of the usually rigorous procedures Yad Vashem follows in the designation process. See also Section 9 of the first paragraph of the "Martyrs' and Heroes' Remembrance (Yad Vashem) Law, 5713–1953," which states that the objective of Yad Vashem is to commemorate "the Righteous Among the Nations *who risked their lives to save Jews.*"

[61] Şorban was informed about the award on November 11, 1986; Rabbi Carmilly-Weinberger was informed on November 20. Şorban File.

Hungary. He paid tribute to the other Romanians who had been involved in the rescue effort and to the members of the Jewish rescue group in Turda, including Finkelstein, Goro, and Hirsch, who, he emphasized, had provided "documents to about 1,200 Jews" enabling them to travel on to Bucharest. He expressed special praise for the activities of Rabbi Carmilly-Weinberger and Ernő Marton.

Şorban did not bother to quote the Turda Jewish rescuers' postwar critical accounts about the latter two—or for that matter about his own role: either he was not acquainted with them or he prudently preferred not to cite them. In tune with the line pursued by the nationalist intellectuals of the Ceauşescu era, Şorban declared that Romania had been not only the least anti-Semitic of the countries under German military occupation [sic], but also the only country that provided safety, identity cards, and the possibility of emigration to Palestine during the war.[62] As is the case with most other Romanian nationalist intellectuals, Şorban also conveniently "overlooked" the massacres committed by the Iron Guard and the mass murders perpetrated by the Antonescu-led Romanian army and gendarmerie during the early phase of the Second World War.

Şorban's chance to elaborate on these themes came on April 7, 1987, the day Yad Vashem bestowed upon him the honors of a Righteous Among the Nations, including the planting of a tree on the Avenue of the Righteous.[63] In his address at the ceremonies Şorban repeated almost verbatim some of the statements in his letter of December 9, 1986, adding some ideas reflecting the Riza "study" as well as expanding on the anti-Hungarian theme. For one thing, he noted in passing that certain "pretentious national

---

[62] Ibid.
[63] Şorban claims that the Ceauşescu authorities refused to issue him a passport for the purpose of accepting the award from Yad Vashem. He was persuaded to change the purpose of his trip to "tourism." Riza, who was allegedly also invited to the ceremony, failed to receive a passport. "Mareşalul Antonescu i-a salvat pe evreii din România."

history treaties" [*sic*] attempted to reduce the Jewish casualties from 400,000 to only 200,000—a clear reference to Hungary. He was more specific in connection with the idea of a Romanian-Jewish symbiosis of suffering, an idea also emphasized in Riza's work. He stated: "The mass of Romanians were not hostile to the Jews, so that the Romanians under the rule of the Hungarian Kingdom and persecuted both by the state bodies and the large majority of the Magyar civilian population set up a common front with the Jews." The most obvious deviation from the contents of the December 1986 letter was the obsequious tribute paid to Rabbi Carmilly-Weinberger. Şorban even provided a new bit of information never before revealed by either: that the Rabbi had not only helped Jewish refugees cross the Hungarian-Romanian border but had also provided the same services to non-Jewish Frenchmen who had escaped from German camps. Şorban claimed that he and Rabbi Carmilly-Weinberger "understood each other not only through words, but especially through invisible links." He recognized in him a man "whose example was compelling ... a man who proved out courageous ... a man I know as my wiser brother."[64]

Sycophantic as he was toward Carmilly-Weinberger in 1986, acknowledging with many others the essential, if not determining, role the Rabbi played in his recognition as a Righteous Among the Nations, Şorban was less than charitable to him in early 1996. In a controversial pro-Antonescu interview, Şorban ignored the Rabbi's involvement and emphasized the decisive role played only by Avraham Ronen and Adrian Riza.[65]

---

[64] Şorban File. This writer was informed that at Rabbi Carmilly-Weinberger's request, the speech was reproduced with some minor deletions in *Martyrdom and Resistance* ("VIP at Yad Vashem: Rumanian Memories"), New York, December 10, 1991.

[65] "Totuşi, unde sunt românii?" (Yet, Where Are the Romanians?" *Totuşi Iubirea*, no. 5, January 1996. This is the third part of Şorban's three-part dialogue-interview with Adrian Păunescu.

Reactions to Șorban's Award. Șorban's recognition as a Righteous Among the Nations was duly celebrated and hailed in the Israeli press, especially the Romanian-language one. Citing the "fact" that Șorban and Rabbi Carmilly-Weinberger "saved several thousands of Jews," one newspaper went so far as to call him a "Romanian Raoul Wallenberg."[66]

Șorban's "rescue" activities were also hailed—and continue to be applauded—by the neo-Fascist ultra-Rightists, who exploit them in their anti-Semitic campaign. Writing in *România Mare* (Greater Romania), a weekly that has published some of the country's most viciously anti-Semitic pieces, Radu Theodoru, a former *Securitate* agent, highlighted Șorban's work on behalf of the Jews to emphasize in contrast "the genocide the Jews practiced on the Romanian people during 1945–1960." Theodoru stated:

> Marshal Antonescu refuses to act like the Horthyites, sends a great part of the Jews to Palestine, not to the frontlines; he uses them for internal labor, and a Romanian organization, acting under the aegis of the authorities and with their support (*see the books and articles by Raoul Șorban*) saves many Jews from Hungary and Hungarian-occupied Transylvania [italics supplied].[67]

Rabbi Alexandru Șafran's Reaction. A few years later, similar sentiments were unwittingly expressed by the former Chief Rabbi of Romania, Alexandru Șafran, the Chief Rabbi of Geneva since 1947 and a bitter enemy of his successor, the late Chief Rabbi Mozes Rosen. Speaking before a plenary session of the Romanian Senate on March 28, 1995, Rabbi Șafran focused his address on a few Romanian "rescuers," largely overlooking the

---

[66] "Un pom pentru Raoul Șorban" (A Tree for Raoul Șorban), *Minimum*, Tel Aviv, vol. 1, no. 1, April 1987.

[67] *România Mare* (Greater Romania), Bucharest, vol. 2, no., 54, June 21, 1991.

martyrdom of close to 270,000 Romanian and Ukrainian Jews who were massacred by units of the Romanian army and gendarmerie during the Antonescu era. It was later revealed that Rabbi Şafran's appearance in Bucharest was orchestrated by the Romanian Foreign Intelligence Service (*Serviciul de Informaţii Externe*), the Romanian version of the CIA.[68] Michael Shafir, a highly respected scholar of Romanian affairs, reminded the Rabbi about the trap he had fallen into:

> From the start it was obvious that the purpose of the invitation was to attempt to use the famous adversity between the deceased Rabbi Mozes Rosen and yourself in order to try to have you join via the back door the chorus of the deniers of the Holocaust. Whatever Rabbi Rosen's sins might have been, in the last years of his life he stood up courageously against these attempts, the attempts to rehabilitate Marshal Antonescu, and the venomous antisemitic publications that spread up after the fall of the former regime.[69]

Apparently unaware of the historical realities of the alleged mass rescue of Jews across the Hungarian-Romanian border during the Second World War and supposedly misled by those who helped him write the speech, Rabbi Şafran paid special tribute to Şorban. He stated: "And those solitary Jews of Northern Transylvania who managed to escape deportation to Auschwitz owe their rescue to the Romanian noble sense of Professor Raoul Şorban...."

Rabbi Şafran's speech was enthusiastically received by the nationalist history-cleansing Romanians. It was reproduced and

---

[68] For details, see Cornel Ivanciuc, "Vizita rabinului Şafran nu şi-a atins obiectivul de partid" (Rabbi Şafran's Visit Failed to Achieve the Party Objective), *Academia Caţavencu* (Catavencu Academy), Bucharest, April 11–17, 1995.

[69] A copy of Shafir's letter addressed to Rabbi Şafran on May 18, 1996 is in the archives of this author.

positively commented upon in most—and especially neo-Fascist, anti-Semitic—national news organs.[70] It was also highlighted in Romanian TV and radio broadcasts.[71] But it also provoked the ire of many Jewish survivors of the Holocaust in Romania and of scholars and laypersons alike. Incensed by Rabbi Şafran's insensitivity to the martyrdom of Romanian and Ukrainian Jewry, several scholars addressed an open letter to him early in April 1995:

> The text of the speech you delivered to a Plenary Session of the Romanian Parliament on March 28 was widely distributed by the Romanian authorities. We read it with great interest and frankly we were shocked and saddened by its content. You lent your prestige as the Rabbi of Geneva and former Chief Rabbi of Romania, to tell the Romanian Senate—and through it to the world of large— what the Romanian nationalists wanted to hear. Through your speech you contributed to the history of the cleansing efforts of those Romanians who are interested in whitewashing Romania's role in the destruction of close to 270,000 Romanian and Ukrainian Jews. These efforts are intertwined with the drive to bring about the rehabilitation of Marshal Ion Antonescu, the man your successor—the late Chief Rabbi Mozes Rosen—publicly and courageously identified as a hangman (călău). The campaign to sanitize Romania's wartime record began during the Ceauşescu era and gained momentum after the collapse of the Communist system in 1989. The politicians, historians, and the pseudo-historians involved in this

---

[70] *Europa* (April 5–19, 1995), one of Romania's most anti-Semitic papers, for example, highlighted Rabbi Şafran's speech under the following headline: "Mr. Alexandru Şafran, the Great Rabbi of Geneva, Succeeded in Shattering the Mendacious Attempts to Falsify Recent Periods in History."

[71] Incidentally, reflecting the nationalists' dominance over the media, even the reference to the Jassy pogrom was left out of the primetime TV and radio broadcasts.

campaign aim—for domestic and foreign political reasons—to portray wartime Romania in exclusively positive terms. While it is true that the Jews of Old Romania
and Southern Transylvania, deprived of their livelihood
and basic liberties, survived the war almost intact, one
cannot overlook the murderous campaign that was initiated and carried out under Antonescu with a brutality that
often shocked the Germans themselves.

By focusing on the few Righteous and ignoring the historical reality of the tragedy of Romanian Jewry you certainly pleased your audience, but unfortunately, let down
the victims—the Jewish martyrs of the Antonescu era.
You may have endeared yourself with the Romanian
nationalists, but unfortunately offered a disservice to both
victims and survivors and above all to historical truth.[72]

Expressing his sadness and worry, Michael Berenbaum,
Director of the U.S. Holocaust Research Center in Washington,
diplomatically rebuked the Rabbi, emphasizing that what he had
said in the Romanian Parliament was "not what they had to hear,
but what they wanted to hear." Reminding Rabbi Şafran about the
strong current of Holocaust denial in contemporary Romania,
Berenbaum stated:

As you well know, the Romanian political elite—both
those in power and in the opposition—are heavily

---

[72] The letter was signed by Jean Ancel, Jerusalem; Randolph Braham, New York;
Victor Eskenasy, Munich; Radu Ioanid, Washington; and Michael Shafir, Prague.
The letter was published, *inter alia*, in the *Newsletter* of the Association of Holocaust
Organizations, August 1995. It appeared in Hungarian translation in *Menóra*,
Toronto, May 5, 1995; *Newyorki Figyelő* (New York Observer), May 5, 1995;
Szombat (Saturday), Budapest, July 1995; and *Romániai Magyar Szó* (Hungarian
Word of Romania), Bucharest, May 31, 1995.

involved in the rehabilitation of Ion Antonescu. Under
your tutelage, they should have heard—at least something—about the Romanian perpetrators of the Holocaust
in Romania.[73]

Rabbi Şafran's response was swift and self-serving. He
attempted to justify the speech by citing the major principles that
guided him, highlighting the fact that he had spoken about the
Jassy pogrom of June 1941. He also emphasized that he had
talked about how the Jews of Romania had been "oppressed, persecuted, and tortured" (*obidiţi, prigoniţi, chinuiţi*) during the war
years.

In a letter dated April 18, 1995, this writer reminded Rabbi
Şafran that the Jews of Romania were not only "oppressed, perse-
cuted, and tortured," but also *murdered*—in Dorohoi, Northern
Bukovina, Bessarabia, Odessa, Transnistria and elsewhere. The
Rabbi was also challenged to prove the accuracy of the statement
relating to Şorban. The letter stated:

As to your comments about the few Righteous Gentiles, I
wonder who was your source because your book—
Resisting the Storm, edited and annotated by Dr. Jean
Ancel—fails even to mention Raoul Şorban, the man you
paid such high compliments to. In this context, I was particularly struck by your reference to the rescue of Jews
across the Hungarian-Romanian border and the role you
attributed to Şorban in that endeavor.

In his response of April 28, 1995, Rabbi Şafran basically
repeated his earlier self-serving stance. Ignoring the thrust of the
letter about Şorban, he laconically stated: "...I based my comments

---

[73] The letter was addressed on April 4, 1995. A similar letter was sent to Rabbi Şafran
by Radu Ioanid of the U.S. Holocaust Memorial Museum on April 21, 1995.

on the decision of Yad Vashem, which accorded him the title of 'Righteous Among the Nations.'" The Rabbi must have taken notice of the inconsistencies, for he made an appropriate "correction" in the Romanian edition of his memoirs published in Bucharest in 1996. He stated in a footnote:

> Raoul Șorban distinguished himself in the operation of saving and aiding [North Transylvanian Jews]; he was supported by his friends, Transylvanian Romanians, and the Chief Rabbi of Cluj, Weinberger. Yad Vashem of Jerusalem conferred upon Professor Șorban the prestigious title of "Righteous Among the Nations."[74]

The Romanians were clearly pleased with Rabbi Șafran's continuing reference to their humanitarianism in general and Șorban's rescue activities in particular, for on March 28, 1997, the second anniversary of his unfortunate speech, they made him an honorary member of the Romanian Academy.[75]

Șorban must have been pleased with Rabbi Șafran's generous comments in the Romanian Parliament, for they appeared to "corroborate" the ever-increasing number of Jews he and Rabbi Carmilly-Weinberger allegedly rescued: In 1945, Șorban boasted only about collaborating in the rescuing of a few Jews, including Rabbi Carmilly-Weinberger and his wife—a "rescue" that even the Rabbi failed to corroborate; in his April 24, 1986, letter to the Rabbi, he recalled only "hundreds of Jews"; then, together with Rabbi Carmilly-Weinberger, he began citing many thousands; in

---

[74] Alexandru Șafran, *Un tăciune smuls flacărilor* (An Ember Plucked From the Flames) (Bucharest: Hasefer, 1996), p. 211.

[75] *Realitatea Evreiască* (Jewish Reality), Bucharest, March 16–31, 1997. The issue also carries fragments of an interview with Manase Radnev, the producer of the TV propaganda documentary on the involvement of Șorban and Rabbi Carmilly-Weinberger in the rescuing of Jews across the Hungarian-Romanian border. For details on the documentary, see chapter 7.

1992, he emphasized the rescue of "tens of thousands";[76] in 1995, Rabbi Şafran talked about his having saved "the Jews of Northern Transylvania who managed to escape deportation to Auschwitz"!

As expected, Şorban's reaction to the open letter addressed to Rabbi Şafran was venomous. In the first of a three-part *ad hominem* attack on this author published in the summer of 1995 in *Timpul* (Time), a weekly published by Adrian Riza (with Şorban serving as "honorary director"), Şorban accused the signers of being both anti-Romanian and supporters of Hungarian revisionism. He reproduced the open letter in Romanian translation to prove the totalitarian [*sic*] mentality of the signers and their failure to understand the humanism and spirit of reconciliation that animated Rabbi Şafran.[77] He resumed the defense of Rabbi Şafran in January 1996 in a controversial interview with Adrian Păunescu which was designed, among other things, to support the drive for the rehabilitation of Marshal Ion Antonescu. Păunescu's Left-Fascist paper reproduced Rabbi Şafran's speech, emphasizing the Rabbi's aura of humanism. Şorban contrasted the "positive" features of the speech with "the foreign literature dealing with the Jewish question in Romania which is based even today on the book by Matatias Carp." Şorban reminded the readers that Carp's book had been "recently published in Hungary in [English] translation." "With this book," he continued, "the Hungarian propaganda wants to demonstrate how anti-Semitic the Romanians were and continue to be."[78]

---

[76] See his "Variante de 'justificare'" (Variants of "Justification"), *Timpul* (Time), Bucharest, July 7, 1992. Interestingly, among those involved in the rescue of the "tens of thousands," Şorban omits the name of Aurel Socol, emphasizing, in turn, the role played by Rabbi Carmilly-Weinberger.

[77] Raoul Şorban, "Incapacitatea de a accepta istoria (I)" (The Inability to Accept History, I), *Timpul*, June 27–July 2, 1995, pp. 9, 11. Interestingly, in the same article Şorban also attacks Yitzhak Artzi, one of his chief supporters at Yad Vashem in 1986, for being involved in the campaign "to perpetuate the memory of the victims of the Romanian Holocaust" though *Ultima Oră* (The Last Hour), a Romanian-language paper published by him in Tel Aviv.

[78] "Confuzia şi neştiinţa sunt mai dăunătoare decât nedreptatea" (Confusion and Ignorance Are More Harmful Than Injustice), *Totuşi Iubirea*, no. 4, January 1996.

Judging by the statements he made during subsequent visits to Romania, Rabbi Şafran appears to have been pleased with the accolades showered upon him by Romanian nationalists. The latter continue to exploit the unwitting Rabbi in their drive to cleanse Romania's wartime history by defaming his old rival, the late Chief Rabbi Mozes Rosen. As M. David, an Israeli of Romanian background, argued, the nationalists are eager "to bury Rabbi Rosen a second time." In connection with Rabbi Şafran's visit to Bacău and Jassy during the summer of 1997, Mr. David had the following to say about the Rabbi's comments in the former centers of Jewish life in Romania: "Not a word about Antonescu, Transnistria, or the Jassy pogrom, except a few confusing words about the dead (without revealing the causes). Nothing about Israel. Not a word about the anti-Semites of today."[79] The Rabbi appears to cling to the political posture he assumed in his infamous speech to the Romanian Senate on March 28, 1995.

[79] M. David, "O dispariţie prematură (A Premature Disappearance), *Ultima Oră*, Tel Aviv, July 18, 1997, p. 18. The letter is also summarized in *Buletin de ştiri* (News Bulletin), Haifa, vol. 1, no. 6, July 20, 1997.

CHAPTER 7

Complementary Rewards and Political Payoffs

ȘORBAN'S REWARDS

On May 3, 1987, less than a month after the tree-planting ceremony, Rabbi Carmilly-Weinberger approached Mordecai Paldiel of
Yad Vashem. Describing Șorban's financial difficulties, he requested
that Yad Vashem recommend that financial support be provided by an
international Jewish institution. He repeated the request on June 19,
1987, suggesting that the money be transferred via the Romanian
Bank for Foreign Trade in Bucharest. On July 30, 1987, Rabbi
Carmilly-Weinberger also contacted Dennis Klein of the Anti-
Defamation League of B'nai B'rith in New York, submitting the documentation relating to Șorban's recognition as a Righteous Among the
Nations. His efforts once again proved successful. On December 28,
1987, Paldiel informed Șorban that, at its meeting five days earlier, the
Commission for the Designation of the Righteous had decided to recommend that assistance be provided due to his "critical financial position." He was also informed that the Claims Conference Organization
in New York would notify him about the schedule of payments.[1]

---

[1] Paldiel contacted the Conference on Jewish Material Claims Against Germany
requesting assistance for Șorban to start on December 28, 1987, i.e., just five days
after he had been designated a Righteous. Saul Kagan, the Executive Director,
informed Paldiel on January 22, 1988, that the Claims Conference "initiated immediate support" to Șorban. Yitzhak Artzi, who played an important role in Șorban's identification as a Righteous, is also a leading figure of the Claims Conference, representing the Association of Holocaust Survivors in Israel, an organization he heads.

In January 1988, the Claims Conference for Material Claims Against Germany began paying Şorban a monthly stipend that lasted until December 1992.[2]   In 1988, Şorban also received $450.00 from the Ostberg Foundation in New York.[3]   When Rabbi Carmilly-Weinberger learned of the financial support being provided to Righteous Gentiles by the Jewish Foundation for Christian Rescuers, a relatively new organization affiliated with the Anti-Defamation League of the B'nai B'rith (JFCR/ADL),[4] he promptly applied for aid for Şorban, bringing along an article— presumably Adrian Riza's—"highlighting Raoul Şorban's heroic deeds."[5]   In July 1988, when Rabbi Carmilly-Weinberger began serving on its allocation committee "authenticating Romanian cases," the JFCR/ADL started paying Şorban a monthly stipend of $125.00.   Upon the urging of the Rabbi, who claimed "that Şorban's life may be endangered because of the precarious political situation (in Romania)," starting in September 1989, the JFCR/ADL increased Şorban's monthly stipend to $250.00, unaware that he was still receiving the smaller stipend from the Claims Conference.   Between March 2, 1989 and August 26, 1992, Şorban received $11,250.00 from JFCR/ADL, an amount that was quite large in inflation-plagued Romania.[6]   However,

---

[2] According to a communication from the Claims Conference, Şorban was given $20.00 a month between January 1988 and June 1991, and $30.00 monthly between July 1991 and December 1992.

[3] Of these, $100.00 were sent on March 28, 1988, $100.00 on October 13, 1988, and $250.00 on November 1, 1988. Communication by Eva Fogelman dated June 11, 1993.

[4] The JFCR/ADL evolved in September 1987 from the Foundation to Sustain Righteous Christians, which was founded by Rabbi Harold M. Schulweis and Eva Fogelman in August 1986 and originally housed at the Graduate Center of the City University of New York. The name of the agency was changed to Jewish Foundation for the Righteous in the summer of 1996.

[5] Communication be Eva Fogelman dated April 11, 1993.

[6] Communication by Eva Fogelman dated June 11, 1993. Reflecting Romania's inflationary spiral, the value of the dollar increased from around 70 lei in 1988 to over 700 lei in 1993.

upon learning of the double-dipping and other details about the Carmilly-Şorban linkage in late fall 1992, the JFCR/ADL reduced the monthly stipend to $50.00—"to reflect the stipend of other Romanian rescuers." Rabbi Carmilly-Weinberger's services on the allocation committee were politely terminated at the same time "because questions have been raised about his personal agenda...."[7]

The termination of the Rabbi's "services" came in the wake of his attempt to provide assistance for other "helpful Romanians" as well. On January 16, 1992, he approached Dennis Klein of the ADL, requesting assistance for Ştefan, Ludovic, and Iuliu Mureşan, three brothers who had, he claimed, "helped him in saving of Jews." He submitted the unsigned English translation of an affidavit allegedly prepared by Ştefan Mureşan. The Rabbi's cover letter stated:

> The Affidavit speaks for itself. It reveals only a part of the great and heroic effort of the Committee of Rescuing Jews initiated by me in Cluj in the years of 1936–1944. A film was prepared by the Roumanian Television of Bucharest of this rescue operation. I think it would be useful for JFCR/ADL.

The affidavit, whose real authorship can only be conjectured, is another unfounded account of rescue that focuses on the "heroic" activities of Rabbi Carmilly-Weinberger. The Rabbi was clearly either unaware of some of the major discrepancies between the affidavit and the propaganda film he offered to the ADL or else

---

[7] Communication by Eva Fogelman dated April 11, 1993. In an undated letter written some time in 1995, Cristina, Şorban's daughter (see below), requested Yossi Sarid, the then Minister of Environment of Israel, that in light of her father's dire economic circumstances his monthly stipend be raised to $150–200. AJDC Archives, New York.

believed that Dennis Klein and the other leaders of the organization would not notice them. For one thing, in the propaganda film discussed below the Rabbi—and Şorban—insisted that the smugglers—reflecting the "humanitarianism of the Romanians"—had received no compensation for their work, while in the affidavit the payment of the smugglers—and of their helpers—is in fact emphasized.[8] Interestingly, the affidavit contains no reference to Şorban and many of its details, especially in connection with the Rabbi's alleged rescue activities, were left unrecorded by the Rabbi himself.

Şorban's pursuit of additional rewards was more successful. Sometime in 1990, he decided to take advantage of a Knesset Resolution of March 25, 1985, under which the Righteous were eligible for Honorary Citizenship. His application, forwarded to Paldiel, was approved and he was named an Honorary Citizen of Israel on December 5, 1990. As a Righteous Among the Nations and Honorary Citizen, Şorban approached President Zehev Tadmor of Technion-Israel Institute of Technology with a request for a favor—a scholarship for his 19-year-old daughter Cristina to study architecture in Israel. In his letter of May 28, 1991, he provided hitherto "unrevealed" details, including his alleged wartime dealings with A. L. Zissu, the highly respected leader of the Romanian Section of the World Jewish Congress, with Ottó Komoly, the former head of the semi-legal Hungarian Zionist Association, and with "the leaders of the Zionist movement of Romania and Hungary."[9]

---

[8] Rabbi Carmilly-Weinberger sent a copy of his letter and of the affidavit to Yad Vashem's Mordecai Paldiel as well. Unfortunately, neither the Yad Vashem nor the ADL files contain copies of the original Romanian-language affidavit, assuming that it ever existed.

[9] File no. 3499 at Yad Vashem's Department for the Righteous Among the Nations. (Cited hereafter as Şorban File.)

Neither Ottó Komoly's diary nor Zissu's writings contain any reference to either Şorban or Rabbi Carmilly-Weinberger. Nor, for that matter, are the two featured in any of the memoirs published by Zionist leaders of Hungary and Romania.

He emphasized that as a result he had helped "thousands of Jews to cross from Hungary to Romania." He explained that his family income was less than 10,000 lei per month, identifying the official rate of the dollar as 60 lei and the "real buying power" as 200 lei, i.e., that he and his family earned only $50.00 a month. However, he failed to mention the generous financial assistance he had been receiving from the Claims Conference, the Ostberg Foundation, and the Jewish Foundation for Christian Rescuers.[10]

Impressed with Şorban's credentials, Tadmor expressed his readiness to Paldiel (June 12, 1991) to go beyond the requested help and solicited some additional specific information about Şorban.[11] On June 24, 1991, President Tadmor, obviously unaware of the Şorban-Carmilly affair, informed Şorban that he was ready to invite his daughter to the Technion "at our expense" and enroll her in the Department of Architecture and Town Planning if she passed some tests for which a pre-university course was available. President Tadmor also informed Şorban of his having forwarded a copy of his letter to Henry Taub, the chairman of Technion's Board of Governors and president of the Joint Distribution Fund, who "will try to secure you additional income through the Joint."[12]

A few months later, when he was asked whether he received

[10] Şorban File.
[11] Ibid. The letter of June 12, 1991, was signed by Leah Milo, the head of President Tadmor's office.
[12] According to a communication from Technion, transmitted by Professor Asher Cohen (August 10, 1995), Ms. Şorban was studying at the Technion for the last four years "on a scholarship (no fees), receiving monthly 500 NIS for living, free housing, and free health insurance." This was confirmed by Dr. Zehev Tadmor, the President of Technion, in a letter dated November 9, 1997. According to a letter from Dr. Ralph Goldman (July 15, 1997), the files at the AJDC headquarters in New York contain no reference to Mr. Taub's involvement in any payments to Şorban. According to a communication by Paldiel early in 1996, Şorban approached Yad Vashem, requesting additional financial assistance for Cristina. It appears that shortly thereafter Cristina, having failed to complete her studies in spite of the generous support received from Technion, dropped out and returned to Romania.

any "pension from the State of Israel," Şorban asserted: "No, I don't receive a penny and I don't even expect any."[13]

Eager to impress upon the world that there had been no Holocaust in Romania and that the Romanians, unlike the Hungarians or the Germans, had helped rather than killing the Jews, some champions of the Şorban-Carmilly-Weinberger "rescue operations" orchestrated a campaign to have Şorban celebrated in the United States "the way Perlasca was."[14] Toward this end, Romanian officials contacted, among others, the U.S. Holocaust Memorial Museum and the Jewish Foundation for Christian Rescuers of the Anti-Defamation League in New York. Rabbi Carmilly-Weinberger also approached the ADL in the fall of 1991. The Rabbi wanted the JFCR to sponsor a United States tour for Şorban and to honor him at official ceremonies. As one of the founders of the JFCR stated, the effort proved unsuccessful primarily because "by early 1992 the real story behind the so-called rescue had become known even to many among those who had earlier believed the Carmilly-Şorban account."[15]

---

[13] Ciprian Banciu, "Interviu cu Raoul Şorban" (Interview with Raoul Şorban), *Nu*, vol. 2, no. 48, September 2–9, 1991. The interviewer presumably was not aware that the State of Israel provides pensions, equal to the average national monthly salary, only to the few dozen Righteous persons and their spouses living in Israel. Those living outside Israel are provided funds by the Claims Conference and other Jewish organizations.

The Banciu interview elicited the publication of an open letter in the subsequent issue of the paper. Written by Valeriu Sabău, it catalogued Şorban's alleged wartime "criminal activities" as originally revealed by Professor Gheorghe Dăncuş, Şorban's former journalist colleague. See chapter 5.

[14] Jorge (Giorgio) Perlasca, an Italian, is credited with saving many lives during the Arrow Cross (*Nyilas*) era (October 15, 1944–February 27, 1945) in Budapest, acting as an "official" of the Spanish Legation. His rescue activities were recognized in the late 1980s and he was honored by Yad Vashem. He was also celebrated in Budapest and Washington. For some details on Perlasca's activities, see Randolph L. Braham, *The Politics of Genocide. The Holocaust in Hungary* 2d ed. (New York: The Rosenthal Institute for Holocaust Studies of the City University of New York, 1994), p. 1243. (Cited hereafter as Braham, *Politics*.).

[15] Personal communication by Eva Fogelman dated April 11, 1993. Romanian officials

THE RABBI'S CONTRIBUTIONS AND REWARDS

The "Historical" Contributions. The chance to repay the compliments Raoul Şorban had showered upon Rabbi Carmilly-Weinberger during the April 7, 1987, award ceremonies at Yad Vashem came a year later, when the Rabbi delivered a lecture at the Nicolae Iorga Institute of History of the University of Bucharest. This was the first of several lectures and interviews that were exploited by chauvinistic nationalists as "historical" substantiation of their anti-Holocaust and above all anti-Hungarian positions. Titled "The Help of Romania in the Saving of Jews During the Era of Nazism," the lecture must have pleased his audience because it emphasized Romania's wartime humanitarianism in contrast to Hungarian barbarism and American-British callousness. As reproduced in the Romanian press, the lecture is an amalgam of the theses advanced by Adrian Riza in his article, Şorban in his letters and speeches, and his own memoirs, complemented by a few new "revelations." To highlight the positive role of Romania, Rabbi Carmilly-Weinberger asserted that "America and England not only failed to hear the desperate cries of the Jews, but also prevented the most modest attempts at intervention in their behalf. This attitude had at its basis a pronounced anti-Semitic policy." After providing details about the suffering of Jews and Romanians during the Hungarian rule of Northern Transylvania, a symbiosis of suffering first developed by Riza, and even hinting at the crimes committed by the Romanian Legionnaires, he wrote:

> Evoking the barbarism of 1941–1944, I believe that it is an elementary moral duty not to forget and to emphasize the fact that during these years the Jews benefited from a ray of

stationed in New York and Washington also approached this writer to have Şorban honored during a planned visit to America.

humanity that existed in Romania. A ray of humanity as
well as a manner of thinking and action that were opposed
to the anti-Semitic formulae then dominant in Europe.

Highlighting his own role in the organization of rescue, Rabbi
Carmilly-Weinberger duly identified the crucial role Şorban had
played in the rescue effort. He provided his Romanian audience
with another detail not previously noted—that 28,000 to 31,000
Jews had been saved from death by crossing the Hungarian-
Romanian border during the 1940–1944 period. He ended his talk
by stating:

> Hungary killed 80 percent of its Jews, whom it sent to the
> gas chambers at Auschwitz-Maidanek [*sic*] while
> Romania wanted to save what could still be saved and
> threw the life-preserver to those who were in danger of
> drowning.... We Jews are and will remain grateful for
> that.[16]

The lecture emerged as a standard source for chauvinistic
nationalists and anti-Semites who used—and continue to use—it
in their campaign for the rehabilitation of Marshal Ion Antonescu.
Three years later it was reproduced in two parts—under the
Rabbi's name—in *Europa*, the most viciously anti-Semitic organ
of the post-Ceauşescu era.[17]

---

[16] The text of the speech was reproduced, *inter alia*, in *Curentul* (The Current), Munich,
November–December 1988; *Europa şi Neamul Românesc* (Europe and the Romanian
Nation), Milan, vol. 17, no. 196, October 1988, pp. 9–16; *Almanah "Luceafărul" 1988*
(Luceafărul Almanac 1988), Bucharest, pp. 47–56. See also footnote 17.

[17] Moshe Carmilly-Weinberger, "Ajutorul României în acţiunea de salvare a evreilor
în timpul nazismului" (The Help of Romania in the Saving of Jews during the Nazi
Period), *Europa*, no. 36, 1991; "Declaraţiile fostului rabin al Clujului din perioada
războiului înfirmă spusele rabinului M. Rosen" (The Declarations of the Former Rabbi
of Cluj Negate the Statements of Rabbi M. Rosen), ibid., no. 37, August 1991. Edited

Rabbi Carmilly-Weinberger's lecture appears also to have made a special impression on Alexandru V. Diţă, a chauvinistic nationalist who edited and wrote the introduction to the wartime memoirs of Radu Lecca, Marshal Antonescu's Commissar for Jewish Affairs. Lamenting Lecca's "oversight," Diţă wrote:

> The rescue operation of Jewish refugees from Northeastern Transylvania and Hungary [was] initiated and organized by Moshe Carmilly-Weinberger (the Rabbi of Cluj) and Raoul Şorban and supported in Bucharest by the governmental authorities as well as the political parties (the National Peasant Party) and the representatives of the Jewish community.[18]

To the delight of the nationalists, Rabbi Carmilly-Weinberger found several other opportunities to contrast the wartime "humanitarianism" of the Romanians with murderous policies of the Hungarians and the apathy of the Americans. In an October 1989 interview, for example, he catalogued the anti-Jewish—and anti-Romanian—measures the Hungarians had implemented in Northern Transylvania during the 1940–1944 era without mentioning the crimes the Romanians had committed during the same

---

by Ilie Neacşu, *Europa* was launched by the Romanian Information Service (*Serviciul Român de Informaţii*), the *Securitate*'s successor organization, and is reportedly supported by *Europa Nova*, the trust headed by Iosif Constantin Drăgan. The lecture was also partially reproduced in *Curierul Românesc* (Romanian Courier; vol. 3, no. 1–2, February 1991 and vol. 9, no. 11–12, November–December 1997) and in *Romanian News* (July 9, 1991), both of Bucharest. In November 1997, it was also reproduced in *Luceafărul Românesc* (Romanian Morning Star) of Montreal. Rabbi Carmilly-Weinberger is also cited extensively by *România Mare* (Greater Romania), another leading anti-Semitic paper edited by Corneliu Vadim Tudor and, until his death, by Eugen Barbu, two of the many Ceauşescu hagiographers with links to the *Securitate*. For some details on Drăgan, see chapters 2 and 3.

[18] Radu Lecca, *Eu i-am salvat pe evreii din România* (I Saved the Jews of Romania) (Bucharest: Roza Vânturilor, 1994), p. 341. For some details on Lecca, see chapter 1.

period.[19] The same theme was the subject of a roundtable discussion in which he participated with Şorban, Riza, and Mihai Ungheanu—all pro-Ceauşescu ethnocentrist nationalists.[20] (The latter became a particularly controversial figure, for it was in his capacity as a Deputy Minister in the Ministry of Culture in the Iliescu regime that he attended and spoke during the unveiling of the Antonescu statue in Slobozia on October 22, 1993).[21] In the course of the roundtable discussion, the Rabbi distorted the historical record, conveniently overlooking that at the time of the Hungarian occupation of Northern Transylvania in September 1940, many (if not most) Hungarian-speaking Jews, appalled by the anti-Semitic measures of the Ion Gigurtu and Ion Antonescu governments[22] and the massacres committed by the Iron Guard,

[19] For the text of the interview, see Moshe Carmilly-Weinberger, "1940–1944. În acele vremuri grele, poporul român şi-a păstrat demnitatea şi omenia" (1940–1944. During Those Difficult Times, the Romanian People Retained Their Dignity and Humanity) *Magazin Istoric* (Historical Magazine), Bucharest, vol. 13, no. 10 (271), October 1989, pp. 42.

Victor Eskenasy identified the periodical as a "voice of the ideological department of the Central Committee of the Romanian Communist Party." Communication dated July 6, 1994. In a letter dated February 11, 1993, Jean Ancel wrote, among other things: "I had a chance to read a few articles published by Carmilly-Şorban in Romanian newspapers and in *Magazin Istoric* and I wish to stress that they lack intellectual integrity; they did not fit the historical truth and are very unilateral."

[20] See "Salvarea evreilor din teritoriul de nord-vest al României, 1940–1944" (The Rescuing of Jews in the Northwestern Territory of Romania, 1940–1944), in *Almanah "Luceafărul" 1989*, Bucharest, 1989, pp. 114–138.

[21] Michael Shafir, "Marshal Antonescu's Postcommunist Rehabilitation. *Cui bono?*," in *The Destruction of Romanian and Ukrainian Jews During the Antonescu Era*, Randolph L. Braham, ed. (New York: The Rosenthal Institute for Holocaust Studies of the City University of New York, 1997), pp. 349–410.

[22] Between September 11, 1940 and January 21, 1941 alone 41 anti-Jewish racial decrees and ministerial decisions were adopted in Romania. Eduard Mezincescu, *Mareşalul Antonescu şi catastrofa României* (Marshal Antonescu and the Catastrophe of Romania) (Bucharest: Editura Artemia, 1993), p. 17. See also *Legislaţia antievreiască* (Anti-Jewish Legislation), Lya Benjamin, ed. (Bucharest: Editura Hasofer, 1993). (*Evreii din Romăcnia între anii 1940–1944*; The Jews of Romania Between 1940 and 1944, vol. 1). See also chapter 1.

looked with less anxiety toward the territorial transfer than did the indigenous Romanians. This was especially true of the older Jews, who still remembered the 1867–1918 "Golden Era" of Hungarian Jewry.

Rabbi Carmilly-Weinberger's writing was also featured in a 1996 memorial volume commemorating the fiftieth anniversary of Marshal Antonescu's death. Titled "Antonescu and ... damnatio mamoriae," the article summarized the rescue activities he, Şorban, and other Romanians had allegedly been engaged in, emphasizing the positive role Antonescu had played in saving the Jews. Unlike the other writings, however, this one also contains a listing of the boats (with the number of Jewish refugees) that left Romanian ports for Palestine during the June 1939–August 1944 periods.[23]

Most of the details relating to Rabbi Carmilly-Weinberger's and Şorban's involvement in "rescue" activities are, as stated elsewhere, missing from the Rabbi's original memoirs, which were first published in 1970 and reissued in *1988*! These appear to have been "discovered" only after the two protagonists established their mutually rewarding relationship in 1985 and published almost exclusively in Romanian outlets.[24] Although basically unfounded, these "rescue" accounts are exploited and perpetuated by sundry nationalist, anti-Hungarian elements, distorting the record of the

---

[23] See his "Antonecu şi ... damnatio memoriae" in *Almanah istoric. Viaţa şi moartea lui Antonescu. 50 de ani de la moartea mareşalului* (Historical Almanac. The Life and Death of Antonescu. 50 Years Since the Death of the Marshal) (Bucharest: Editura Tess-Express, 1996), pp. 88–90.

[24] See, for example, Constantin Mustata, "Convorbire cu Moshe Carmilly-Weinberger fost Şef-Rabin al Clujului" (Discussion with Moshe Carmilly-Weinberger, the Former Chief Rabbi of Cluj), *Almanahul "Flacăra" 1989* (Flacăra Almanac, 1989), Bucharest, 1989, pp. 140–148. See also Adrian Riza, "Arhivele încep să vorbească" (The Archives Begin to Talk), ibid., pp. 139–162, an article consisting of footnotes explaining the "meaning" of three letters by Şorban with emphasis on Romanian rescue and humanitarianism.

Holocaust.[25]   Like a computer virus, these basically invented "accounts" are also spread by well-meaning writers and pseudo-historians who were not acquainted with these particular aspects of the Holocaust in Hungary and Romania.[26]

Deferring to the Hungarians. A man steeped in Hungarian language and culture, Rabbi Carmilly-Weinberger is presumably aware of the differences in the history of the Jews in Hungary and Romania since the mid-nineteenth century. Yet, he clearly distorted this history, especially that relating to the Jews of Transylvania, to suit his personal interests. The attitude of the Jews in this region were more honestly and accurately described by Ernő Marton, the late editor-in-chief of the *Új Kelet* (New East) of Kolozsvár, whom he and Şorban boastingly identified as their close collaborator.[27]

In a lengthy memorandum addressed to all members of the Hungarian Parliament in September 1940, i.e., almost immediate-

[25] See in this category, Vasile T. Ciubăncan, Maria I. Ganea, and Ion V. Ranca, *Drumul holocaustului* (The Road to the Holocaust) (Cluj-Napoca: Editura Ciubăncan, 1995), and Oliver Lustig's *Blood-Bespotted Diary* (Bucharest: Editura Ştiinţifică şi Enciclopedică, 1988), pp. 239–247, and the original Romanian version *Jurnal însîngerat* (Bucharest: Editura Militară, 1987), pp. 255–263. Although much of the account in the book reflects awareness of this author's works, Lustig singled out a single quote dealing with the Hungarian gendarmes' brutality in the ghettos. See pp. 145–146 and 155–156 of the English and Romanian versions, respectively. See also Ion Şuţa, *Transilvania. Himera ungarismului iredentist* (Transylvania. The Chimera of Irredentist Hungarism) (Bucharest: Editura Academiei de Inalte Studii Militare, 1995), pp. 118–126.

[26] The Carmilly-Şorban story of rescue was accepted at face value by a number of authors who apparently failed to double-check its veracity. See, for example, I. C. Butnaru's *Waiting for Jerusalem. Surviving the Holocaust in Romania* (Westport, CT: Greenwood Press, 1993), and Marius Mircu's *Oameni de omenie în vremuri de neomenie* (Men Who Retained Their Humanity in Times of Inhumanity) (Bucharest: Editura Hasefer, 1996), pp. 113–116.

[27] For some details on Marton's alleged dealings with Rabbi Carmilly-Weinberger and Şorban, see chapters 4–6.

ly after the Hungarian annexation of Northern Transylvania,
Marton emphasized not only the cultural and linguistic identification of the Jews with the Hungarians, but also how the Jews shared
the fate of the Hungarians during the interwar period and resisted
all exhortations to assimilate coming from the Romanians and
even the Union of Romanian Jews (*Uniunea Evreilor Români*), the
central organ of Romanian Jewry.[28]

The intellectual versatility and opportunism of Rabbi
Carmilly-Weinberger served him well. In contrast to the lectures
and interviews he gave in Romania, his comments for the
Hungarian press appear to be closer to the historical truth. For
example, in a 1989 article published in *Magyar Hírek* (Hungarian
News), a Hungarian magazine published by the *Magyarok Világ-
szövetsége* (World Federation of Hungarians), Rabbi Carmilly-
Weinberger identified only Emil Hațieganu, Bishop Áron Marton,
and Bishop Iuliu Hossu as Romanians who were helpful to the
Jews; Raoul Șorban was left out. Moreover, in contrast to the
claim made in interviews published in Romanian journals, he stated that only hundreds—not many thousands—of Jews had been
helped across the Hungarian-Romanian border during the
1936–1940 period. In this same article the Rabbi was also more
forthright about the Romanians' involvement in the Holocaust.
He wrote:

> In Romania, which pursued a "swing policy" but refused
> to yield to the Nazis' demand for the deportation of the
> Jews, around 300,000 Jews lost their lives in the wake of
> the pogroms and murders committed in Bukovina,

[28] Titled *Az erdélyi zsidóság a román uralom alatt* (The Jews of Transylvania During
Romanian Rule), the memorandum and the background of Marton were subjected to
close scrutiny by the Hungarian authorities and even brought to the attention of
Ferenc Keresztes-Fischer, the Minister of the Interior. *Magyar Országos Levéltár*
(Hungarian National Archives), Budapest, File 149–651(2) 1941–6–15091.

Bessarabia, and Transnistria. Who can forget the three-day bloodshed in Bucharest, the "death train" of Jassy? The blood of Jews ran in brooks in the wake of the bestialities committed by the Legionnaires and even the Romanian military. In Romania, anti-Semitism did not search for "scientific" theories. Without this, they instinctively took the scythe and the gun in their hands to kill innocent Jews.[29]

In an interview published in another Hungarian-language paper, Rabbi Carmilly-Weinberger even exaggerated the responsibility of Romania during the Holocaust. He stated: "Here too 350,000 Jews were killed in Transnistria."[30]

The Rabbi's Rewards. Presumably, Rabbi Carmilly-Weinberger's new Romanian friends were unaware of the inconsistency between the Rabbi's interviews in the Romanian and Hungarian media. They were in a hurry to express their gratitude for the oral and written statements made in Romania—and above all for his efforts in having Şorban identified as a Righteous Among the Nations. On October 22, 1990, a " 'Moshe Carmilly' Institute for Hebrew and Jewish History" was established at the Babeş-Bolyai University of Cluj-Napoca presumably on the initiative and with the help of the *Fundaţia Culturală Română* (Romanian Cultural Foundation) of which Şorban was reportedly then Vice President.[31]

---

[29] Moshe Carmilly-Weinberger, "Szülőhelyem és bánataim földjén" (On the Land of My Birth and Sorrows), *Magyar Hírek* (Hungarian News), Budapest, vol. 42, no. 2, January 22, 1989, pp. 18–19.

[30] Júlia Németh, "Anyanyelvem magyar, de a zsidó néphez tartozom. Interjú dr. Moshe Carmilly professzorral" (My Mother Tongue is Hungarian, but I Belong to the Jewish People. Interview with Professor Moshe Carmilly), *Szabadság* (Freedom), May 3, 1991.

[31] *Studia Judaica*, Cluj-Napoca, no. 1, 1991, pp. 9–10. The Romanian Cultural Foundation succeeded the *Asociaţia "România"* ("Romania" Association) that was Ceauşescu's agency for "maintaining contact with Romanians abroad," reportedly with links to the *Securitate*.

The question of why the local Romanian authorities consented to naming an institute in honor of the former Rabbi of a small
Hungarian-speaking Neolog congregation—a man steeped in
Hungarian culture and language—rather than in honor of Mozes
Rosen, a native Romanian who as Chief Rabbi of the country
served his nation and the Jewish community loyally and effectively for close to forty years, has baffled many individuals. The
project appears to have received the blessing of Gheorghe Funar,
a fiercely anti-Hungarian politician, who is chairman of the Party
of Romanian National Unity (*Partidul Unității Naționale
Române*—PUNR), one of Romania's largest ultranationalist parties.[32] With the full support of his party, Funar, who was elected
mayor of Cluj in 1992, is actively involved in the building of two
anti-Hungarian monuments in the Transylvanian capital: a statue
of Marshal Ion Antonescu[33] and a Holocaust museum, presumably to focus on the oppression of Romanians and the destruction
of the Jews of Hungarian-ruled Northern Transylvania.[34] The
idea of such a museum was, in fact, first advanced by Şorban at
the June 1993 county meeting of the anti-Hungarian *Vatra*

[32] The party was founded in early 1990 as the political arm of *Vatra Românească*
(Romanian Hearth), the vehemently anti-Hungarian "cultural" organization. For
some additional details on the party and Funar, see "Nationalist Transylvanian Mayor
Kindles Romanian-Hungarian Animosity," *Research Bulletin* (Radio Free Europe),
vol. 10, no. 5, March 2, 1993, and *East European Reporter*, November–December
1992. See also chapter 3.

[33] Details about the planned erection of an Antonescu statue in Cluj were brought to
the attention of this author by Alex Sándor Kolozsy (June 10, 1996), a sculptor associated with the Sydney Branch of the Transylvanian World Federation, presumably a
Hungarian nationalist organization.

[34] Funar announced his plans for the building of such a museum in the spring of 1996,
when he also boasted about having conferred an award on two survivors of the
Holocaust, Harry Maiorovici and Oliver Lustig. The latter is a writer recognized in
Romania for his accounts on the destruction of the Jews in the Hungarian-ruled terri-
tories. "Doresc să înălțăm un Muzeu al Holocaustului la Cluj-Napoca" (I Wish To
Erect a Holocaust Museum in Cluj-Napoca), *Realitatea Evreiască* (Jewish Reality),
Bucharest, June 16–July 15, 1996.

Românească (Romanian Hearth).[35]

The primary reason for Funar's and the other nationalists' preference for the institute to be named for Carmilly rather than Rosen is simple. In contrast to Chief Rabbi Rosen, Rabbi Carmilly-Weinberger played into their hands by providing "personal and historical accounts" for the "documentation of Romanian humanitarianism"—accounts exploited by deniers and distorters of the Holocaust pursuing the rehabilitation of the Marshal. In the printed version of his inaugural lecture Rabbi Carmilly-Weinberger apparently felt it necessary to document the cultural losses of North Transylvanian Jewry by citing an article from *Revista Fundaţiei Drăgan* (Review of the Drăgan Foundation), the organ of the chief supporter of anti-Semitic and neo-Fascist activities in post-Communist Romania.[36]

Shortly after his return from the inauguration, *The Jewish Week* of New York unwittingly published (November 30, 1990) a basically unfounded account of Rabbi Carmilly-Weinberger's wartime rescue activities. The paper informed its readers that "while serving as Cluj's Chief Rabbi [*sic*] from 1934 to 1944, the Hungary native coordinated an underground rescue operation that helped smuggle some 4,000 Jews to safety in Palestine." His return to Cluj in 1990, the article emphasized, "marked the rebirth of Jewish scholarship ... [and] ... may herald the renaissance of one Jewish community nearly destroyed in the Holocaust." The readers were, of course, not informed about the reality of Jewish life in Cluj or the historical background of the Institute. The few hundred mostly elderly Jews left in the city represent not the "renaissance" but the end of the once flourishing Jewish commu-

---

35 "Vátra konferencia. A pánikkeltés nagymesterei" (Vatra Conference. The Grand Masters of Panic), *Szabadság*, Cluj, June 3, 1993.
36 *Revista Fundaţiei Drăgan*, Rome, no. 3–4, 1987, pp. 281–310. His lecture ("The Development of Hebrew Language and Literature in Transylvania") was reproduced in the first issue of *Studia Judaica* (1991), the Institute's journal.

nity of Cluj, reflecting the state of Jewish life in the other Jewish communities of Transylvania and Romania as a whole.[37]

Rabbi Carmilly-Weinberger was more candid in an interview he gave to a Hungarian-language paper published in Cluj shortly after the conference. When asked why the Jewish young people of Cluj and elsewhere in Romania were emigrating to Israel, he correctly stated that they had no future in Romania. In contrast to *The Jewish Week*'s reference to a *renaissance* of Jewish life, he asserted that the once flourishing Jewish culture was "at an end." When asked whether it should be allowed to die out completely, his response was once again honest: "The process goes on by itself. You cannot halt it. This is a natural process. There are no more young people."[38]

The Jewish leaders of Cluj greeted the establishment of the Institute with considerably less enthusiasm than Rabbi Carmilly-Weinberger and his nationalist supporters. They were particularly upset that neither they nor the representatives of the Israeli Legation nor the national leaders of Romanian Jewry had been invited to the Institute's inauguration.[39] They were also chagrined over Rabbi Carmilly-Weinberger's lecture, which reflected his Hungarian cultural background and orientation. They expressed their views in writing to the national Jewish leadership in Romania as well as to the president of Babeş-Bolyai University in

---

[37] It took the *Jewish Week* close to four years to correct this unverified and misleading account by publishing a more realistic article by David Tobis. See his "Last of a Breed. Soon There May Be No Jews Left in Cluj, Romania" in the September 16–22, 1994 issue of the paper.

[38] Júlia Németh, "Anyanyelvem magyar, de a zsidó néphez tartozom. Interjú dr. Moshe Carmilly professzorral," op. cit. Rabbi Carmilly-Weinberger was even more blunt in an article published in a Hungarian journal: he asserted that "Cluj, the center of religious Jewry and of Jewish cultural and political life is dead today." See his "Szülőhelyem és bánataim földjén" cited above.

[39] The failure to invite Chief Rabbi Rosen and other dignitaries of the central Jewish leadership was not an oversight. Since early 1990, the former Chief Rabbi had been looked upon as a *persona non grata* by Romanian chauvinistic nationalists.

Cluj.[40] They also shared their views with Radu Ioanid and this writer in December 1990.[41] Similar views were also expressed by Agota Kuperman, the then Cultural Attaché of the U.S. Embassy in Bucharest, and several intellectuals, including a professor emeritus at Babeş-Bolyai University.[42]

The Carmilly Institute organized its first international conference on April 15–16, 1991.[43] The noncontroversial program included no Holocaust-related papers. These were later published in *Historia Judaica*, the Institute's journal published with the financial support of the Memorial Foundation for Jewish Culture, a creation of the Claims Conference. The Institute-related events were apparently well received by the Romanians, since Rabbi Carmilly-Weinberger was invited after the conference to a private meeting with President Ion Iliescu.[44] However, the Rabbi must have been less pleased with the reaction to the interview in the Hungarian-language paper cited above. In the interview, while forthright in connection with the inevitable end of Jewish culture in Cluj-Napoca, the Rabbi was quite disingenuous in his respons-

[40] Iosif Weintraub and E. Tischler, the Vice President and Secretary of the Jewish Community of Cluj-Napoca, expressed their anger in letters to Theodor Blumenfeld, a university professor who also serves as general secretary of the Federation of Jewish Communities in Romania (January 31, 1991), and to Ionel Haiduc, the president of Babeş-Bolyai University of Cluj-Napoca (February 25, 1991). In a letter addressed to Radu Ioanid of the U.S. Holocaust Memorial Museum (February 26, 1991), these leaders quoted Haiduc as having said: "The problem was posed very correctly by you and you are quite right."

[41] In December 1990, this writer and Radu Ioanid spent close to two weeks in Romania, including Cluj-Napoca, on an archival mission for the U.S. Holocaust Memorial Museum. Our reports to the Museum summarized the state of the Jewish community as well as the local leaders' view of the "Carmilly Institute." See Ioanid's memorandum of December 26, 1990, addressed to Brewster Chamberlin, the Museum's director of archives.

[42] See Radu Ioanid's memorandum cited above.

[43] The travel expenses of Rabbi Carmilly-Weinberger and of a "professor" from New York were covered by the then Princeton-based International Research and Exchange Board (IREX).

[44] *The Jewish Week*, New York, May 17–23, 1991.

es to questions relating to Şorban. When he was asked about
Şorban's vehemently anti-Hungarian positions, he stated that he
had never discussed this issue with Şorban nor had he inquired
about his political views. Rabbi Carmilly-Weinberger also used
the occasion to attack Chief Rabbi Rosen, calling him "a sickly
megalomaniac man," again playing into the hands of Romanian
ultra-Rightists. The response to the interview was provided by a
survivor of the Holocaust, who not only alleged inaccuracies and
depicted what he perceived to be something akin to megalomania
on Rabbi Carmilly-Weinberger's part, but also provided some
details about his controversial wartime attitude and the postwar
reaction of the survivors.[45]

THE "DOCUMENTARY" FILM

Exploited by the nationalist press, the Carmilly-Şorban story
of rescue was also utilized by Romanian "information specialists"
for a slick, propaganda-type TV documentary. The film, "The
Road to Life" (*Drumul vieţii*), was produced by Ioniţa Dincu and
Cornel Ştefănescu and directed by Manase Radnev. It was first
shown on Romanian TV in April 1992 to the delight of an audience unfamiliar with the historical realities of the wartime era.[46]
(A few months after the film was first shown on Romanian TV,

[45] László Erős, "Dr. Moshe Carmilly interjújának margójára" (In the Margins of Dr.
Moshe Carmilly's Interview), *Szabadság*, Cluj-Napoca, May 16, 1991. The paper
refused to publish Rabbi Carmilly-Weinberger's response to Erős. In a letter
addressed to the Rabbi dated July 13, 1991, Erős provided extraordinary details about
his (Rabbi Carmilly-Weinberger's) questionable wartime activities and identified the
specific pages in the Rabbi's memorial volume—*A Kolozsvári zsidóság*—that
allegedly were plagiarized. A copy of the letter is in possession of this writer.

[46] The film is shown on Romanian TV periodically, especially during the worldwide
Holocaust remembrance period, as part of the campaign to "prove" the country's
wartime "humanitarian" record in contrast to that of Hungary's. It was re-broadcast,
for example, on April 18, 1996. Zoltán Tibori Szabó, "A Weinberger-Sorbán legenda" (The Weinberger-Şorban Legend), *Szabadság*, Cluj-Napoca, April 24, 1996.

Manase Radnev also published the "story" with all its exaggerations and falsehoods.)[47] Copies of the "documentary" later reached Israel and the United States.[48]

The film was shot at the various "historical" locations (Cluj, Turda, Jerusalem, and, reportedly, the site of the border crossings). It includes detailed interviews with the *dramatis personae*, including Rabbi Carmilly-Weinberger, Raoul Şorban, and Arieh Hirsch.[49] Focusing on the alleged Romanian-Jewish symbiosis of suffering during the Hungarian occupation of Northern Transylvania, the documentary is based largely on the "stories" earlier detailed in the articles, letters, and interviews by Rabbi Carmilly-Weinberger, Şorban, and Riza.

A skillful and persuasive concoction of facts, fiction, and outright lies, the film is fused by a narrative aimed to demonstrate Romania's "positive and humanitarian" record as against Hungary's "barbaric maltreatment" of its Romanian and Jewish minorities during the Nazi era. It reveals its propagandistic nature by omitting the "embarrassing" parts of Şorban's "rescue" activities, focusing on the unsubstantiated accounts of the heroes, and including scenes "borrowed" from other ghettos.[50] For example,

---

[47] See his "Drumul vieții. Mărturii recente din România și Israel" (The Road to Life. Recent Testimonies from Romania and Israel) *Magazin Istoric*, vol. 26, no. 9(306), September 1992, pp. 50–52; no. 10 (307), October 1992, pp. 27–30. A detailed, critical response to the Radnev pieces was written by László Erős, one of the Jewish survivors of Cluj, but *Magazin Istoric* reportedly refused to publish it. The alleged Romanian record of exclusive wartime humanitarianism with emphasis on the Şorban-Carmilly rescue stories has also been featured in Adrian Riza's *Rețelele omeniei* (The Networks of Humanity) (Bucharest: Editura R.A.I., 1995).

[48] The film was shown and introduced by Rabbi Carmilly-Weinberger, among others, at the Romanian Cultural Center (March 28, 1993) and Congregation Shearith Israel (April 18, 1993) in New York.

[49] Arieh Hirsch talked about the Turda rescue operation that he organized with Arnold Finkelstein and Carol Moscovits. Interestingly, he talked neither about the Rabbi's escape nor about his and Şorban's "rescue activities."

[50] The film shows a picture from the ghetto of Zalaegerszeg, Western Hungary, to illustrate a scene in the ghetto of Kolozsvár.

Éva Semlyén is not mentioned at all although Şorban devoted considerable effort to her and her family's failed rescue. The "omission" was probably necessitated by the untruthful statements made by both Rabbi Carmilly-Weinberger and Şorban that no groups of refugees were caught crossing the Hungarian-Romanian border by smugglers who received no compensation. Both of them, of course, were fully aware of the tragic fate of Éva Semlyén's group, which was caught and returned to the Hungarian Fascists by Romanian border guards, as well as of the fact that the smugglers were paid.[51]

The documentary begins with its opening credits superimposed over a Romanian archive full to overflowing with folders of documents—an obvious attempt to subliminally persuade the viewers of its authenticity. The story's perspective is established by a rosy portrayal of life in Romanian-ruled Transylvania (1918–1940). The harmony that prevailed among the many nationalities of the region is depicted as matching Romania's generosity toward the refugees fleeing the Nazis.[52] The flight of the refugees toward Romania is dramatized by the background of battle scenes, air attacks, and Hitler's reviewing of marching troops.

The film proceeds to the worsening of the situation in August 1940, when the Axis Powers allotted Northern Transylvania to Hungary. Pointing to the alleged horrors to which the Jews were immediately subjected by the Hungarians, Rabbi Carmilly-Weinberger refers in the same sentence to the immediate application of Hungarian anti-Jewish laws and to Auschwitz. The "doc-

---

[51] The lies were revealed by the liers themselves. Carmilly's admission was recorded by Yehuda Bauer, citing the Rabbi's statement about his rescue activities in Kolozsvár, p. 99. Şorban also admitted paying the smugglers during a January 1996 dialogue-interview with Adrian Păunescu. See "Confusia şi neştiinţa sunt mai dăunătoare decât nedreptatea" (Confusion and Ignorance Are More Harmful Than Injustice), *Totuşi Iubirea* (Love, Nevertheless), Bucharest, no. 4, January 1996.

[52] In the film interview, Rabbi Carmilly-Weinberger asserted that about 20,000 refugees passed through his synagogue in Cluj before August 30, 1940.

umentary" generally fosters the impression that life in Romania then was ever so much better for the Jews, which is patently false.[53]

In an open letter addressed to Rabbi Carmilly-Weinberger shortly after the film was first broadcast in Bucharest, a group of Holocaust survivors living in Cluj referred to it as a "fairy tale" which, in their view:

> (1) Serves the interest of those who, continuing the Ceauşescu policy of forced amnesia, refuse to accept the historical truth;
> (2) Adds water to the mill of those occult political circles that openly use the press to propagate an exacerbated form of anti-Semitism which, after Auschwitz, should be legally forbidden and mercilessly punished in any civilized country in our time.[54]

The "story" apparently had an impact outside Romania's borders. Şorban's "achievements" appear to have been recognized for a while at least at an international conference of Righteous Gentiles from East Central Europe, which was held in Athens on November 17, 1992. Organized with the support of Harvey Sarner, a successful Jewish-American attorney and businessman who is not himself a Holocaust survivor,[55] the conference brought about the establishment of a stillborn organization, the International

[53] For a critique of the film, see Randolph L. Braham, "A TV Documentary on Rescue During the Holocaust. A Case of History Cleansing in Romania," *East European Quarterly*, vol. 28, no. 2, June 1994, pp. 193–203. In a Romanian bibliography, the article is identified as anti-Romanian. See *Revista Istorică* (Historical Review), no. 1–2, 1995.
[54] See *Scrisoare deschisă prim-rabinului Moses Weinberger-Carmilly* (Open Letter to Chief Rabbi Mozes Carmilly-Weinberger) a copy of which they sent to this writer. The letter was signed "Without Respect, Group of Cluj Survivors Who Don't Forget."
[55] For some details on Harvey Sarner, see Eva Fogelman, *Conscience and Courage* (New York: Doubleday, 1994), pp. 310–311.

Association of the Righteous Among the Nations. It elected Şorban as its president.[56] The delegates were apparently unaware of Şorban's wartime rescue record, just as they were clearly unacquainted with his vehement anti-Hungarianism—an intolerant stance that goes counter to the concept of righteousness.

UPDATED AND NEW FANTASIES OF RESCUE

While some "historians" and lay persons have accepted the rescue accounts advanced by Rabbi Carmilly-Weinberger and Raoul Şorban at face value since the mid-1980s, others became alarmed over the falsification of the historical record of the Holocaust. With the passage of time, more and more pseudo-historians have incorporated the "rescue account" in their own often tendentious writings. The danger that these "rescue accounts" would spread like a computer virus became clearly discernible. Among the first to express this concern was Eszter Goro (Fränkel), one of the heroines of the wartime rescue group in Turda. In an attempt to stem the tide of falsehood, this writer brought the sordid affair to the attention of Mordecai Paldiel of Yad Vashem, prepared and deposited a document collection in some of the major Holocaust-related archives,[57] and published a critique of the propaganda film described above.[58] The legend of

[56] The conference was attended by delegates from Albania, Bulgaria, Czechoslovakia, Greece, Hungary, Romania, Ukraine, and Yugoslavia. Alecos Kalidopoulos of Greece and Leonard Glinski of Poland were elected vice-presidents, and Sándor Kopácsi of Hungary was elected secretary. According to a telephone communication by Kopácsi in early April 1996, the Association never met after its founding.

[57] *The Rescue of Jews Across the Hungarian-Romanian Border During the Nazi Era: Facts and Fiction.* Dated May 1993, it consists of 168 p. of documentary evidence preceded by a 61-page essay. Copies have been deposited at the archives of Yad Vashem, Haifa University' Holocaust Institute, the U.S. Holocaust Memorial Museum, and the Institute of History and the Institute of Judaistic Studies of the Hungarian Academy of Science.

[58] See footnote 53.

the Carmilly-Weinberger-Şorban "rescue" was also unmasked in a Hungarian-language paper in Romania.[59]

It is apparent that both protagonists became familiar with these writings; judging by their reaction, they were not favorably impressed. The Rabbi became rather defensive and published several "updated" versions of his "rescue" story. He presumably realized that the critics' observations about his memoirs and many aspects of his ever more grandiose "rescue" accounts had some validity and required further "explanations." Raoul Şorban gave vent to his anger by publishing a three-part *ad hominem* attack and, going beyond the Rabbi's "scholarly" effort, provided new and even more fantastic accounts of rescue than those revealed earlier. Judging by the content of the new revelations, he clearly did not allow his title of Righteous Among the Nations to detract him from advancing the cause of Marshal Antonescu.

THE RABBI'S "UPDATED" ACCOUNTS

Reflecting familiarity with the criticism directed against him since the early 1990s, Rabbi Carmilly-Weinberger updated the various and often conflicting accounts of rescue in 1994–1995. The updated information was provided in three books, which, judging by their content and interpretation, were designed to please different audiences: an English-language work, *The Road to Life*, which is clearly designed for the world at large, and two books—one in Hungarian and the other in Romanian—on the history of the Jews of Transylvania, which appear to be geared to Hungarian and Romanian audiences, respectively.[60]

---

[59] See Zoltán Tibori Szabó, "A Weinberger-Şorban legenda."

[60] See his *The Road to Life* (New York: Shengold Publishers, 1994), 189 pp. (Cited hereafter as Carmilly, *Road*); *A zsidóság története Erdélyben (1623–1944)* (The History of the Jews of Transylvania, 1623–1944) Géza Komoróczy, ed. (Budapest: MTA Judaisztikai Kutatócsoport, 1995), 390 pp.; *Istoria evreilor din Transilvania (1623–1944)* (The History of the Jews of Transylvania, 1623–1944). Translated by Ladislau Gyémánt (Bucharest: Editura Enciclopedică, 1994), 190 pp.

The Road to Life. Bearing the title of the Romanian propaganda film, this is by far the most defensive of the Rabbi's explanatory works. Published by a New York-based vanity press, the work was edited by Ladislau Gyémánt of the Babeş-Bolyai University of Cluj-Napoca, the administrator of the Institute that bears the Rabbi's name.[61]

This book is a selective compendium of the essentially unfounded accounts originally published in Rabbi Carmilly-Weinberger's self-serving "memoirs" and the many, often conflicting, unsubstantiated stories of rescue he and Şorban have related since the mid-1980s. Reflecting the content of the interviews and articles published in Romania, the first three chapters juxtapose the wartime "humanitarianism" of the Romanians with the "barbarism" of the Hungarians. While the Rabbi identifies the casualties incurred by Romanian Jewry during World War II—the book after all is designed for English-speaking readers—the tendency is to place ultimate responsibility for the massacres on German units, the Gestapo, and ethnic Germans.

Notwithstanding the murderous role Marshal Ion Antonescu and Mihai Antonescu had played during the first phase of the anti-Soviet war, Rabbi Carmilly-Weinberger goes out of his way to identify the "positive" achievements of the Romanian leaders. Deputy Prime Minister Mihai Antonescu is described in especially glowing terms. He is portrayed as a courageous statesman who had often lectured Manfred von Killinger, the German Minister in Bucharest, and stood up against the Germans in defense of the Jews. Rationalizing the crimes committed by the Romanians, the Rabbi asserted that Romania had, after all, been under German occupation for four years[62]—a claim denied even by Gheorghe Buzatu, one of Romania's leading Holocaust-deniers working for the rehabilitation of Antonescu. Buzatu was

[61] The book is identified as Volume 2 in the Bibliotheca Judaica series of the Institute.
[62] Carmilly, *Road*, p. 15.

clearly more accurate in stating: "During the 1940–1944 period Romania was not in the situation of a country occupied by the Fascist Axis and its allies; the regime that operated at the time was that of a satellite."[63]

Rabbi Carmilly-Weinberger is particularly charitable about the "Jewish policies" of Mihai Antonescu, citing his alleged warning to the Germans (October 1942) that he would not tolerate "the excessive and barbaric acts against the Jews." The Rabbi identifies the additional mitigating element: "Those atrocities were committed by German units but, at the same time, the Romanian government assumed responsibility."[64]

Without providing the historical context, the Rabbi tries to prove that Mihai Antonescu was actively involved in supporting the Jewish refugees in Romania and in their emigration to Palestine. The Deputy Prime Minister was reportedly so concerned with the fate of the Jews that after the sinking of the Bulgarian ship *Struma*, he insisted that only "safer" Romanian ships carry the Jewish refugees to Palestine. In the best interests of the Jews, he is also said to have tried to heal the internecine rift between the Jewish leaders, expressing special concern over the ideological rivalry between W. Filderman, the President of the Federation of Jewish Communities, and A. L. Zissu, the Zionist leader. The rivalry, the Rabbi emphasizes, had been exploited by Radu Lecca, the Commissar on Jewish Affairs, "for his own destructive purposes," implying that Lecca had the power to act without the consent of the Antonescus.[65]

---

[63] See his "Mareşalul Antonescu şi problema evreiască" (Marshal Antonescu and the Jewish Problem), *Revista de Istorie Militară* (Review of Military History), vol. 6, no. 28, 1994, p. 22. The units of the German armed forces stationed in Romania had in fact been invited by Antonescu in October 1940 to help train and restructure the Romanian army along the Wehrmacht.
[64] Carmilly, *Road*, p. 20.
[65] Ibid., pp. 28–29.

The anti-Jewish policies of the Hungarians during the Nazi era in general and the German occupation in particular are described as being basically the reverse of those attributed to the Romanians. Generally overlooking the pre-German occupation record of the Hungarians and the post-Voronezh policies of the Kállay government in particular,[66] Rabbi Carmilly-Weinberger focuses almost exclusively on the crimes that were committed by the Hungarian authorities, citing exaggerated statistical data on the losses of Hungarian Jewry. Following in the footsteps of the nationalists, he identifies Admiral Miklós Horthy, the nemesis of the Romanians, as the person whose hatred of the Jews was reflected in the horrors of the Holocaust.[67]

The eagerness with which Rabbi Carmilly-Weinberger aimed to juxtapose the wartime record of the Romanians with that of the Hungarians is reflected in the many serious historical errors in the book. To cite just some of the most glaring ones in connection with Romania, the Rabbi asserts that:

– The Jassy pogrom of June 1941 was due to the machinations of Horia Sima.[68] But by that time, the Iron Guard leader was already in the Reich, having fled Romania after the crushing of the Legionary rebellion by Antonescu in January.
– After the Hungarian Jewish labor servicemen were evacuated from Bor on September 16, 1944, Mihai Antonescu "granted asylum" to those who managed to flee to Romania.[69] But by that time, both Mihai and Ion Antonescu were in prison in Moscow, following their arrest in the wake of the coup of August 23.

---

[66] The lot of the Hungarian Jews changed considerably for the better during the second half of 1943, when the Kállay government was actively involved in seeking an honorable way out of the Axis Alliance. For some details, see Braham, *Politics*, chapter 8.
[67] Carmilly, *Road*, p. 37.
[68] Ibid., p. 4.
[69] Ibid., p. 42. For details on the suffering of the labor servicemen withdrawn from the copper mines at Bor, see Braham, *Politics*, pp. 343–352.

– The turning point in the Romanian government's emigration policy came "in November 1942 when the German army suffered its greatest loss at Stalingrad."[70] One does not have to be a historian to know that the Stalingrad debacle of the German and Romanian armies took place in January–February 1943.

– On December 17, 1941, Radu Lecca was appointed "director" of the newly established Center of the Jews of Romania (*Centrala Evreilor din România*), and in January 1942, "with the German influence penetrating into Romania," he became its "head."[71] But Lecca, who was Marshal Antonescu's Commissar on Jewish Affairs, was neither the "director" nor the "head" of the Center.

In connection with Hungary, Rabbi Carmilly-Weinberger wrote, among other things, that:

– Béla Imrédy was succeeded as Prime Minister in February 1939 by Count Béla Teleky [*sic*].[72] Béla Teleki was a centrist parliamentarian representing Northern Transylvania; Imrédy was succeeded as Prime Minister by Count Pál Teleki.

– Hungary attacked the Soviet Union on June 23, 1941.[73] Hungary joined the Reich in the anti-Soviet war only on June 27, 1941.

– The "alien" Jews were deported in June 1941 to Kamenets-Podolsk and murdered.[74] The deportation and murder of most of the 16,000 to 18,000 "alien" Jews took place in August 1941.

[70] Carmilly, *Road*, p. 23.
[71] Ibid., pp. 8–9.
[72] Ibid., p. 33.
[73] Ibid., p. 34.
[74] Ibid., p. 34.

– *"The great majority of 800,000 Jews in Hungary (618,000) was sent to the gas chambers in only 46 days* by the German and Hungarian Nazis" (italics supplied).[75] The massive deportations that took place during May 15–July 9, 1944, involved, in fact, "only" around 438,000 Jews.[76]

– "On August 19, 1944, László Baky, State-Secretary of the Ministry of Interior, deported 1,200 Jews from Kistarcsa."[77] It was on July 19, 1944, that 1,220 Jews were deported to Auschwitz through the connivance of Adolf Eichmann and the other members of his *Sonderkommando*, defying Regent Horthy's decision to halt the deportations.[78]

In a change from his memoirs published in 1970, Rabbi Carmilly-Weinberger, apparently confronted by evidence, now acknowledges the role Hannah Ganz (Grünfeld) played in his and his wife's escape to Romania on May 2, 1944.[79] But he continues to be silent about Eszter Goro and Arnold Finkelstein, two of the leading figures of the Turda-based Jewish rescue group that helped in the escape: these two had undermined the Rabbi's postwar "explanations" about his "mission." The book also appears to "correct" a lie the Rabbi and Şorban insisted upon in the TV-documentary, namely that the smugglers involved in the rescuing of Jews across the Hungarian-Romanian border in 1944 received no compensation, i.e., their services were just another example of Romanian humanitarianism. The Rabbi felt compelled to admit that the smugglers were paid 500 pengő per capita, which at the

[75] Ibid., p. 95. The exaggerated figure of 618,000 is used by anti-Hungarian Romanian nationalists, including Şorban.

[76] For details on the massive deportations from Hungary in May–July 1944, see Braham, *Politics*, chapters 17–22.

[77] Carmilly, *Road*, p. 81.

[78] For details on the Kistarcsa tragedy, see Braham, *Politics*, pp. 890–893.

[79] Carmilly, *Road*, pp. 104–105. The Rabbi presumably saw Hannah Ganz's statement in this author's documentary collection. See footnote 57.

time was quite a lot of money.[80]

Aside from the many other basic mistakes, inconsistencies, and misspelling of names,[81] the book is also memorable by reflecting the author's selective memory. For example, in connection with the Semlyén case and the story about Şorban's alleged plans to leave for Palestine, the Rabbi provided the following twisted account:

> Two days before the ship was supposed to leave, Şorban received a message from Cluj-Kolozsvár concerning Éva Semlyén-Pamfil's escape from the ghetto. She asked Şorban to help her cross the border to Romania. Şorban returned to the border-zone and succeeded in transporting Éva Semlyén-Pamfil to Turda.[82]

The Rabbi, apparently, not only failed to double check Şorban's account of the story, but also falsified it by intimating that Ms. Semlyén had been rescued. He even felt emboldened to "prove" that, in addition to Ms. Semlyén, Şorban had also helped "save" Ernő Marton, Edith Andrási-Hirsch, and Vera Simon.[83] To demonstrate his own role in rescuing a fellow Jew, the Rabbi cites

---

[80] Ibid., p. 108. The official value of the pengő in the early 1940s was $0.20. Under the conditions of the anti-Jewish laws, especially after the German occupation of Hungary on March 19, 1944, when the Jews had to surrender their valuables, very few Jews had that much money.

[81] For example, Carmilly-Weinberger claims, contrary to the historical record, that the Antonescu regime had protected the Jewish nationals in German occupied Europe (p. 39); the first step in the tragedy of Hungarian Jewry was ghettoization (p. 75), overlooking the many anti-Jewish measures that preceded it, including the isolation and expropriation of the Jews; the Jews of Kolozsvár were driven into the ghetto on May 3, 1944 (p. 98). The ghettoization, in fact took around 10 days.

[82] Ibid., p. 113.

[83] Ibid., p. 143, n. 20. The record is clear that Marton, the former editor-in-chief of *Új Kelet*, found his own avenue of rescue, and the others ended up, like Ms. Semlyén, in Auschwitz.

a statement by Ernest Nimberger, a former resident of Kolozsvár.[84] However, the historical record indicates that Nimberger and his family were in fact saved through the controversial deal Rudolph (Rezső) Kasztner had struck with the SS in April 1944.[85]

In his eagerness to demonstrate the wartime "humanitarianism" of the Romanians, the Rabbi is particularly manipulative in describing the alleged appeal Bishop Iuliu Hossu, a leader of the Uniate (Greek-Catholic) Church, made in April 1944 on behalf of the persecuted Jews of Northern Transylvania. The Bishop is quoted as having said:

> We firmly appeal to all of you, Venerated Brothers and Beloved Sons: Help the Jews not only in your thoughts, but also with your sacrifice, having in mind that today we cannot do more than this Christian and Romanian duty of assistance resulting from warm human love. Let this duty of assistance be the first preoccupation of the present hour.[86]

These were noble thoughts, but unfortunately the evidence that the Bishop ever expressed them is not provided. The Rabbi's footnote reference to the quotation is misleading: it refers to a page in Aurel Socol's book, which, however, lists Bishop Hossu only as one of several Romanian ecclesiastical leaders in Northern Transylvania, without any reference to any actual appeals.[87] The Rabbi, apparently realizing the inadequacy of such a reference, adds the explanation that the "quotation" was based on something

---

[84] Ibid., p. 92.

[85] For details on the Kasztner group, see Braham, *Politics*, pp. 1069–1112. On the list of the "Kasztner refugees" admitted into Switzerland in December 1944, Ernest Nimberger is listed as no. 853.

[86] Carmilly, *Road*, p. 77.

[87] Aurel Socol, *Furtună deasupra Ardealului* (Storm Over Transylvania) (Bucharest: Biblioteca Tribuna, 1994), p. 31.

remembered by Şorban. Interestingly, the same quotation is reproduced without a reference in Rabbi Carmilly-Weinberger's contribution to a book generally eulogizing Marshal Antonescu and in *Istoria evreilor din Transilvania*.[88] The *A zsidóság története Erdélyben*, a book designed for the Hungarian-speaking world, omits the quotation altogether.

Two Histories of the Jews of Transylvania. Rabbi Carmilly-Weinberger's "explanations" about his alleged wartime "rescue" activities were also included in two versions of his history of Transylvanian Jewry. Clearly geared to two different audiences, they differ considerably in scope and content. As the treatment of the Hossu quote reveals, they appear to reflect the Rabbi's perception about the possible political impact of his "history" in Romania and Hungary, two countries locked in a historical rivalry over Transylvania. The Rabbi's account of the pre-World War I history of the Jews in Transylvania is more informative and honest in the Hungarian version. In the Romanian edition the "positive" elements of the Jews' identification with the Magyar cause since the Revolution of 1848–1849 are virtually emasculated. On the other hand, the account of the Romanians' involvement in the wartime "rescue" of Jews is more exaggerated and embellished.

The Hungarian version was published as volume nine in the *Hungaria Judaica* series of the Center of Jewish Studies of the Hungarian Academy of Sciences. It is well documented, thanks largely to the editorial contributions of Professor Géza Komoróczy, the head of the Center. The scholarly nature of the work would have been enhanced had the editor decided to end the history of the Jews in Transylvania with 1918, when the region was annexed by Romania—an annexation subsequently sanctified

---

[88] See his "Antonescu...şi damnatio memoriae," p. 89, and *Istoria evreilor din Transilvania*, pp. 174–175.

under the terms of the Trianon treaty of 1920. The post-World War I account of the history, covered in the last chapter, suffers from politicizing. Thus the events of the pre–1940 era, when the entire region was under Romanian rule, are merely summarized, focusing on the Rabbi's activities on behalf of the refugees from Nazi-dominated Europe; on the other hand, the 1940–1944 period, when Northern Transylvania was part of Hungary, is described in greater detail, with emphasis on the ever harsher anti-Jewish policies of the Hungarians. Although there are fewer unfounded details and exaggerations than in *The Road to Life*, the Rabbi devotes the bulk of this self-serving chapter to his "rescue" activities. Apparently the editor failed, for a variety of reasons, to insist on the historical integrity of this part of the book as well.

The Romanian version of the history of the Jews of Transylvania, published as volume one in the *Bibliotheca Judaica* series of the "Dr. Moshe Carmilly Institute for Hebrew and Jewish History" at the Babeş-Bolyai University in Cluj-Napoca, is much shorter, clearly because many parts of the Hungarian edition were deemed unpalatable for the Romanians. Thus, for example, chapters 4 and 7 in the Hungarian edition dealing with the reforms of the eighteenth and nineteenth centuries, respectively, are consolidated into one relatively short chapter (6) in the Romanian version. The latter virtually ignores the reform measures initiated by Joseph II, including the issuance of the Edict on Tolerance in 1787, and emasculates the advances made by the Jews of Hungary following their identification with the revolutionary cause of Lajos Kossuth in 1848–1849. It largely "overlooks" the sections dealing with the spectacular achievements of Hungarian Jewry in the country's economic, financial, and cultural life and their general identification as "Hungarians of the Israelite faith." The Romanian version also downplays the important role Jews played in the advancement of Hungarian culture in Transylvania, omitting the section on their leading role in the Hungarian press.

The contrast between the Hungarian and Romanian versions

is particularly glaring in the last chapter, dealing with the end of Transylvanian Jewry. In the Romanian version, the anti-Semitic climate and the anti-Jewish policies of the Romanian governments during the interwar period are generally toned down. The chapter fails to reveal that throughout this period the Jews of Transylvania remained basically Hungarian in both language and culture—a source of conflict between the Jews and the Romanians. This facet of Jewish life in Transylvania was more honestly and accurately described by Ernő Marton (see above).

While the Romanian version virtually ignores the specifics of Antonescu's Final Solution program, focusing instead on the humanitarian activities of the regime, it concentrates on the anti-Jewish measures of the Hungarian governments in Northern Transylvania, failing to reveal that prior to the German occupation the bulk of Hungarian Jewry survived under the protection of the Kállay regime. Both versions of the final chapter of the Jews in Northern Transylvania emphasize the "rescue" activities of the author, but to a lesser extent than *The Road to Life*. But in this connection, too, there are basic differences. To cite but a few examples, the Romanian version clearly aims to corroborate the "rescue" accounts the Rabbi had been advancing since the mid-1980s. Bent on proving the humanitarianism of the Romanians, it fails to note that the Romanian smugglers were paid for their services. The Rabbi also ignores the role Hannah Ganz (Grünfeld) had played in his and his wife's rescue. The Hungarian version provides a more honest account: it reveals that the smugglers were paid 1,500 pengő per capita, a sum which, in fact, is two-thirds higher that the one disclosed in *The Road to Life*.[89] and provides a relatively detailed account of Ganz's role. But here, too, the active involvement of Eszter Goro and Arnold Finkelstein in the rescue of Jews across the Hungarian-Romanian border is ignored.

---

[89] *A zsidóság története Erdélyben*, p. 307. See also Carmilly, *Road*, p. 108.

Rabbi Carmilly-Weinberger's questionable handling of sources and texts in the three books is reminiscent of the deplorable practice he used in his memorial volume on the Jewish community of Kolozsvár.[90]

ȘORBAN'S NEW FANTASIES OF RESCUE

Șorban's reactions to the revelations about his unfounded rescue accounts differed from those of the Rabbi. In contrast to Rabbi Carmilly-Weinberger's attempt to justify the questioned parts of his story by revising and updating his account, Șorban decided to defend his position by engaging in crass *ad hominem* attacks and advancing new invented stories of rescue.

Șorban expressed his anger over the criticisms directed against him in three articles published in *Timpul* (Time), a weekly managed by Adrian Riza[91] on which he also serves as "honorary director." He was particularly chagrined over the critique of the TV-documentary, the accusations directed in an open letter against Chief Rabbi Alexander Șafran,[92] and his critics' alleged "inability to accept history" in connection with his and Rabbi Carmilly-Weinberger's "rescue" activities. He identified the critics, especially this author, as "agents of Hungarian revisionism" and "Communists" for failing to recognize the wartime "humani-

---

[90] By far the most informative chapters of his book—*A Kolozsvári zsidóság emlékkönyve* (The Memorial Book of Kolozsvár's Jewry) (New York: The Editor, 1970)—were taken without proper attribution from Imre Szabó's *Erdély zsidói* (The Jews of Transylvania) (Cluj: Kadima Kiadás, 1938). Compare, for example, pp. 127–144, 145–146, 146–148, and 151–60 in Szabó's book with pp. 31–42, 56–59, 95–96, 42–44, and 96–104 in the Rabbi's book. The Rabbi was reminded about this plagiarism by Dezső Schön and László Erős in their letters of December 10, 1970, and July 31, 1991, respectively. Copies of the letters are in this author's files.

[91] For some details on Riza, see chapter 6.

[92] See chapter 6.

tarianism" of the Romanians.[93]

Şorban's stories about his involvement in large-scale wartime rescue activities became ever bolder with the passage of time, feeding the needs of chauvinistic nationalists bent on distorting or denying the Romanian chapter of the Holocaust. His virtual fantasies of rescue climaxed in a three-part interview with Adrian Păunescu, a former Ceauşescu hagiographer and "court poet," published in the weekly *Totuşi Iubirea* (Love, Nevertheless)"—a nationalist-socialist organ owned by Păunescu. One of the main objectives of the dialogue was clearly to help bring about the rehabilitation of Marshal Antonescu.

A fervent nationalist, Păunescu had so well served the late Romanian dictator as editor-in-chief of the weekly *Flacăra* (Flame) and also as a propagandist, that a mob almost lynched him during the uprising of December 1989. Shortly after the fall of Ceauşescu, Păunescu managed to make a spectacular comeback, launching his weekly as well as a daily called *Vremea* (The Time). In 1992, he joined the Socialist Party of Labor, the Left-Fascist party that succeeded the defunct Communist Party, headed by Ilie Verdeţ, a former premier and Politburo figure during the Ceauşescu era. Păunescu quickly rose to a top leadership position and won a seat in the Senate in 1994, and ran as his party's candidate for the presidency in the elections of fall 1996.[94]

---

[93] See his "Incapacitatea de a accepta istoria" (The Inability to Accept History), *Timpul*, Bucharest, June 27–July 2, July 3–9, and July 10–16, 1995. The articles were translated into English, presumably with the involvement of Rabbi Carmilly-Weinberger (he first contacted one of his former students to do the translation), and mailed to many students of the Holocaust the world over. Most of the recipients, this writer's friends and colleagues, were already familiar with the "rescue" story.

[94] Reflecting the maturity of the Romanian electorate, Păunescu and his party suffered a devastating defeat. In the elections of November 3 and 7, 1996, Păunescu received only 0.69 percent of the vote. His party obtained only 2.16 percent of the vote for the Senate and only 2.15 percent for the House of Representatives, failing to attain the 3.0 percent required for representation in the Parliament.

Păunescu is in the forefront of the drive to bring about the rehabilitation of Marshal Antonescu. With reference to the wartime ordeal of Romanian Jewry, Păunescu has consistently emphasized that Antonescu "did not have a policy of exterminating Jews, and that, furthermore, he opposed Hitler each time he was asked to hand over Romanian Jews for extermination in concentration camps." The deportation of the Jews to Transnistria, he argues, "had been an attempt by Antonescu to save them from starvation and the illnesses prevailing under the conditions of the war." He fails to explain why the Marshal was so "good" to the Jews and, above all, why he refused to extend the same benefits to the Romanians.[95] He claimed, moreover, that the wartime suffering of the Jews in Romania was not greater than that of the Romanians.[96]

Reflecting its major objective, the first of the three-part Păunescu-Şorban interview was headlined "Marshal Antonescu Saved the Jews of Romania." The dialogue was clearly designed not only to help bring about the rehabilitation of the pro-Nazi dictator, but also to defend the nationalist rule of Ceauşescu, and, above all, to whitewash the crimes committed against Romanian and Ukrainian Jews. It also serves as a vehicle for Şorban to attack Chief Rabbi Rosen, and provide new, hitherto "unrevealed"—though glaringly false—details about the wartime rescue operations he was allegedly involved with other Romanians and Rabbi Carmilly-Weinberger. As usual he provides no docu-

---

[95] Michael Shafir, "Marshal Antonescu's Postcommunist Rehabilitation: *Cui bono?*"
[96] Ibid. For some additional background information on Păunescu in general and his involvement in the drive for the rehabilitation of Marshal Ion Antonescu in particular, see also Shafir's "The Men of the Archangel Revisited: Anti-Semitic Formations Among Communist Romania's Intellectuals," *Studies in Comparative Communism*, Autumn 1983, pp. 223–243, and "Anti-Semitism in the Postcommunist Era," in *The Tragedy of Romanian Jewry*, Randolph L. Braham, ed. (New York: The Rosenthal Institute for Holocaust Studies of the City University of New York, 1994), pp. 333–386.

mentary or other evidence, expecting the readers to accept his "authoritative" assertions.

Şorban claimed, among other things, that the rescue of Jews across the Hungarian-Romanian border was organized with the cooperation of Mihai Antonescu and the consent of Marshal Ion Antonescu—a "fact he could not reveal in 1987, when Yad Vashem had recognized him as a Righteous Gentile." The rescue was initiated, he asserted, in the winter of 1942–1943, when he learned that Rezső Kasztner—working in tandem with Ottó Komoly, the head of the Zionists of Budapest—had reached an understanding with the "celebrated" Eichmann for the freeing of Jews against the delivery of trucks and other goods for Germany. The difficulty was, Şorban continues, that nobody, not even the Americans, wanted to accept the Jews and the delivery of such goods would have helped the enemy. He revealed this scheme by Kasztner and Komoly to Emil Haţieganu, who had agreed with him that these Jewish leaders were not normal. Thereupon he reverted to his "traditional relations with Rabbi Carmilly-Weinberger and the head of the Transylvanian Zionists, Ernő Marton." They, together with some other Romanians, including Haţieganu, Bishop Iuliu Hossu, Eugen Filloti, the Romanian Minister in Budapest, and Mihai Marina, the Romanian Consul in Oradea, had formed a "conspiracy" to save the Jews—Hungarian and other Jewish refugees—by helping them first across the Hungarian-Romanian border, then from the border towns to Bucharest, and finally for them to move on to Palestine. The first part of the trip was organized by the Transylvanian Zionists, i.e., Rabbi Carmilly-Weinberger and Marton. (In contrast to his previous statements, Şorban does not even mention the role played by such Jewish and Halutz leaders in Turda as Arie Hirsch, Arnold Finkelstein, and Eszter Goro.) The second part of the rescue operation was his and his group's responsibility, a task they performed with the aid of the Romanian authorities, including the Ministry of the Interior, the police, the security and counterintelligence services, and the army. These authorities, in turn, enjoyed the approval of the "great ones," Mihai Antonescu and Ion Antonescu. In another context, Şorban boasted to Păunescu that the smugglers involved in the taking of Jews across the border, including a Legionary woman named Letiţia Papu, were paid by him, for he was rich—contradicting the lie he and Rabbi Carmilly-Weinberger propagated in the TV propaganda film.[97] To highlight the success of their rescue activities, Şorban noted that Kasztner managed to rescue only some 800 to 1,000 Jews against payment—an act for which he was shot.[98]

Any serious student of general history, let alone Holocaust history, knows that the so-called Kasztner-Eichmann negotiations took place only shortly after the Germans had occupied Hungary on March 19, 1944. Moreover, as indicated elsewhere, Marshal Antonescu and Constantin (Piki) Z. Vasiliu, the head of the Romanian gendarmerie and State Secretary in the Ministry of the Interior, were reportedly never aware of any Jewish refugees in Romania. According to Radu Lecca, Antonescu's Commissar on Jewish Affairs, who obviously was more informed about these matters than Şorban was in 1996, "if the Marshal had known about the presence of such refugees from Hungary, he would have given the order to shoot them (in accordance with the law then in effect) in order to prevent other Hungarian Jews from trying their luck in Romania."[99]

In a second fantasy account, Şorban informed Păunescu about "another sensational thing nobody knows anything about": his

---

[97] "Confuzia şi neştiinţa sunt mai dăunătoare decât nedreptatea," op. cit.

[98] "Mareşalul Antonescu i-a salvat pe evreii din România. Un dialog Raoul Şorban-Adrian Păunescu, Bucureşti, 17 Ianuarie 1996" (Marshal Antonescu Saved the Jews of Romania. A Raoul Şorban-Andrei Păunescu Dialogue. Bucharest, January 17, 1996), *Totuşi Iubirea*, no. 2, January 1996.

[99] See his *Eu i-am salvat pe evreii din România*, p. 289. Lecca claims that General Nicolae Diaconescu, the General Director of the Police, protected a few Hungarian Jews without the knowledge of Vasiliu. Ibid.

involvement in another major rescue operation effectuated with the aid of Ion and Mihai Antonescu! This time, Şorban takes credit for having played a key role in the rescue of the leaders of the Jewish Orthodox community of Hungary—Jews, he emphasized, who had nothing to do with either Romania or Transylvania. He boasts about having served a vital intermediary role in getting Romanian passports for Fülöp Freudiger and other leaders of the Orthodox Jewish community of Hungary—an act for which he has "moral pangs." He regretted the fact that 80 leaders of a community were selected on the basis of wealth and service. Şorban and Păunescu concurred that the disappearance of the entire leadership of a community was immoral![100]

This account of rescue is still another product of Şorban's fantasy and part and parcel of the campaign to sanitize Romania's wartime history. No historical source dealing with this episode in the tragedy of Hungarian Jewry even hints at Şorban. The background and the means by which Fülöp Freudiger, a leading figure of the Budapest Jewish Council, and his family and close friends escaped to Romania on August 9, 1944, are authoritatively described elsewhere.[101] Moreover, Şorban's account is refuted even by Rabbi Carmilly-Weinberger, who asserted that the Freudiger group managed to come to Bucharest with passports acquired through the intervention of Filderman, the head of the Romanian Jewish community.[102]

Asked to identify Antonescu's place in history, Şorban reminded Păunescu of Rabbi Carmilly-Weinberger's talk at Bucharest University's Nicolae Iorga Institute of History in 1988. He paraphrased the Rabbi as having said: "During the war, there

---

[100] "Mareşalul Antonescu i-a salvat pe evreii din România."
[101] See Braham, *Politics*, pp. 455, 911–912. See also Fülöp Freudiger, "Five Months," in *The Tragedy of Hungarian Jewry*, Randolph L. Braham, ed. (New York: Institute for Holocaust Studies of the City University of New York, 1986), pp. 237–294.
[102] See his "Antonescu şi...damnatio memoriae," p. 90.

were only two ways to escape from Nazism's circle of fire: through the Pyrenees and through Romania. Both ways were unusual. Franco accepted the Jews, housed, fed, clothed, and kept them in Spain until the end of the war. And this is what the Romanians did as well." Şorban concurred with Păunescu that the term "Romanians" meant in fact Antonescu and the Romanian State, which had saved "tens of thousands of Jews." "It is an obligation, a national duty of maximum importance," he emphasized, "for [the world] to know in a true way what Antonescu had done and why."

Upon reading Şorban's account of the alleged active role the Romanian dictator had played in the "saving" of so many thousands of Jews, Michael Shafir, a noted expert on Romanian affairs, facetiously wondered whether Şorban ought not in fact to surrender his title of Righteous Gentile to Marshal Antonescu![103]

Quixotic as Şorban's inventions about his involvement in the Kasztner and Freudiger-related "rescues" may be, his comments about the Holocaust are absolutely outrageous. Şorban insisted that there was no Holocaust in Romania, notwithstanding the exhibit at the U.S. Holocaust Memorial Museum in Washington, which he visited only because he "was invited to the opening with President Iliescu." He assured Păunescu that he had informed Iliescu that the depiction of the Romanian part of the exhibit was in contradiction with his own views. To substantiate his view, he told Păunescu that the "deportations" to Transnistria were in fact only resettlements and the losses of Jews were due primarily to "poor organization." The resettled Jews could receive food, clothing, and drugs from Romania, and could communicate with each other via mail. As to the Jassy pogrom of June 25–26, 1941, he tried to convince Păunescu and the world that he only heard about it and was not really informed about its details. He concurred with Păunescu that the massacres at Odessa and in Bessarabia were not

<hr>

[103] See his "Marshal Antonescu's Postcommunist Rehabilitation. *Cui bono?*," p. 350.

ethnic, but political in nature and necessitated by military considerations. Păunescu added that the Jews affected by these measures in the former Soviet held territories were Bolsheviks.

True to the position of the other Romanian history-cleansers, Şorban claimed that the Holocaust took place in Hungary "where no one survived." "The Hungarians worked systematically. And they have acknowledged their guilt with precision: 618,000 Jews killed, deported and killed in 2 months."

Şorban insisted that he could "prove" statistically that the Jews of Romania, in contrast to those of Hungary, survived the war. He stated:

> Not even today do I know what Transnistria was. They speak about 400,000 Jews having been exterminated there. Mr. Păunescu, 800,000 Jews lived in Romania. Approximately 200,000 remained in Northern Transylvania. About 200,000 remained in Bessarabia, who did not return. Thus, there remained 400,000. And they speak about 400,000 victims. For over 25 years, 400,000 Romanian Jews live in Israel. An additional 50,000 live in the West. There are many of them in Latin America as well. There was also the postwar increase. There are 700,000 Jews of Romanian origin in the world today in various diasporas. How, then, did these 400,000 Jews die?[104]

Şorban's and Păunescu's depiction of the wartime achievements of Antonescu was matched by their highly positive evaluation of Nicolae Ceauşescu. They concurred that the former dictator had protected the national sovereignty and advanced the national reconstruction of Romania—achievements that will grow

---

[104] "Mareşalul Antonescu i-a salvat pe evreii din România." See also parts 2 and 3 of the dialogue in *Totuşi Iubirea*, no. 4, February 1–8; and no. 5, February 8–15, 1996.

with the passage of time. Ceauşescu was murdered, Păunescu emphasized, "not because of what he did bad but because of what he did good." Şorban agreed with the assessment of a friend of his, concluding that Ceauşescu "will remain in the memory of the country as a great builder."[105]

The interview, most probably well received by nationalists within Romania, engendered a critical reaction in democratic circles, especially abroad. Radu Ioanid, an expert on Romania associated with the U.S. Holocaust Memorial Museum, expressed his outrage in letters to Mordecai Paldiel of Yad Vashem and Ken Jacobsen of the Anti-Defamation League in New York. The letters included excerpts from the interview. His May 23, 1996, letter to Paldiel stated, among other things:

> It is unbelievable to see a Righteous Gentile from Romania who tries hard to rehabilitate Ion Antonescu, lowers dramatically the number of the Jews killed under the Romanian administration and confuses (the already confused) public opinion about the Romanian responsibility in the destruction of the Jews from Iaşi, Bessarabia and Transnistria. It is outrageous to see Antonescu presented as a savior of the Jews from Romania and Hungary.[106]

HISTORY-CLEANSING IN HIGH GEAR

Şorban's involvement in the pro-Antonescu history-cleansing campaign has become intertwined with the propaganda drive to safeguard his own tarnished reputation as a "rescuer." He has

---

[105] Şorban-Păunescu dialogue, part 3. Ibid.
[106] Copies of the letters are in the archives of this author. See also Michael Shafir, "Marshal Antonescu's Postcommunist Rehabilitation. *Cui bono?*" The leaders of Yad Vashem were also alerted about the Şorban-Păunescu pro-Antonescu dialogue via Jean Ancel.

been pursuing this objective since 1986 by protecting himself with the mantle of respectability bestowed upon him by Yad Vashem. His image-saving drive included the use of propaganda techniques developed during the nationalist-socialist era as further refined by the neo-Fascists following the elimination of Ceaușescu in 1989. Working in tandem with fellow history-cleansing chauvinists, he appears to have been instrumental in publishing a propaganda booklet under the authorship of Dan Dungaciu.[107] The author reportedly is an associate of Ilie Bădescu, a pro-Fascist sociologist and former chief ideologist of the anti-Semitic Movement for Romania Party.[108] In tune with Șorban's position, the author not only embraces the cause of nationalism but also pretends to be "scholarly." Like Șorban, he identifies those who criticize Antonescu's wartime role or question Șorban's "rescue" activities as anti-Romanian. His pretentions of scholarship are reflected in the "documentation" of the wartime "humanitarianism" of the Romanians, the "rescue" activities of Șorban and Rabbi Carmilly-Weinberger, and the "anti-Romanian" position of their critics. He provides footnote references, many of which are sheer inventions, cites texts from the writings of the "rescuers" and their critics, usually out-of-context, and offers "historical" interpretations that are clearly both psychopathological and political in nature. Most of his sources consist of the self-serving writings of Șorban and Rabbi Carmilly-Weinberger in various nationalist and neo-Fascist organs.

The introduction to Dungaciu's work is written by Șorban. It is basically a rehash of his anti-Hungarian positions, highlighting Romania's wartime "humanitarianism" by focusing on his and his friends' "rescue" activities. In contrast to his many earlier accounts,

---

[107] See his *"Reţelele omeniei" şi reţelele mistificării* ("The Networks of Humanity" and the Networks of Mystification) (Bucharest: Editura Romanitatea Orientală, 1997), 89 p. (Cited hereafter as Dungaciu.)
[108] For some details on the party, see chapter 3.

however, Şorban's introduction does not even refer to Arieh Hirsch, Eszter Goro, or Éva Semlyén—Jewish heroes of the Holocaust era who have publicly questioned his and the Rabbi's post–1985 rescue accounts.[109]

The first part of the work—The Networks of Humanity—is devoted to a detailed description of the wartime "rescue" activities of a number of Romanians, especially those of Şorban. Here, too, the activities of the above-mentioned Jewish heroes of the rescue campaign are overlooked. The author's goal is clearly to counteract Şorban's critics and "prove" that he rightly deserved the identification as a Righteous Among the Nations. The documentation sources are as familiar as they are questionable: in addition to the accounts by Şorban and the Rabbi, the author relies on the writings of Andrei Riza, the speech by Rabbi Alexander Şafran in the Romanian Senate on March 28, 1995, and the comments by Yad Vashem officials during Şorban's designation as a Righteous in 1986. Dungaciu is carried away. Some of his exaggerations exceed even those advanced by the "rescuers." For example, in quoting Rabbi Carmilly-Weinberger's 1988 speech at the Nicolae Iorga Institute, Dungaciu felt it necessary to inflate the Rabbi's reference to the number of Jews who flocked to the Transylvanian capital. He cites the Rabbi as having said that "hundreds of thousands of Jewish families came to Cluj from the provinces" during the Hungarian rule of Northern Transylvania.[110] Even *Europa*, the viciously anti-Semitic weekly which also found the speech worthy of reproduction, quoted the Rabbi as having referred to "hundreds of Jewish families."[111] The section is replete with propagandistic references to the "network of humanity" that allegedly permeated

---

[109] Among the addenda to the book is the text of Şorban's speech accepting the award from Yad Vashem on April 7, 1987. It omits the name of Eszter Goro, prominently identified in the original.

[110] See p. 17 of his booklet. In 1942 the population of Cluj was about 100,000.

[111] *Europa*, no. 37, August, 1991.

Romanian life during the Antonescu era. Just like his text, Dungaciu's "documentation" is also suspect. To highlight Şorban's achievements, for example, Dungaciu cites Chief Rabbi Şafran's comments about his and Rabbi Carmilly-Weinberger's rescue activities as if Şafran had published them in the 1989 French version of his memoirs.[112] In that version, like in the original 1987 English-language edition of his book, Rabbi Şafran does not even mention Şorban. The Rabbi first noted Şorban's "achievements" on March 28, 1995, when, duped by the Romanian Foreign Intelligence Service, gave an unfortunate speech in the Romanian Senate—"achievements" he felt compelled to note in a footnote in the Romanian version of his memoirs.[113]

The second part of the work—The Networks of Mystification—is devoted to an "evaluation" of Şorban's critics, who are identified as pro-Hungarian and by definition enemies of Romania and the Romanian people. Apparently, no one taking issue with the lies and falsified accounts of rescue advanced by Şorban and his cronies can escape the label of being either an agent of Hungarian revisionism or an enemy of Romania. Among those so labeled is Tudor Bugnariu, the postwar mayor of Cluj and a former good friend of Şorban's. In several of his cogent writings, Bugnariu took issue with the unfounded rescue accounts and unbridled anti-Hungarian positions Şorban had taken since 1986. The author attempts to counteract Bugnariu's criticism and expose his "hypocrisy" by citing a letter of recommendation written by Bugnariu on Şorban's behalf *in 1955*! One does not have to be a student of logic to recognize the propagandistic nature of the argument. Only a fellow neo-Fascist will accept a letter written on behalf of a presumably destitute friend in 1955—during the era of the Stalinist Gheorghe Gheorghiu-Dej—as evidence that a criti-

[112] Dungaciu, pp. 19–20.
[113] See chapter 6.

cism advanced after 1986 was "unfounded."[114] The author also "unmasks" the anti-Romanian, i.e., anti-Şorban, positions of Dr. Ernő Gáll, a professor emeritus at the Babeş-Bolyai University, the late Dr. Radu Florian, a former associate of the Institute of Sociology of the Romanian Academy, and Zoltán Tibori Szabó, the former editor-in-chief of *Szabadság* (Freedom), the Hungarian-language daily of Cluj.[115] He repeats Şorban's accusations against Yitzhak Artzi, the very person who as head of the Commission at Yad Vashem recommended Şorban's recognition as a Righteous Among the Nations. But Artzi, like the other "accused," committed the unpardonable error after 1986 of getting more deeply involved in documenting the catastrophe that befell Romanian Jewry during the Antonescu era.[116]

The most venomous part of Dungaciu's, i.e., Şorban's, accusations are directed against this author. He is singled out for his critical review of the Şorban-Carmilly "rescue" story as portrayed in the TV documentary and for his alleged role in publishing the open letter to Rabbi Alexander Şafran.[117] To emphasize the alleged pro-Hungarian bias of the author, Dungaciu cites the November 1994 issue of *Szombat* (Saturday), a Hungarian-Jewish monthly as the source for the review. While one can be grateful that Dungaciu's

---

[114] For some details on the attack against Bugnariu, see Dungaciu, pp. 24–33.

[115] Professor Gáll is accused of having produced an audio-cassette with personal accounts that minimize the role Romanians played in the rescue of North Transylvanian Jews (pp. 33–34); Dr. Florian is lambasted primarily for his role as editor of *Societate şi Cultură* (Society and Culture) that published, among others, a piece by Bugnariu (pp. 49–50); Mr. Tibori Szabó is attacked for his series of articles on "The Weinberger Şorban Legend" in *Szabadság* (pp. 51–52).

[116] Ibid., p. 44. Dungaciu's comments about Artzi are almost identical with those used by Şorban in *Timpul*, June 27–July 2, 1995, p. 9. This did not prevent the author from including as an addendum the text of Artzi's speech of April 7, 1987, when Şorban received Yad Vashem's award.

[117] The co-signers of the letter—Jean Ancel, Victor Eskenasy, Radu Ioanid, and Michael Shafir—also receive failing marks. Dungaciu is particularly pugnacious in dealing with Ancel's role in the "distortion" of Rabbi Şafran's position (pp. 42–43).

selective citations may in fact acquaint some of his readers with the history-cleansing technique used by Şorban and his ilk, these readers will be unable to read the entire text simply because it is not in that journal.[118]   To denigrate this author's scholarship, Dungaciu, like Şorban before him, used an out-of-context quotation from a review of *The Politics of Genocide* by the late Professor György Ránki, the former head of the Institute of History of the Hungarian Academy of Science.   Clearly, neither Şorban nor his neo-Fascist "scholar" ever read Professor Ránki's review: it is in fact part of the introduction to both the first and second editions of the Hungarian-language version of *The Politics of Genocide*.

The lies and innuendoes directed against this author by Dungaciu are verbatim copies of those originally published by Şorban in *Timpul*.   To cite but one example of their chicaneries, they cite a letter by Zev Rotice [*sic*], an Israeli high school teacher who once worked for the Institute for Holocaust Studies at Haifa University.   In a February 14, 1988, letter Rotics, who was probably awed by his contact with a Righteous, informs Şorban that he (Rotics) had sent him some documents from the Institute files concerning his outstanding work of behalf of the Jews of Transylvania, and that he forwarded copies of the same to this writer.   Unfortunately, he never did, and apparently those "documents" were not thoroughly convincing for Şorban would certainly have long published them.   This author received copies of the same documents through the courtesy of Kate Nemes, a volunteer worker at the Haifa Institute.[119]   The few letters by Şorban to Ernő Marton (no trace of any response by Marton) reveal primarily Şorban's character.   In one of them Şorban informs Marton of the

---

[118] The original English version (see footnote 53) appeared in Hungarian translation in *Kommentár* (Commentary), vol. 2, no. 1, 1993. *Kommentár* was at the time identified as a quarterly supplement of *Szombat*.

[119] These copies were sent with a cover letter date September 29, 1995.

false statement he gave to the police authorities in Turda;[120] in the others he asks for monetary support, a practice he continued quite successfully after he became a Righteous Among the Nations.[121]

Reflecting Şorban's position, Dungaciu argues that the main objective of the critics is not only to question and deny the involvement of Romanians in the rescue of Jews from Transylvania, but also to distort—mystify—the situation of Romanian Jewry during the Second World War. In almost paranoiac fashion, he argues that Hungary seems to play an important role in the worldwide drive of mystification and that "Jews of Hungarian origin have a massive influence in the leading circles of the Jewish world." The argument comes close to the standard anti-Semitic accusation of Jewish conspiratorial machinations.

The direct and indirect attempts by Şorban and his fellow history-cleansers to falsify the record of the Holocaust have now been unmasked. The reaction of the falsifiers of history to those dedicated to preserve the integrity of the historical record in general and the Holocaust in particular is both saddening and potentially harmful to the evolution of Romania along the path of democracy. As to Şorban, the more he "explains" the more he corroborates the wisdom of the French proverb: *Qui s'excuse s'accuse!*

---

[120] See p. 136.
[121] For details of the anti-Braham diatribe, see Dungaciu, pp. 34–49.

CHAPTER 8

Overview and Conclusions

The tragic fate that befell the Jews of Romania and the Romanian-occupied areas of the Ukraine during the Second World War constitutes one of the most neglected and controversial chapters of the Holocaust era. While the Jews of Old Romania and Southern Transylvania survived the war almost intact, close to 270,000 Romanian and Ukrainian Jews were killed, mostly by units of the Romanian army and gendarmerie, often acting in concert with German security forces. While the Germans were genuinely impressed with the speed and resolve with which the Romanians were "solving" the Jewish problem, they were often appalled by the disorganization and barbarism that characterized their killing operations.

The Romanians were particularly eager to liquidate the Jewish communities of Bessarabia, Northern Bukovina, and some parts of Moldavia which they identified as "alien" and "pro-Soviet." The Romanian version of the Final Solution program was planned and partially implemented by the regime of Marshal Ion Antonescu without any prodding on the part of the Germans. The pro-Nazi regime began the "cleansing of territory" (*curăţirea terenului*)— the Romanian euphemism for the Final Solution program—almost immediately after joining the Reich in the war against the Soviet Union on June 22, 1941. Launched during the euphoric era of the war, when the Antonescu regime shared the Nazis' conviction in the ultimate victory of the Axis, the territorial cleansing was envisioned to be completed in two distinct phases. The first called for the elimination of the Jews of Bessarabia and Northern Bukovina, the territories the Soviets had occupied the year before, and from certain parts of Southern Bukovina and Moldavia. This phase was largely completed within a relatively short time, concurrently with the campaign of mass murder the *SS-Einsatzgruppen* were waging against the Jews in the German-occupied parts of the Soviet Union.

The second phase called for the extension of the Final Solution program to the rest of the country. The Antonescu regime had formally agreed with the Germans in the summer of 1942 to carry out the nationwide program in accordance with the details worked out by the Nazi experts at the Wannsee Conference of January 20, 1942. The plans called for the initiation of the program in Southern Transylvania, an area inhabited by Jews whose language and culture were basically Hungarian. The aspirations of the ultra-nationalists—a Romania free of Jews—failed to be realized primarily because the tide of war had in the meantime changed in favor of the Allies. By the time the program was to be launched in late summer 1942, the Romanian leaders, realizing that the Axis might not win the war after all, shifted gear. They decided to exploit the surviving Jews to advance both their economic and national interests. Guided primarily by political expediency, they decided to permit a considerable number of indigenous and foreign Jews to emigrate to Palestine against the payment of high per capita fees and use the newly evolving "humanitarian" record as a bargaining chip with the Allies after the war. As a consequence of this shift in policy, close to ninety percent of the Jews of Old Romania and Southern Transylvania, while subjected to ever harsher anti-Jewish measures, survived the war.

Like many other states in former German-dominated Europe, Romania has failed to come to grips with its historical past. With the exception of the brief immediate postwar period, the subject of the Holocaust in Romania, i.e., the mass murder of Jews in general and the responsibility of the Romanian army and gendarmerie units in particular, became taboo until after the dissolution of the nationalist-socialist system late in 1989. While anti-Semitism was officially condemned during the Communist era, the age-old scourge was kept alive, as in the other Soviet bloc nations, by a persistent campaign against Zionism and cosmopolitanism.

The issue of the Holocaust was brought to the fore in a controlled fashion in the mid-1970s. The nationalist-socialist regime of Nicolae Ceauşescu decided to exploit the wartime suffering of the Jews for political ends. One of the primary but not openly articulated objectives was to gradually bring about the rehabilitation of Marshal Antonescu and thereby assure the national continuity and legitimacy of his own regime. The other was to advance Romania's case against Hungary on the issue of Transylvania and the treatment of the relatively large Hungarian minority in Romania by juxtaposing the wartime record of the two countries. The idea was to demonstrate Romania's "humanitarianism" against Hungary's "barbarism" in handling the Jewish question during the war.

The guidelines for refurbishing the historical past were issued by Ceauşescu himself. In accord with these guidelines, party-affiliated "intellectuals," including a considerable number of pseudo-historians, artists, military figures, and professional propagandists, launched a systematic history-cleansing drive to convince the Romanian people—and the world—that there had been no Holocaust in Romania. The only part of the country in which the Final Solution was applied, they claimed, was Northern Transylvania, an area that had been under Hungarian occupation at the time. According to these history-cleansers, Marshal Antonescu had been unjustly tried and executed in 1946 by Soviet agents bent on vengeance rather than the pursuit of justice. The drive for the rehabilitation of the Marshal gained momentum after the systemic change of December 1989.

The nationalist-socialist regime of Ceauşescu not merely tolerated but actively supported chauvinistic nationalists whose political-ideological views were clearly rooted in the doctrines and policies of the viciously anti-Semitic Rightist movements of the interwar period. During the last 15 years of its existence the Ceauşescu regime became increasingly Left-Fascist in character: its nationalist-socialist ideology gradually incorporated some of the main themes of the prewar Right radical movements. These were further advanced and politically exploited after the 1989 revolution by chauvinistic nationalists many of whom had previously been closely associated with the Ceauşescu regime. Having played leading roles in the army, party, government, and the dreaded *Securitate*, these nationalists found the transition from Left-Fascism to Right radicalism both easy and profitable.

Taking advantage of the political opportunities offered by the post-Communist regime, the nationalists organized a series of new Right radical political parties and movements. Some used the pro-Nazi Iron Guard as a model. Increasingly vocal and politically active, the nationalists have launched a concerted drive not only to bring about the rehabilitation of Marshal Antonescu, but also to lay the foundations of a new political and social order that would reflect his nationalist stance: the reestablishment of a Greater Romania which is ethnically homogeneous, national-Christian, anti-liberal, anti-democratic, and anti-parliamentarian. The ideology of these neo-Fascists includes a nebulous amalgam of views that fuses religion, ethnicity, common descent, and consanguinity. Reflecting the ideological tenets of the Antonescu regime, their doctrine rejects the principles underlying the modern civic state and civil society, namely those of democracy, tolerance, and pluralism.

In pursuit of their objectives, the chauvinistic nationalists are engaged in a history-cleansing process that distorts, denigrates, and actually denies the Romanian chapter of the Holocaust. Using the mass media outlets placed at their disposal, the history-cleansers began to whitewash the crimes of the Antonescu regime during the Ceauşescu era. The pro-Antonescu campaign has usually been coupled with a contrasting of Romania's "humanitarian" and Hungary's "barbaric" wartime record.

While the Romanian nationalists' description of the Holocaust in Hungary in general and Northern Transylvania in particular, its occasional exaggerations notwithstanding, is basically correct, it usually fails to provide the appropriate historical context. The nationalists consistently fail to differentiate between the anti-Jewish policies of the various Hungarian governments during the pre- and post-German occupation periods. They also fail to present a comparative evaluation of the treatment of the Jewish question in Hungary and Romania for the entire Nazi era. Such a comparative treatment, if objectively pursued, would not substantiate their claims.

The history-cleansing campaign acquired new momentum in the mid-1980s. It was reinforced by largely unfounded accounts of rescue of Hungarian and other Jewish refugees across the Hungarian-Romanian border, spread by the media of mass communication. These were advanced by two individuals ostensibly motivated by their particular personal interests: Dr. Moshe Carmilly-Weinberger, the former Chief Rabbi of the small Neolog Jewish community of Cluj (Kolozsvár), and Dr. Raoul Şorban, a painter and professor of art history at the University of Bucharest. In the course of time, their rescue accounts became ever more grandiose, consisting of facts, fiction, and outright lies and, since they were often geared to different audiences, contradictory on some crucial aspects.[1]

The interests that bound them, the ever more grandiose stories of rescue they advanced, and the rewards they consequently reaped have been detailed in this work. It is one of the tragic

---

[1] To cite just a few examples: 1. Şorban claimed that he had saved the Rabbi and his wife; the latter insisted that they went to Romania on a "mission" assisted by others; 2. Şorban asserted that he had played a leading role in rescuing the Orthodox Jewish leadership of Budapest; the Rabbi insisted they were saved by the Romanian Jewish leaders; 3. Rabbi Carmilly-Weinberger stated that he never heard about the extermination of the Jews in Auschwitz; Şorban had reminded him that he, too, had informed him about it.

ironies of history that the cause of chauvinistic nationalists bent on whitewashing Romania's wartime record and rehabilitating Marshal Antonescu is being advanced by a Rabbi and a Righteous Among the Nations: inadvertently by the former, consciously by the latter. While the Rabbi continues to emphasize the positive role of the Romanians in apparent gratitude for the positive spin Şorban and others provided for his escape from Kolozsvár prior to the ghettoization of the Jews on May 3, 1944, Şorban has emerged as one of the leading champions of Antonescu and his regime.

The possession of the coveted title of Righteous Among the Nations and of an honorary citizenship from the State of Israel did not prevent him from distorting and denigrating the Romanian chapter of the Holocaust. The twisting of the historical record of the Holocaust is reflected in many of his politically oriented writings. Whether in interviews, dialogues, personal recollections, or political commentaries, Şorban generally overlooks the many increasingly severe anti-Jewish measures the various Romanian governments adopted starting in 1937, the Iron Guard pogroms of 1940–1941, the expropriation of the Jews, and especially the mass murder of Romanian and Ukrainian Jews by units of the Romanian army and gendarmerie during the Antonescu era. Bent on demonstrating the "humanitarianism" of the Romanians and the Antonescu regime, Şorban, like other nationalists, consistently tries to convince the world that Romania was the only country during the war which prevented the application of the Final Solution, brought back the deportees from camps, allowed the emigration of Jews to Palestine, desisted from requiring Jews to wear a distinctive badge, and allowed its officials to issue false identification papers and passports to Jews.[2] Many of these assertions are patently false, others are half-truth, and all are presented out of context and without documentary substantiation.

---

[2] See, for example, his "Variante de 'justificare' " (Variants of "Justification"), *Timpul* (The Time), Bucharest, July 7, 1992.

Şorban, who has emerged as an active champion of Marshal Antonescu's rehabilitation, misses no occasion to emphasize the Marshal's protection of the Jews of Romania and support for the Jewish refugees. He even claims that the rehabilitation drive enjoys the sympathy of many Jews in Israel who owe their survival to the Marshal's resistance to Hitlerite pressures.[3] In recent comments he also emphasized that his own wartime "rescue activities" were carried out with the knowledge and protection of the Marshal. These comments induced Michael Shafir, an astute student of Romanian affairs, to ask a question concerning Şorban: "If [Şorban's] deeds during the war were so well protected, why does he deserve the title of Righteous Gentile? The usurper should pass it on to the one who should have received it, Marshal Antonescu!"[4]

Şorban's exploitation of the coveted title of Righteous highlights another potential danger. While the title is sometimes exploited for the advancement of personal pecuniary interests it can also be misused in the pursuit of political objectives, falsifying the historical record of the Holocaust.

The preoccupation with the Righteous Among the Nations in recent years is both welcome and disturbing. It is welcome when dealt with by scholars devoted to the clarification and documentation of the many complex facets of the Final Solution. It is disturbing when it is exploited for pecuniary and, above all, political reasons. This is particularly the case in East Central Europe, where the Nazis found many willing accomplices during the war. To counteract their dismal record during the Holocaust, the nationalists in these states virtually encourage a numbers game about

---

[3] Gabriel Ţepelea, *Însemnări de taină* (Secret Notes) (Bucharest: Editura Fundaţiei Culturale Române, 1997), p. 357.

[4] See his "Marshal Antonescu's Postcommunist Rehabilitation. *Cui bono?*," in *The Tragedy of Romanian and Ukrainian Jews During the Antonescu Era*, Randolph L. Braham, ed. (New York: The Rosenthal Institute for Holocaust Studies of the City University of New York, 1997), p. 350.

their Righteous. Highlighting the number of the Righteous recognized by Yad Vashem and focusing almost exclusively on their rescue activities, however, inevitably distorts the record of the Holocaust. This practice tends to denigrate the Holocaust by minimizing the number of victims, emphasizing the number of rescued, and occasionally inflating the number of rescuers.

Unidimensional, politically oriented accounts of this type often play into the hands of Holocaust deniers. As Rabbi Marvin Hier, Dean of the Simon Wiesenthal Center in Los Angeles, correctly observed, "stress on the Righteous is a victory for revisionists" as it deflects attention from the large number of perpetrators—the Nazis and their accomplices all over Europe—and "young people might come to accept the notion that the relatively few practitioners of righteous conduct were the dominant characters of the Holocaust."[5] The unilateral preoccupation with the Righteous is clearly even more questionable in cases involving largely unfounded wartime rescue activities. Awards based on basically unsubstantiated accounts of rescue, moreover, also tarnish the record of the men and women who *really* risked their lives to save Jews during the Nazi era.

History is a formidable weapon. It is particularly corruptive and dangerous in the hands of chauvinistic nationalists bent on shaping history. Romanian nationalist ideologues, like their counterparts elsewhere, are engaged in an Orwellian attempt to obfuscate the past in order to shape a future of their own liking. They are engaged in what the noted American historian Arthur M. Schlesinger, Jr. calls exculpatory history, sedulously defending Antonescu's wartime record, including his policies toward the Jews. The political-ideological objectives of these nationalists are enhanced not only by the governmental officials who tacitly agree

---

[5] Rabbi Marvin Hier, "Remembrance Needs to Emphasize Villains, not Heroes," *Martyrdom and Resistance*, March–April, 1995, p. 12.

with them, but also by those who contribute to the falsification of history through unfounded accounts of rescue.

It is the responsibility of scholars and persons of good will everywhere to counteract them. For unless the falsifiers of history are unmasked and the drive of the history-cleansers is stopped or counteracted, the historical record of the Holocaust will be tarnished. If false accounts of rescue and benevolent portrayals of the wartime behavior of Nazi leaders were left unmasked, they would spread like computer viruses, affecting genuine historical writing. The historical record of the Holocaust must be preserved untarnished and protected from history-cleansers, whatever their background and "public recognition."

The linkage between anti-Semitism and the Holocaust has been established beyond any doubt. The denigration, distortion, and denial of the Holocaust by Romanian "historical revisionists"—and their counterparts elsewhere in the world—are part and parcel of their deep-rooted anti-Semitism. These falsifications of history represent a new virulent strain in postwar anti-Semitism. The logic behind the linkage between Holocaust denial and anti-Semitism was cogently summarized by Walter Reich, Director of the U.S. Holocaust Memorial Museum in Washington, D.C. Writing about "the perverse ingenuity" of the Holocaust deniers, he stated:

> The primary motivation for most deniers is anti-Semitism, and for them the Holocaust is an infuriatingly inconvenient fact of history. After all the Holocaust has generally been recognized as one of the most terrible crimes that ever took place and surely the very emblem of evil in the modern age. If that crime was a direct result of anti-Semitism taken to its logical end, then anti-Semitism itself ... is inevitably discredited.... What better way to rehabilitate anti-Semitism, making anti-Semitic arguments seem once again respectable in civilized discourse

and even make it acceptable for governments to pursue anti-Semitic policies than by convincing the world that the great crime for which anti-Semitism was blamed simply never happened— indeed that it was nothing more than a frame-up invented by the Jews, and propagated by them through their control of the media.[6]

With respect to the Romanian anti-Semites, Silviu Brucan, a former leading figure of the Romanian Communist Party, provided a complementary and more specific explanation:

The revival of anti-Semitism in Romania is part and parcel of the Right-wing nationalist chauvinistic current that re-emerged in all former "Communist" countries with the collapse of Marxism-Leninism and the ideological vacuum left by that collapse.... The need to find 'scapegoats' for the failures suffered under the new historical experience of the transition from "socialism" to a market economy is so acute that anti-Semitic diversion is being encouraged even where there are no Jews left. In addition, there is also a phenomenon that is specific to Romania: since the overwhelming majority of Romania's intellectuals had collaborated with the Ceauşescu dictatorship, one encounters among them what could be termed "retroactive dissidence," meaning that while they lacked the courage to stand up against the dictatorship, they are trying to display "courage" now, when there are no risks. And one of the handiest ways is to be a nationalist anti-Semite.[7]

---

[6] See his "Erasing the Holocaust," *The New York Times Book Review*, July 11, 1993.
[7] Quoted from an interview published in *Minimum*, Tel Aviv, no. 51, June 1991, as cited by Michael Shafir, "Anti-Semitism Without Jews in Romania, "*Report on Eastern Europe*, June 28, 1991, p. 29.

In view of the current intertwining of the denigration, distortion, and denial of the Holocaust with the contemporary manifestations of anti-Semitism, it is clear that the struggle against the age-old scourge must entail a resolute stand against the falsifiers of history. Judging by the attitudes of the various regimes since 1947, the content of textbooks used at various levels of education, the position of many political and governmental leaders, and the writings of most intellectuals, the near-term prospects of victory in the struggle against the twin evils of anti-Semitism and Holocaust denial in Romania are quite disheartening.

But, Romania's historical record notwithstanding, there are some encouraging signs that things may be headed for a change in this regard. The national elections of November 1996, the first in which the Romanians changed their head of state through the ballot box, bodes well for a more positive future. One can only hope that President Emil Constantinescu and the members of his regime will one day not only formally express their opposition to the rehabilitation of Marshal Antonescu and condemn manifestations of anti-Semitism, but also take a resolute stand against the distortion of the Romanian chapter of the Holocaust.

A significant step in this direction was taken in April 1997. Speaking on the occasion of the annual Holocaust remembrance day in Bucharest, President Constantinescu presented a "balanced" account of the wartime tragedy of Romanian Jewry. Without specifying the number of casualties, the Romanian President emphasized that while "the planners of the unforgivable genocide were not Romanians ... and many Romanians on every social level risked their lives [and] some even gave their lives to rescue Jews from the ruthless extermination mechanism, ... other Romanians engaged in the implementation of the infamous Nazi project of the "final solution." Without identifying Marshal Antonescu and the other top wartime leaders by name, President Constantinescu continued his assessment as follows:

Romania's wartime authorities tried more than once to resist Nazi demands for a total annihilation of the Jewish population, arranged the emigration of Jewish groups to Palestine, openly defended a number of leading personalities of the Romanian Jewish community. Yet it was these selfsame wartime authorities that organized deportations, set up labor camps, and issued racist legislation. Today, we feel responsible for this terrible inconsistency. The sacrifice of thousands of Jews from all over Romania weighs heavy on our hearts. The killing of innocent people can neither be forgiven, nor corrected, nor forgotten. It is our duty over and over to commit a place in our memories for the Holocaust victims, and make sure that nothing, no fact, no name will ever be forgotten.[8]

There was no open condemnation of the Marshal as a war criminal, let alone an apology. The murderous role that units of the Romanian army and gendarmerie played in the liquidation of 270,000 Romanian and Ukrainian Jews was left unmentioned. Yet the President's words were courageous—words never before heard from a Romanian head of state. They represent a long step forward in Romania's coming to grips with the Holocaust, a tragic chapter in the history of Romanian and Ukrainian Jewries that was also one of the darkest chapters in the history of Romania. Only time will tell whether the Romanians will actually commit themselves to the advancement of historical truth and the preservation and perpetuation of the memory of the Holocaust. An hon-

---

[8] "The Message of President of Romania, Emil Constantinescu," *Realitatea Evreiască* (Jewish Reality), Bucharest, April 18–May 15, 1997, p. 19. In light of the above statement, one is puzzled by the reaction of President Constantinescu to the October 22, 1997 initiative taken by Sorin Moisescu, the Prosecutor General, for the judicial rehabilitation of six members of the Antonescu government. The President referred to the six individuals convicted for "crimes against the peace" as "outstanding Romanian cultural figures." For details see chapter 3.

est confrontation of the historical past is, along with the protection of basic rights and the advancement of social justice, a basic requirement for the establishment of the genuine democracy the President and most Romanians are striving for.

Statement by
Eszter (Fränkel) Goro

June 3, 1992

My name is Eszter Goro (Mrs. David Fränkel). I was born in 1924 in Turda, where I lived until 1946. My father, Ferenc Goro, was the chief engineer of the railway office there; he died in 1934. Both he and my mother (née Elza Brunner) were emancipated, liberal members of the intelligentsia, and were not involved in politics. My older brother, Ferenc Goro, Jr., (born in 1914) was a Zionist during his student years in Kolozsvár and after the Vienna Award he sympathized with the Communist movement in Turda. It was through him that I became acquainted, during the war, with the then Communist leaders of Turda—Arnold Negrea (Schwartz) and Zoltán Eidlitz; within a short time I became an active member of a Turda Marxist circle of young people.

In the summer of 1943 Eidlitz told me and my brother that a young man of Leftist orientation called Ari Hirsch had arrived in Turda, the police was pursuing him, and he was ill—we should persuade our mother to hide him in our home. This in fact happened. In accordance with the Jewish laws then in effect, our family home (Piaţa Andrei Şaguna—later Ecaterina Varga, 31) had been expropriated and we lived in three small rooms in the underground part of the house. In the greatest secrecy, we gave one of these to Ari Hirsch, who throughout his stay in Turda (over two years) lived and ate with us. To this day I wonder how my mother, widowed with three children as she was, admitted a man like this to the house, a man who represented a major and constant danger to all of us politically and also was suffering from acute tuberculosis. I cannot understand why Ari Hirsch, in his statement discussing his experiences in Turda (Strochlitz Institute, University of Haifa, R3c7) doesn't even mention her name although there is so much for which he must be thankful to her. The risk was even greater because immediately above us in the house there lived a scoundrel of a police commissar named Balosu, and in the neighborhood there also lived the military commander of Turda, in front of whose house a police sentry was posted day and night. That I and my brother, who were young and enthusiastic, risked the hiding of Ari Hirsch was normal; but that my mother did so was extraordinary.

Within a short time a close and intimate friendship developed between me and Ari Hirsch. I know that he was concerned with the threatening future of the Jews of Transylvania, as he always reported about his plans and concerns. Because of his status and serious illness, he rarely went out; I helped him to transmit messages and maintain contact with Eidlitz and Negrea, etc.

In the meantime the Germans occupied Hungary, and the Jews of Kolozsvár were placed into ghettos and later deported. My mother's entire family lived in Kolozsvár; my grandfather (Elek Brunner, then 80 years old) as well as his sons (Sándor and Jenő) were taken away with their wives and none of them returned. But Jews who had hid before people were taken to the ghetto whose addresses we somehow discovered could be saved—it was at this time that the campaign whose soul was Ari Hirsch was started.

I know for sure that Zoltán Eidlitz had reliably good connections with peasants living in a community near the border (if I remember correctly, the name of the place was Pata) who could cross the border into Kolozsvár—a part of their land was on the other side of the border. These peasants went in carts to the addresses we gave them and brought the refugees, dressed as peasants, to Turda in the carts. Here they were met by young people who took them to apartments where they stayed one or two days, after which, supplied with false papers, they were moved on by train to Bucharest, usually with an escort. (I could draw well, so the forging of signatures was my task.) We maintained contact with Bucharest by telephone as well; Commissar Balosu frequently amused himself elsewhere, so we organized his maid and Ari frequently spoke from his place. I am not aware that there were any means other than this route to take people across, but it is by no means impossible that there were other attempts as well. At any rate, this route was safe. I don't remember exactly how many people came across, the number could be 100 to 200. I know that it was over this route that Rabbi Weinberger and his wife also came across. He too, like everyone else, went on to Bucharest after one or two days. I never heard that Weinberger had any role in rescuing the Jews of Kolozsvár or that he organized or was involved in any activity of this type—that he did not do so in Turda is certain. I am not aware that there were other organized rescue crossings in other localities in Turda County but this does not mean that there couldn't have been. I don't know with whom Weinberger could have organized such an operation—the congregation and the official Jewish leadership of Turda at first viewed the activities of Ari's and my group with great disapproval, and later with passivity at best. Many people took part in this operation who were neither Zionists nor Communists but simply Jews who were ready to help—but they helped individually, not at the urging of the community or the Jewish leadership. Besides, when Weinberger came the operation was already underway, and I find it inconceivable that he could have accomplished anything during the one or two days that he was hiding in Turda before he went on to Bucharest. Ari Hirsch never mentioned to me that Weinberger had played any role—he was no more than one of the people being transferred, like many others.

About Raoul Şorban I know the following: He was a

Romanian living in Kolozsvár, a democratically oriented young
man belonging to the Maniu party (I think he was about 30 to 35-
years old during the war) whose fiancée, Éva Semlyén, belonged
to a well-known wealthy Jewish family in Kolozsvár. Both of
them tried to escape across the border to Turda. They were caught
and returned to Kolozsvár. Éva Semlyén was deported (she survived and returned to Kolozsvár as far as I know she still lives
there). After a while Raoul Şorban came to Turda—I don't know
how but I believe it was also through our group—and stayed in
Turda for a longer while. He was in contact with both Ari and
Negrea/Eidlitz, so I got to know him as well. He appeared to have
a confident, well-intentioned, daring, and adventurous nature. I
remember hearing the Eidlitzes talk smilingly about the energy
with which he was looking for the valuables of the already deported Semlyén family which had previously been transferred to
Romania for safekeeping.

Şorban was a man who enjoyed considerable influence in the
police circles of Turda (as a Romanian Transylvanian refugee),
and had free access everywhere. It was at that time that something
that involved him about which I already gave a Declaration in
Israel (János Kun in Haifa, an associate of Yad Vashem). A young
Jewish Communist sympathizer named Jakab (Busu) Abraham,
who took part in the rescue operation, was caught by the police
and they tried to find out what he knew through beatings.
(Luckily, they didn't know much about him, and he kept silent.) I
also was summoned to the police as they knew that he was often
at our place, but of course they didn't find out anything. We were
afraid, however, that Busu might be tortured and it was at this time
that Raoul Şorban undertook to settle the case. He went to the
police with a previously well-planned story, and he in fact succeeded in freeing Busu. Although he himself did not assume any
great risk, this nevertheless was a very positive deed. On the other
hand, however, I never heard anything about Raoul Şorban having
any organizational role in the rescuing of Transylvanian Jews to

Romania or that the entire operation was under his, i.e., the Maniu party's, initiative and leadership.

I was still living in Romania (which I left in 1987 when I and my husband went to Germany on a tourist passport and remained there) when I read with great indignation a long article (in interview form) by Raoul Şorban in the 1985 or 1986 edition of *Flacăra Almanac* (at least that's how I remember the name), where he reports on the rescue of Northern Transylvanian Jews as the Maniu party's and his own personal operation. He also mentions Ari Hirsch as someone who "helped" and mentions my name as well. I didn't understand the whole thing, but at the same time I immediately thought that perhaps I had not been accurately informed, as I did not know everything at the time and it's not impossible that the Maniu party had indeed had a more important role in Kolozsvár than I had been aware of. But it was obvious from this article alone (many others followed, becoming increasingly exaggerated) that things were portrayed in a slanted, distorted, and false way. When I last was in Israel in 1989 I saw Ari Hirsch for the first time in decades. I asked him: "What role did Şorban have in the rescuing of Jews?" His reply was brief: "None."

I would like to make three important points in this connection:

1. For decades following August 23, 1944, the whole Jewish rescue operation was hushed up. Nowhere did a single line appear in connection with this. I became a member of the Romanian Communist Party in 1945, and in all my resumes I wrote in detail about it—no one ever asked me what it was all about. I know for sure (personally from Zoltán Eidlitz) that the Romanian Communist Party did not acknowledge this operation, it identified the participation of Eidlitz and Negrea as individual initiatives and did not approve either of it or of participation by Communists and Communist sympathizers. Zionism was, for a long time, looked upon as an enemy i.e., as an anti-Communist movement, and mentioned in conjunction with Fascism. This position was then offi-

cially changed, I believe in the early 1970's, but in practice every-thing remained as before—no serious material appeared anywhere about the Romanian Jewish question.

2. At the same time, the Romanian Communist Party con-sidered the Maniu party as the principal enemy. It is conceivable that the active role of the Maniu party in the Turda operation also played a role in the hushing up of the operation. But I know one thing for sure: when Arnold Negrea was expelled from the Communist Party in the 1950's, one of the accusations against him was that he actively collaborated with the Maniu party. In retro-spect, I don't think it impossible that this collaboration of which Negrea was accused referred to the Jewish rescue operation in Turda. The fact is that certain members of the Maniu party helped Jews in Kolozsvár—we heard (I believe from Ari Hirsch) that Ernő Marton was brought to Turda in the trunk of the car of Hațieganu, one of the party's leaders. I repeat, it is not impossi-ble that Raoul Șorban made a more serious contribution to the res-cue operation than I knew; however, it is impossible that this con-tribution was what he and Weinberger, glorifying each other, claim.

3. It is not an accident that after decades of silence Romania suddenly awoke to the fact that there was a Jewish rescue opera-tion in Turda in 1944, and that the press exaggerated the Romanians' positive role in it. This was part of the nationalist anti-Hungarian politics incited by the Ceaușescus, who at the same time wanted to prove that Romanians had nothing to do with (persecuting) the Jews but rather did everything possible to rescue them from the murderous Hungarians. It is this policy that is being pursued by the "Vatra" movement of Romania, of which Raoul Șorban is an active and zealous member. Unfortunately only a few people are still alive who could give more accurate information in connection with the Weinberger and Șorban cases.

They are:
1. Naturally, Ari Hirsch (Eldar).
2. Arnold Negrea (Schwartz). He lives in Jerusalem, Dr. Tibor Lusztig knows his address (Mizrah Talpiot 108, Reh. Meir Naqquar 10/11, Jerusalem).
3. Mrs. Negrea, née Zita Weinberger—same address.
4. Simion Someşan (Goldman). Retired, lives in Bucharest.

P.S.—I heard not long ago that a "documentary" film was prepared and is being shown in the movies in Romania in which various scenes are cleverly edited in—Raoul Şorban and Weinberger also have a role in it, and what's more there is an interview with Ari Hirsch.

Eszter Goro-Fränkel
(signed)

"*I Have Never Dreamt about the Camps*"

A Conversation with Mrs. Éva Pamfil Semlyén

My Dear Good Father: Yesterday a telegram came from Tivadar in which you note your arrival together with Pista. One must still have faith, and living through so much suffering was also worthwhile because fate has provided some meaning for going on with life as well. I hope that your health did not suffer too much from last year's ordeal ...

By coincidence when I arrived in Auschwitz I was put in the same bloc from which Mother and Juci had left with a transport three days earlier. Later they took us to Workcamp B, where I stayed until November 1.

(Excerpts from a letter which Éva Semlyén wrote to her father from Sweden on July 22, 1945)

Where does your family come from?

I know more about my father's side; they settled in Iklód [Iclod in Romanian]. They were large landholders until the expropriation of landholdings near the end of the last century. My great grandfather had 13 children, from whom I have many relatives. Later my grandfather settled in Szamosújvár [Gherla in Romanian], where he established a distillery. I also was born there, in

Szamosújvár, on August 28, 1918. I am not sure how the distillery ceased production. I do know that my father brought the family to Kolozsvár [Cluj in Romanian], where he was a bank director until the economic crisis that started in the late 1920s. That crisis ruined the banks, and us as well. Later, in the late 1930s, my father rebought the failed distillery in Szamosújvár on a corporate basis and put it back into production. My mother, Irén Klärmann, came from a business family in Dés [Dej in Romanian].

Where did you go to school?

Here in Kolozsvár, in the Saxon Evangelical School, because at that time this was the school for good bourgeois families. I also had a German *Fräulein*, so I already became proficient in German at that time. Later, when the necessity of learning Romanian appeared unavoidable, I got into the Romanian Regina Maria Gymnasium. This was a great shock for me, because my parents made the mistake of registering me in the school from one minute to the next, when we had no idea what happens in such a school. I did not know the language at all and this had a negative impact on me. I didn't even try to study. So I was unable to go beyond the fifth year of gymnasium and then I declared that I wanted to learn a trade. I wanted to become a ladies' fashion stylist and designer, so I learned sewing and cutting. I was hoping to open my own salon later because I thought I had the requisite good taste. But then came "the events."

How did these "events" start for you?

As a young person I was part of a large social group and since minorities generally seek each other out there were many Hungarian young men in our group. This was strange in those days, because by then the Jews already lived a kind of ghetto life. I don't mean that we were excluded, but outside relations were quite few. I was not involved in politics of either the right or the left, but many of our friends and in general many of the children of the very well to do became Communist. This also was the case during the interwar period; it was a rather romantic leftism, feeling sorry for the poor and that was about it. It was fashionable. At the same time there was another important group among the young: the Zionists. With these I had less contact.

When did you start working?

Around 1935–1936. I hired a girl to sew, doing the cutting and fitting myself. Everything could have gone very well, but on the one hand I was very young and very busy, and on the other hand I really didn't have any financial need, so this period was relatively short. Meanwhile, one of my uncles who lived in England invited me and I went there. Then this activity of mine also came to an end. We were young. At that time we concentrated on socializing, having a good time, going on excursions, and being involved in sports.

When did the atmosphere begin to change?

There was a brief period in my gymnasium years when the Iron Guard movements were active, when we felt that we were Jewish. In our class one of the girls declared that she would not speak to Jews. This lasted a short time, perhaps two to three months, but left an imprint nevertheless. Then this passed and after the Vienna Award [of August 30, 1940] we had a different rather mixed social group. My older sister was a university student and we had had many young Romanian student friends. Following the Vienna Award, things changed in a different direction. At that time we personally didn't yet feel any discrimination or persecution, but there were demonstrations against us. This is exactly like my daughter's case. Since my husband was Romanian,

her classmates considered her Romanian, but when a Jew was
molested she always intervened, saying that she too was Jewish.
The response she received then was "yes, but you are different!"
In other words, this otherness was in operation at that time as well.

When did you feel that it would be necessary to escape?

As a matter of fact, between 1940 and 1944, aside from the
fact that we had to confront the consequences of the anti-Jewish
laws, we came to that realization rather late. Some stores bore the
inscription "Hungarian Christian store" or "We do not serve
Jews." We avoided these stores with great consternation. For
example, there was the old Leitersdorfer cosmetics-perfume store
where we had used to shop, or the Gallia silk store, where we had
also shopped in the past. We no longer went in there. Until 1944,
we were free to move about. We went to Pest and attended con-
certs and plays; from this point of view there were no restrictions.
But I had a school colleague who later married an Imrédyst, and
during an encounter on the street she did not greet me. On the
other hand, my father once came home and told us quite excited-
ly: "Imagine, I met Jenő Szentimrei, who was in uniform, and he
stopped and shook hands with me." At that time such things suddenly became important. Szentimrei was a newspaperman who
was a lieutenant at the time, whom we had always known as a
decent person. I always said that if the Germans hadn't occupied
Hungary in March 1944 perhaps everything would have developed differently, perhaps we would have escaped.

*Did you know during the early 1940s what was happening
with the Jews of Romania?*

Yes, we were informed about the pogroms in Bucharest, but
we did not know about the horrors of Bessarabia and Transnistria.
We only learned about these later. There were also people who

were helped by the Romanian authorities. For example, this was the case of Mrs. Sándor Farkas who died recently in Paris, and her husband, who came from Bucharest at the time of the Vienna Award and settled in Pest. After the German occupation they received Romanian passports from the Romanian Legation in Budapest which enabled them to return to Bucharest. But the situation of the Jews in pre-March 1944 Romania was worse than that of those in Hungary, so it was not wise to seek refuge there.

How and when did you reach the big decision to cross the border into Romania?

As soon as the Germans came into Kolozsvár, everything changed. The people deluded themselves even when the Germans were already in Pest. There was a rumor that the Germans would not come into Transylvania and thus not to Kolozsvár. But one had the feeling that an invisible noose was tightening. It was subjectively a bad feeling but at the same time, thanks to the instinctual will to live, we hoped that everything would be alright and that somehow we would escape. However, a few days later the Germans came into Kolozsvár and we awoke to the fact that we had to escape to somewhere, and while there was still time to rescue whatever we could from the apartment. At that period we lived in one of the Péter Pál villas [today Arges Street—Z. T. Sz.] behind the doublebranched church. After we managed to safeguard a few things from the apartment, we were just waiting for Raoul Şorban, whom we had sent for a horse-drawn carriage, so we could salvage some more things from the apartment. The *Sicherheitsdienst,* the SD-men, came directly to our house. Presumably they picked this house by themselves, or it may have been suggested to them. Only Jews lived there. They also liked the place, and the fact that there were no other houses next to the villas. We were just having lunch when suddenly two officers ran into each of the apartments and asked if we were Jewish. We said

yes. Then they ordered us to pack what we needed for two days
and leave the apartment, within 10 minutes. At that time—this
happened in March—the ghetto wasn't in existence yet. They let
us go on our own and they said we should go to the Jewish
Community which was under obligation to place us somewhere.
Of course there could be no question of this since we had no contact whatever with the community, but even if we had had such a
connection.... At that time the Jews had not yet been rounded up,
so everyone went where he could go. As we left the house Raoul
Şorban arrived with the carriage. In the next few days the thought
was born that it would be wise to escape, that it would be necessary to cross over into Romania. Raoul Şorban, who was our close
friend and my fiancée, was here. At the time of the Vienna Award
he had left for Romania, but had come back to Kolozsvár towards
the end of 1940. His mother came from a Magyarized Armenian
family. Her maiden name was Bogdánffy. Our family also knew
Raoul's father very well, since in his youth he had taught my
mother to play the piano in Dés. I got to know Raoul in the winter of 1940 in Kolozsvár. He was staying in a sublet place. Later
he worked for the university; he was Zoltán Felvinczy Takács's
teaching assistant and also had a studio. We used to go there and
sketch, paint, draw. Many people went there, including Miklós
Elekes, Korvin, Francisc Păcurariu, and Vaszi (Vasile) Moldovan.
I also met Aurel Bernáth in his studio. Then Raoul became associated with Hațieganu at the *Tribuna*. He had been previously
married; his wife was Olga Kaba, who later sympathized with the
Iron Guard. In perhaps 1943, the Hungarians called Şorban up for
labor service, together with Bubi (Aurel) Socol and three other
Romanian lawyers. They were put together with the Jews and,
wearing yellow armbands with black dots, were interned and were
supposed to be taken to a labor camp. I traveled there to help
them. They were taken to an army barrack, and shortly thereafter
the Romanians were freed. I was asked to go, and went, to the
Romanian Legation in Pest carrying a letter from them, and here I

also went to Milea, the lawyer, for them to intervene. Şorban returned briefly to Kolozsvár, where he was referred for psychiatric observation, and came home from there shortly thereafter. Thus it was natural that I and my older sister went to Raoul Şorban's studio on Király Street. Şorban's mother also lived there, in the same house on the same hallway. The Germans caroused all day in front of the house and on our hallway as well; we on the other hand, were reading *The Good Soldier Schweik* and laughed a lot. We were young.... Our parents had a garden in Török-vágás [a section of Kolozsvár] with a two-room furnished summer cottage and they went there. In the next few days, I also began to think very seriously about a possible escape to Romania. One of the Haţieganu brothers visited Şorban and it was then that the idea of my crossing the border to Romania first came up. We had already heard by then that several people had made the crossing successfully, although we did not believe the news. István Semlyén also sent a letter from labor camp in which he warned us about ghettos and gas chambers. The letter was passed around in the family but nobody believed it. All this was far away from us, in the Ukraine, Poland....

Did they hear such news among your circle of friends?

The news and rumors spread quickly among the Jews. László Salamon, the poet, was a good friend of my father's; we also heard this from him and from Jewish circles in general. And then, I remember clearly, I went with Şorban to Bubi Socol, Dr. Aurel Socol, who had an office here in Kolozsvár on Kossuth Lajos Street near the Katona bakery, and they discussed the escape. I placed my trust in them. They discussed the details. They said that there was a peasant from Monostor [Mănăştur in Romanian] named Crişan, who perhaps later was recruited by the Hungarian counterintelligence, and when he had to take us across he left us in the dark forest and disappeared. Crişan left not only us in the lurch but the next group as well; thus actually he really didn't take us across.

How many people were planned to be included in the group with which you finally crossed?

At the time it was only a question of me. My parents were not considering it yet, and perhaps didn't even want to. My mother was still preoccupied with household matters, what to store for the winter and things like that. My older sister, too, remained with my parents. Socol said that there was another young woman, Eszter Salamon, who also had a Romanian friend, Teodoru, whom she later married, and that we would be two. So just the two of us left. However, at first Şorban wanted to persuade Teodor Harşia, the painter, to take us across the border. He thought that if somehow they managed to capture us I would assume the identity of Harşia's wife. Şorban acquired some personal identification of a Romanian peasant girl named Veronica. But Harşia, though very decent, was a very indecisive man and rejected the plan. He asked why Raoul didn't accompany me across. But Şorban didn't have the courage to do it, and he said that if something should happen to me he would come across the border officially and be of help. I fully agreed with Harşia—why should he really risk his freedom and life for me? He had second thoughts at the last minute. Thus we had to find a different way and it is like this that Vaszi Moldovan, the journalist and later theater director and a diplomat in Hungary, agreed to come with me. The three of us left: Moldovan, Eszter Salamon, and I. For Moldovan it was quite dangerous, since if he were caught he would be punished as a military deserter. Moldovan agreed to take us across and to go back later.

When did all this happen?

It was before the establishment of the ghetto. We were at Socol's about the middle of April and left one or two days later.

We went by taxi to Crişan at Monostor; Şorban also accompanied us for this part of the trip. It was already dark. We left and Crişan disappeared a short while later in the darkness of the pitchdark night and left us there. He didn't say anything, just left suddenly. We found a gypsylike person in the forest who at the end led us across into Romania. If I had known the Bükk Forest as well as I know it today I could have walked across by myself. We were supposed to reach a house, Socol had told us, the house of a peasant named Gligor, who was to take us to Torda (Turda in Romanian). I trusted Socol's good faith, but looking back I must say that they organized the escape very superficially. Gligor was reluctant. He said he could not take us further because his horse was under requisition and he had no carriage. This was already near the Romanian border, but by then we already knew in what direction we had to go, so we left. We in fact arrived in Erdőfelek [Feleac in Romanian] village in Romanian territory. We made a mistake: we went into a peasant's house. I was exhausted and we were afraid we might be stopped for identification and land in trouble. So we sent Vaszi Moldovan to Torda with the intention that he would come back with a car. Eszter and I went into the peasant's house. At that time my Romanian was still rather poor, and my clothing also revealed that I was not a Romanian peasant girl. The peasant left a short while afterwards, and came back after us with a Romanian border policeman.

Were you taken into the border-control station?

Yes, and we stayed there overnight. Apparently they were waiting for instructions. Moldovan returned for us with a car but couldn't find us any more. The Romanians next took us to Torda, where they first kept us for a night at the police, interrogated us, and shouted that they would intern us in Jilava. We thought as long as they didn't send us back this would be alright. Perhaps we would have gotten away with internment, but in the meantime another, much larger, group arrived; it included my parents, my older sister, and many good friends and acquaintances. They were about 40, and they also had been caught in Felek.

Wasn't it possible to bypass Felek and go to Torda directly?

We would not have had any problem if we hadn't gone into the peasant's house. They, on the other hand, were probably already expected, that is the authorities already knew a group was going to come. I don't know, you see, these are important issues, and really we never cleared up where and how they were caught. At the time I found out in a horrible way that they had been caught. I was downstairs in a cell, and suddenly I heard the voices of my mother and sister talking from the floor above. I didn't even know that they were going to come across. We met later at the gendarmerie.

Was there no talk about their departure as well, before you left Kolozsvár?

Yes that they might consider it, but they had not decided yet.

Was their crossing also organized by Socol?

Yes, Socol organized it through Şorban.

How much did Socol ask for such an escape?

I didn't pay anything but of course Crişan had to be paid, Socol having written about how much it would be. It was natural that one would have to pay, no one expected it for free. I heard about agreements where a note had to be sent back and those still in Kolozsvár would only pay after receiving it, but I don't know anything concrete.

What happened in Torda?

After the police station I was taken to headquarters, where a very decent officer was in charge of our case. I must note that I was extremely inexperienced and stupid. Except for this escape I had never dared to make an independent decision. This officer told us he was sending us to a house where we were to sleep and told us to report back the next morning. We should have disappeared then and there ... but I had neither money nor anything with me. So that's how I crossed.

Did you know at the time about the activities of Arieh Hirsch?

At that time I didn't know anything. Şorban came across the border because we had agreed that if he did not hear from me within two days he would come. He came officially, with a passport, perhaps two or three days later. He then established contact with his acquaintance at city hall and perhaps with the Jewish community as well, and it was the hope and promise that they would send us to Szeben [Sibiu in Romanian] where the military tribunal would convict us of illegal border crossing. This is what was customary up to that time. But something must have changed. Perhaps Antonescu issued a decree under which alien citizens illegally crossing the borders would have to be shot at the border or pushed back.

So the following morning you went back to the police...?

Yes, and the following day we were taken from there to the gendarmerie, where we met the family. There were my parents, Hugó Semlyén and his wife, my older sister, Judit Schleifer, Ernő Fischer and his wife, Edit Fischer, who later married the artist Zoltán Andrásy, Pista Semlyén's wife, also named Éva Semlyén, the young lawyer Bandi Klein who had escaped by himself, and

Vera Simon. These are the ones I remember. Only Vera Simon is
still alive, in Israel.

What did they say at the gendarmerie?

I don't even know today how I dared to enter Colonel
Craioveanu's office. But I did walk in, to ask him what would
happen to us. I felt his disdain. He did not ask me to sit down, he
did not look me in the eye, and said they would be sending us to
Sibiu. This was what I wanted to know. He lied, of course,
because the following day at dawn, about 5 A.M., they put me
along with Eszter and Bandi Klein into the Colonel's car and we
left along with an adjutant and the driver. The adjutant began talking to us sarcastically. He knew Yiddish because he came from a
poor Moldavian background, and in Moldavia where many Jews
lived he had learned Yiddish as a child. I could not speak to him
in Yiddish. He said they were taking us to the forest, where we
could leave the car and go anywhere we wanted. Of course this
was not the truth. They took us back to near the village of Felek,
they locked us into a large barrack. A guard kept watch while we
spent three or four hours in horrible anxiety, as we did not know
what would be happening to us. Bandi Klein, I remember, lay
down, pulled his hat down over his eyes, and slept. I felt he was
betraying me, but like the men in general he tried to live through
the events with less emotion. After a while they herded us out-
doors, where I also found the other group, my family, who had
been brought there by truck. Then we were taken over by the SS.
This was our first encounter with the SS. Shouts and lining up....
This was near Ajton [Aiton in Romanian], somewhere near the
main highway. There was a moment when I thought they would
shoot us, because they ordered us to take everything out of our
pockets. They turned their weapons toward us but didn't shoot.
Meanwhile, another truck arrived from Kolozsvár. They stopped
it and after the canvas cover was removed a group of Jews wear-

ing the yellow star got off; among them was my cousin András Semlyén.

Where did they come from?

They also wanted to escape with a German Wehrmacht driver, who I believe was later executed by the Germans. But by that time the roads were already being watched, and there were many denunciations. There were quite a few people in this group but I recognized only two, my cousin and a man called Kro. We got into the trucks and took us into the cellar of the Péter Pál villas, to the SD. At that time coal was still being used for heating there; they locked us into a very small enclosure in the basement. We were lots of people and most had only enough room to stand; someone would always have to get up so someone else could rest for a while. The SS soldiers with their machine guns guarded us. They kept us there for about a day while the SS prepared the basement of another villa with great thoroughness and speed, put up plank beds, and took us over. The Germans interrogated us one by one. I was interrogated by a primitive sergeant who wanted to know why I crossed the border. I said I did because I no longer had a place to live here and I had an aunt living in Romania. He claimed that we wanted to escape to the Soviets. Across the front?, I asked. But he wrote down what he wanted and they probably already knew what awaited us. We were there for two days; then they took us into the ghetto where there was "a full house" already.

Did you meet Şorban in Torda?

Yes, he came into Romania and looked for me at the gendarmerie. He spoke with Craioveanu, who told him the same thing he had told me, that they were sending us to Szeben. Şorban said that he established contact with some members of the Jewish community of Torda as well. He was given the same information by them as by Craioveanu, namely that we would be taken to Szeben where they would probably convict us of having crossed the border illegally. In other words, he tried to do something. He also knew a civil servant at the prefecture of Torda. It was this man, a person who had actually been found by Moldovan, who was supposed to help us during our escape.

In the years before my escape, Şorban was engaged in painting and art history; later he became an editor of the daily *Tribuna Ardealului* and organized a number of exhibitions. To the best of my knowledge he was not involved in political activities at the time. He was before 1940, because he worked with Coriolan Tătaru, the king's representative; we only met later.

Many people mention nowadays that Şorban was involved in rescue activities ...

I can only talk concretely about our group, but it is clear that with the passage of years this rescue activity has been greatly exaggerated and there are many contradictions. I see this as someone personally involved; an outsider perhaps doesn't understand anything about it. I tell you, but.... This is what I don't want to talk about. I am not aware of this rescue.

But it's a fact that he tried to save you?

This is a fact. And what's more, his attitude in those times.... There are those who did nothing, but he tried to do something. He publicly walked with us wearing our yellow stars. There were those who avoided us. Professor Braham also wrote that at that time it was not yet legally punishable for someone to lodge Jews, but people were not pleased to do it, and most avoided taking in Jews. And last but not least, he was the liaison to Socol.

But whether Şorban allegedly participated with Rabbi Weinberger in rescue activities...?

I know nothing about it, he never spoke of it to me. When I raised this question later, he answered that I couldn't have known about everything. Later I was also asked about it by Yad Vashem, but then also I could only state that Raoul Şorban had helped me escape to the border, had spoken to Socol, and had asked Vaszi Moldovan to accompany me.

Is it possible that he participated in such activities without your knowledge?

Did you see the film about it on television?

Yes.

Şorban and Weinberger said there that there was a peasant's house at Felek that belonged to Vaszi Moldovan's father, where the border crossing of the Jews was organized and they even were able to rest. Did you hear this? In that case, why did his son have to shiver while taking me across? Because he was as terrified as I was. And he took us to a stranger's house, not that of his father.

Was there never any talk about Şorban personally accompanying you across the border?

No. I did not raise the question with him. He had tried so hard to convince me that should my border crossing fail he would have to cross the border officially to free me that I believed it. He was not a hero. There are people who under certain circumstances become heroes; others, on the other hand... I didn't tell him, because under certain circumstances I am quite uncommunicative and fearful, but there was great sorrow within me. I felt a certain repressed reproach which, however, I did not reveal. I felt this especially when he took me by taxi to Crişan at Monostor and then turned back.

You ended up in the ghetto of Kolozsvár. What were the conditions there?

We were under the open sky. In the drying shed of the brickyard. We hung blankets on the girders but there were so many of us that we could barely lie down side by side. There was a Jewish leadership in the ghetto. From time to time the authorities would take away those they thought they might be able to extract some wealth from. At first local Hungarian policemen guarded us, but these were found insufficiently reliable and were soon replaced by gendarmes from Hungary proper.

Did the people around the IRISZ Plant try to help?

We were totally surrounded. But there were cases when they helped. In my father's office staff was a young woman, Emilia Wertlen nicknamed Mici, who was a very good friend of ours and helped us a lot. She also brought in food. She helped me a lot later on as well.

In there, what did you know about the future?

They spread the news that they would take us to Kenyérmező, where we would be in a World War I camp. The internal leadership was not truthful either. But I decided to escape from the ghetto. It was only possible to leave if one was declared sick, as groups of sick people were taken to the Jewish hospital for examination or treatment. I had an acquaintance among the Jewish leadership, László Fenyő, who was in our social circle, and I thought I could be truthful with him. I asked him to put me on the list. He wouldn't do it. You know, it was the kind of atmosphere where everyone was afraid for their own life, their own position, and even if they knew what the future would be like they kept it a secret. They were probably promised that if they assured order they would enjoy an advantage and would not be deported. As a matter of fact they were left to the end, and were saved with the Swiss group.

In the ghetto, was there talk about the possibility of escape?

No, even the case of the Swiss group was kept secret. Later I did not fault so much the fact that Rabbi Weinberger saved his life, but what they subsequently created out of it. We could not demand of anyone that he become a hero and sacrifice his life, since even if someone had told us that we would end up in Auschwitz it would have been in vain. Had I known it in advance, I would perhaps have felt even worse. Anyway, not everybody could have escaped because this was impossible. It would be useless to accuse people individually, because here it was the system that was wrong. For example, Tibor Simon, a former bank official, escaped from the ghetto. He then fled across the border, but perhaps not here near Kolozsvár but rather somewhere in the Gyalu [Gilău in Romanian] region. I escaped before him, and I don't know whether anyone noticed his escape because no records of any kind were kept.

In the ghetto of Kolozsvár, did you hear any news about anyone having fled or crossed across the border into Romania?

There were individual escapes across the border, but I only found out about it afterwards. For example, this was the case of the Julika Szilágyis, who crossed on foot. I also heard about Ernő Marton, who was smuggled to Torda by the driver of the Romanian consul, in the trunk of the car. Then the German

Gauleiter of Torda intervened and established contact with the Germans here, which made escape more difficult.

In the ghetto, did you hear about the Swiss group?

No. We knew nothing. All the while the ghetto was getting progressively emptier. I thought that since they were being taken to Kenyérmező there should have been some means of communicating with someone. My instincts started working again and a bad feeling enveloped me. We only saw that those selected for the Swiss group moved into a barrack, and since I escaped before this, I only heard later that my former brother in law, who had a good friend among those who stayed behind as a part of the Swiss group, went to this friend before he was taken away and slapped him in the face. They didn't tell anyone, people only saw that they were keeping some kind of secret. The Swiss group stayed there to the end, and then they were taken to Pest and from there to Switzerland.

How did you manage to escape from the ghetto?

After my friend failed to help me by putting me on the sick list, when the group of patients left I attached myself without being noticed and succeeded in getting out. No recordkeeping or rollcall or anything of that kind was being done in the ghetto yet. They took us to the Jewish hospital, where I met the wife of Tudor Bugnariu, Kató, who also was Jewish; since her husband was a Romanian Christian, she had not been taken into the ghetto. She told me not to go back, and for the time being took me to her home. I cannot tell you how decent Tudor was. I stayed there for three days. At the time there were constant air raids, but I could not go into the cellar shelter; Tudor stayed upstairs with me so I wouldn't be afraid. He was very decent. In the meantime Kató established contact with someone—to this day I can't recall the name. I only know that he was a Reformed Church minister who had a garden in Török-vágás. There was a wooden shed there. At Kató's request, he allowed me to stay there. Thus this became my next stopping point. Staying alone in the woodshed was horrible; I was afraid to leave and in constant fear that they would come for me. The hours passed very slowly. I didn't have my wristwatch and never knew what time it was. Kató would bring me food every other day. From there I went to the other side of Török-vágás, where our former cook lived, and I spent a few days there too. I always felt that everyone was afraid because at that time there were constant threats. It was a horrible feeling to stay with someone about whom you knew that they could hardly wait to get rid of you.

What was the name of the cook?

Ilona Botár. She had a house there, in Török-vágás, at the Donát Road side. I was there one or two nights but Mici, from my father's office staff, took me to a friend of hers who also lived in the same area, someone called Rappaport. This woman's husband was Jewish and had been taken away. When she came home and looked at me, the poor thing cried all the time. It was awful; her face reflected the question as to why she did not hide her husband instead of me. I could have survived there for I spent almost three weeks with her. It was already June. Things were so chaotic at the time that a stranger would have great difficulty in grasping what happened next. I had a friend, Vera Simon, whose fiancée, István Gábor, was a journalist. They were also in hiding somewhere. Mici visited them too, as well as me, when she brought me food. This couple had the idea for us to write to my cousin in Pest, László Devecseri, who is still alive, and to ask his help, since as a builder he did a lot of work for the Hungarian army. He also had a Hungarian officer among his friends through whom he had managed to have his mother in law sent to Pest at the very beginning. In other words, the suggestion was for us to ask my cousin to try to do something because we were in a desperate situation here, and if he could he should send someone for us. They wrote a letter, which I also signed as "Éva." Pista Gábor gave the letter to a friend of his. We never found out whether this person was captured or whether he denounced us: Pista Gábor was deported and never came back—he died. Vera and Pista were arrested and were interrogated on where "Éva" was staying. They knew nothing about me except what they had assumed from the signature on the letter; they did not know where I was but revealed Mici's name and address. A civilian gendarme appeared at Mici's, saying he was Devecseri's driver coming to take me to Pest. Mici gladly took him to me. He told me as well that he was the driver who would take me to Pest, and that Vera and Pista were already in the car. At the same time, the Bugnarius also tried to find Şorban in Torda to take me once more across the border. On the same day, Mrs. Bugnariu brought Şorban's answer hidden in a two-sided mirror; he wrote that I should wait and a peasant woman would come to take me into Romania again. Thus this coincided with the trick of the Hungarian gendarme. I even started to tell him that I wasn't sure if I should go with him because if the same thing were to happen in Pest as here, it would be better for me to go to Romania. He answered that I should think about it because he would be back in an hour, and I would have to decide what I wanted to do by then. On his way out he parenthetically asked if I had any valuables. This whole game revolved about this question and this is why he did not reveal himself immediately. By that time I had nothing left, as they had taken everything from me in the ghetto. He left through the door, but at the same moment someone rang the doorbell. It turned out that his associate was waiting outside, and right away they both came in with revolver in hand. They informed me that I was under arrest. At that point I felt this was the end, there was no escape from there any more, and I did not even have the strength to attempt it. They took me to the gendarmerie on Monostor Road and locked me up in the cellar. A gendarmerie colonel interrogated me. I wasn't interested enough to find out his name during the 50 years since. He was very polite, offered me a cigarette, and complimented me by saying he had never seen a Jewish woman as beautiful as I was. He said the trouble was that the Jews didn't know how to work and Hitler would teach them, in other words that those who had a trade had nothing to fear because they would be able to continue to work where they were being taken. Was he crazy too, or did he think that I was? I don't know. My friends were taken away separately. I was placed on a train with two armed gendarmes and taken to Nagyvárad [Oradea in Romanian], where the last provincial ghetto was still in operation. We were in a barn, from which, if I remember correctly, we were entrained on June 14 and we left. This was one of the last transports from this region. Although my friend and her fiancée were there too, I was left all by myself. There was a very beautiful young pregnant woman there who had heard something. She told the rest of us, but the human survival instinct prevented us from accepting reality. I too rejected her news—we didn't want to believe them. What's more, after I went through all the examinations and we were inside the camp, and asked for the first time where the old people and the children were, and the old-timers pointed at the chimney, even then I believed that the people there made up such stories because they had become bad and evil. This reality could not be accepted.

Was your girlfriend in the freightcar as well?

Yes, but she was with her fiancée. So I was completely alone. A person's life depended entirely on accidents. One could never figure out where to turn and what means what. The technique of the Germans was that the weaker ones should perish as quickly as possible. They assigned the stronger people to the easier jobs and those who looked weak to the harder ones. The accidents notwithstanding, I also had the advantage of being alone. In such times people concentrated all their energies exclusively on saving their own lives, and did not waste their energy on saving their loved ones and such things. Furthermore, there all human emotional resources stopped functioning. I always had associates from whom I was occasionally separated, but this was not as great a tragedy as when a mother was separated from her children

Were you taken to Auschwitz?

Yes. It was my first piece of luck there that somehow I got into the work camp. In the camp where I was supposed to stay people were frequently subjected to selections. I got into the Birkenau work camp, where, according to a document that I received in 1980, I was tattooed on July 8, 1944, with the number A9661. We believed that this was a good sign because this meant they would be keeping track of us, but there was no logic in it whatever. On November 1, when they started to evacuate Auschwitz, they took us from there because the front was approaching. This was the second selection I went through. I had already lost a lot of weight, and when we were lined up in the nude I already knew what it could mean for me. I was completely apathetic.... They took us to Bergen-Belsen, which was also a notorious camp. I immediately saw that there were no gassings going on there, but that death by starvation awaited us. In Auschwitz we had one or two friends who worked in the kitchen, occasionally we were taken into the fields for work where you could dig something from the ground and eat it raw, which did not matter. In Bergen-Belsen, however, we received only the same rotten turnip broth every day. I felt I couldn't survive on it. Before Christmas 1944 they took us to Braunschweig, where the city was completely bombed out. We had to clear the rubble. We spent a whole month there and I had a very beautiful experience there. There was such a thing in the midst of misery as well.... It was Christmas and we were working on the streets. There was an older lady standing in the midst of the ruins, who looked at us with tears in her eyes. She pointed to where she lived in the ruins: the house was bombed out but a laundry room was left. She said I should go there later if I could. I asked if I could take my friend along, the young woman with whom I was always together at the time. She said yes. When we went she gave us a Christmas lunch. It was a fantastic thing to be in a house and be given lunch under humane circumstances! it was indescribable! We went to her a few days, and told her what had happened to us. Her husband was there too and she told him: "You see, it's true?!" They didn't know what was happening either. After we thanked her for the Christmas lunch she said she was thankful to us because it had enabled her to do this good deed on Christmas day. And this woman too was a German! However, the guards were terrible. They cursed the Jews, saying we were responsible for the war and everything was because of us. They avenged themselves for having been sent to the front by beating us.

How long were you in Braunschweig?

We were completely infected with lice, and the population had started to protest. We lived in a horrible stable, where the straw was rotten and there was only a single water tap for 600 people. One could not undress. It was cold because it was winter. From there they took us to Helmstedt, a small town near the old East German/West German border, where a man came and looked at our hands. The following day they took us to an airplane parts plant in an underground salt mine that had been transferred there along with its workers from Łódź in Poland. The work was very strenuous, as they did not take us down in an elevator—we had to walk down and back up every day. Only on the moon could there be another unbelievable place like that.... The air was very heavy. We had to make screws. Polish women worked there, who warned us: "nicht arbeiten," in other words that there was some sort of silent strike going on. They didn't work and the German

supervisors did not interfere. It was not even that the work was
hard; it was the lack of food and the heavy air. We were already
completely weakened. But even from there they took us further.
My next stop was the camp at Beendorf. We naturally heard the
news that we were completely surrounded and they would no
longer be able to take us anywhere; nevertheless they put us on a
train. It was horrible, they took us for about 10 days. There was
no food, we did not eat for days on end, and the guards didn't
know what to do with us. There I again took a risk which turned
out to my advantage. I went among the sick people in a special
freight car, although it was known not to be good for someone to
declare himself sick. But there were fewer of us in this freight car
than in the others into which they crowded 120 people in each one
and many perished during this trip. One could already see the
British or American tanks, the SS people began to cry, jumped off
the train, but in the end the train zoomed away from the area and
they managed to take us to Oxenzoll, another camp near Hamburg.
From there we were taken to Hamburg, also into a camp, and saw
the bombed-out city. This was already almost May 1. It turned out
that we got into the group which Himmler handed over to the
Swedish Red Cross. We still spent April 30 in the camp. We
thought they would again look us over because, I remember well,
we rouged our faces with beet juice so we would appear healthier.
But there was no inspection. We were put on a train, the SS no
longer came with us, and an old Wehrmacht man who was with us
told us that we would now end up in freedom. Of course we did
not believe him, because we no longer believed anything. This
was the height of our dreams, that perhaps some day the Red Cross
would take us over. When I saw the burning chimney in
Auschwitz I told myself that they would never let us leave alive so
there should be no witnesses. At the same time, following my survival instinct, I did not feel that I personally would not survive. I
always believed that I had to continue living.... We crossed the
border at Padborg into Denmark, where we were transferred to

Pullmann cars and taken over by the Swedish Red Cross people. We were taken to Sweden. We arrived at Malmö, where we were taken care of—and deloused several times over. The crossing was humorous because we were taken across the sea in a luxury ship, and we were still in our striped inmate clothing but were served lunch by waiters in toxedoes. The near-starved deportees only had eyes for what there was to eat. It must have been a very strange picture.... In Sweden we were told that Northern Transylvania no longer belonged to Hungary but had once again reverted to Romania, and Romania would have to deal with us.

Who came back of your family members?

My father, who had a weak physique and could not do hard physical work. My mother and my sister, who was an athlete, ended up there. Physical strength was not the decisive element. And of the extended family? I have a large family photograph from a picnic on which I noted who ended up where. One of my uncles, Károly Semlyén, did not return. One of his sons, András, also died while deported; another son, who was a labor serviceman, survived. The other part of the family survived in Temesvár (Timişoara in Romanian). The Devecseris of Pest got into the Swiss group. Pista Semlyén was a labor serviceman in the Ukraine; he returned, his wife was deported but she also survived and returned.

Who died in your family?

My mother, whom I never met again. My mother and my sister remained in the camp there for a while. I later found out from someone who had been with them for a while where they were. But I don't know what happened to them after that, but in a general way I know how people died there: by force or through starvation. I went through many camps....

Eszter Goro declared that in Torda Şorban had searched with great energy for the valuables of the already deported Semlyén family, valuables that had previously been taken to Romania. What do you know about this?

A few fairly valuable pieces of jewelry were indeed taken safely to Torda, but I no longer remember how. These survived the difficult time with Mrs. Erzsébet Engel Gergely. Presumably Eszter Goro found out something about these pieces. Aside from this, we didn't take anything into Romania. Whatever we had remained with Mici. I gave Raoul a necklace and some other pieces so he would have something to sell in case he needed money. But this was an absolutely personal and normal thing because we had that kind of relationship.

Why did your proposed marriage fail to happen?

Because Raoul did not wait for me.

Was he already married when you came back?

He was already married to a woman, whom he also left. I came back in 1946, but I wanted to return to the West. However they took away my passport. Later, in 1947, I married Gabriel Pamfil, a pharmacist. We have two children: Judit, born in 1951, and Gabriel, born in 1959. My daughter now lives in Canada, in Toronto, while my son was living for seven years in Israel but came back last year for family reasons.

In 1945 there was a trial...

That denunciation by Glück? Why they were angry at Şorban I don't know. They truly wanted to break his neck, but what they stated was absurd. I also was called to the *Securitate,* in the 1950s, and they asked me how I had crossed the border. And if I didn't think

Şorban had intentionally led us into the hands of the Gestapo. I asked what his objective could have been for doing this. He answered: "To get rid of you." I told them there was no need for him to do that, because if he had left me he could have broken with me without any complication, and moreover our relationship was not the kind that he would have needed to get rid of me in this way. If Raoul had told me at the time that he thought we ought to end the relationship, we would have ended it. Glück stated that he heard this from my father in Kassa. This is absurd, that someone in a deportation freight car would have a conversation like this. There was no such thing and it would have been impossible. My father also denied the statement. I always tried to separate these things from each other, as I did not feel the need to avenge myself as a woman and had no other feelings of this kind. For a long time I still believed that he was an honest man and a good and sincere friend. I don't like to talk about this.

According to this, was the 1945 trial unjust?

If he was being accused of this, yes. It is unlikely that Laci (László) Glück, a labor serviceman/physician, could have talked with the entrained deportees at the Kassa station. He stated that Raoul and I had a marriage contract, which also is not true.

Was there any relationship, did you or your family know anything about Rabbi Weinberger and his rescue activities jointly with Şorban?

No. We were not temple-attending Jews. I saw him once or twice but we knew nothing about things of that kind. They said they had rescued Poles and Slovaks across the borders.

Do you know of any persons still alive who know about the rescue across the Hungarian-Rumanian border?

No.

Later, did you talk about these things with Aurel Socol?

No. He was in jail for perhaps 14 years; we met but we never talked about this. There were years here when one didn't talk a lot. That's what times were like, and there were so many things that put me under stress.

What is your opinion about the Holocaust commemorations of recent years?

It was characteristic of these commemorations that they consisted of little more than standard text. They were also such that one immediately felt that they mostly served political objectives. Those who did not live through the events have no idea.... A short while ago my son took me to the area of the brickyard. It was the first time I saw the site of the ghetto again. Everything changed. After the war, the Gyár Street of today (Str. Fabricii in Romanian) was known as Road of the Deportees (*Deportáltak útja*). They could have kept the name.... There is no memorial plaque. Nothing is there to remind one.... You know, I am a very lucky person! During the decades that have passed since those days, I have never dreamt about the camps.

Recorded by
———————
Zoltán Tibori Szabó

Approved by
———————
Éva Pamfil Semlyén

May 5, 1997
Cluj-Napoca
Arges Street, 20, Apt. 6

Index